Fighting Fraud and Corruption at the World Bank

Stefano Manacorda • Costantino Grasso

Fighting Fraud and Corruption at the World Bank

A Critical Analysis of the Sanctions System

Springer

Stefano Manacorda
University of Campania
"Luigi Vanvitelli"
Caserta, Italy

Costantino Grasso
Coventry University
Coventry, United Kingdom

ISBN 978-3-030-08863-7 ISBN 978-3-319-73824-6 (eBook)
https://doi.org/10.1007/978-3-319-73824-6

Printed on acid-free paper

This Springer imprint is published by the registered company Springer International Publishing AG part of Springer Nature.
The registered company address is: Gewerbestrasse 11, 6330 Cham, Switzerland

To my PhD students, who made my academic life a collective experience and an enjoyable adventure.

Stefano Manacorda

To my loving wife, Anna Maria, because of her continued support and love, and our three children, Aurora, Luna and Leo, because of the joy they have brought in our lives.

Costantino Grasso

Foreword

The Important Role of the World Bank's Sanctions Regime in Deterring Foreign Corruption

Public corruption and fraud are among the most important impediments to economic development. Corruption also fundamentally undermines the rule of law. Deterring bribery requires a concerted effort to punish both those who pay bribes and those who receive them. To achieve this goal, we cannot rely only on enforcement by nation-states. In addition, deterrence requires active intervention by intergovernmental organizations, such as the World Bank.

Countries' Efforts to Deter Foreign Corruption

The World Bank sanctions regime is vital to the battle against corruption because enforcement by government authorities alone is not enough to deter corruption. Although many bribe-paying countries are improving their efforts to deter corrupt payments made by companies under their jurisdiction, countries vary considerably in their commitment to, and the effectiveness of their legal regimes for, deterring corruption. Countries where public corruption remains a serious concern—and an impediment to economic development—also often remain unable, and in some cases unwilling, to take the steps needed to prevent and punish corruption by public officials.

How Have Things Improved?

The picture has improved. In the 40 years since the United States adopted the Foreign Corrupt Practices Act (FCPA) and the more than 20 years since the Organisation for Economic Co-operation and Development (OECD) adopted the

Anti-bribery Convention, many countries have made great strides in reforming their laws and enforcement practices to aggressively pursue, and deter, public corruption. Prior to the OECD convention, only one country, the United States, had an explicit law criminalizing foreign bribery (OECD 2016, p. 14). Indeed, many countries, such as Germany, even allowed companies to deduct bribe payments on their taxes. By contrast, today most countries have laws criminalizing foreign bribery.

In addition, prior to the OECD convention, almost 40% of the OECD parties did not have an established system for holding corporations liable for the bribes paid for their benefit (OECD 2016, p. 14). In addition, some countries, such as Japan, Poland, Norway, and Iceland, had corporate liability to a subset of crimes, not including foreign corruption (id.). By contrast, today, almost all the parties to the convention have adopted some form of corporate liability for foreign bribery (OECD 2016, p. 14). Corporate liability is essential to deterring bribery[1] because companies directly determine their employees' incentives to bribe through control over compensation and promotion policies and internal corporate culture; corporations also are often better able than government officials to detect bribery by their own employees and obtain evidence needed to convict those responsible (Arlen 2012). Corporate liability is important to the effort to deter bribery because it can induce corporations to work actively to deter their employees from bribing and may even induce firms to help the government detect and sanction misconduct (Arlen 2012, 2018).

Of course, corporate liability is only effective to the extent that it is structured to include firms to deter bribery by employees. Given corporations' comparative advantage in detecting and investigating their own corruption, this implies that liability should be structured to incentivize corporations to adopt compliance programs that are effective at detecting bribery, genuinely investigate suspicious transactions, self-report detected misconduct, and cooperate with government enforcement officials to provide them with evidence of corruption that can be used to sanction bribe payers and bribe recipients (see Arlen 2012, 2018).

Historically, most countries failed to provide these incentives. Some deterred firms from detecting, obtaining evidence about and self-reporting misconduct by using *respondeat superior* to hold corporations criminally liable, whether or not they detected and self-reported this misconduct and fully cooperated. Others failed to incentivize either effective compliance or self-reporting and cooperation by restricting corporate liability to bribes paid by employees "in the directing mind" of the firm. Yet recently, more and more countries are considering approaches to corporate enforcement that deter bribery by providing companies with incentives to adopt genuinely effective compliance programs, to investigate suspicious activities, and to self-report detected misconduct to government enforcement officials and provide them with the evidence needed to sanction the individuals who paid the

[1]The OECD convention recognized the essential role that corporate liability plays in deterring corruption in the requirement, included in Article 2, that each country must "take such measures as may be necessary, in accordance with its legal principles, to establish the liability of legal persons." See 'Convention on Combating Bribery of Foreign Public Officials in International Business Transactions' (*OECD*, 2011) art. 2 <www.oecd.org/daf/anti-bribery/ConvCombatBribery_ENG.pdf>.

bribes (Arlen 2018). These approaches include laws that require companies to adopt effective compliance programs, as well as those that enable companies with actionable bribery to avoid formal conviction by entering into a deferred prosecution agreement[2] if the firm self-reported the misconduct and cooperated.[3]

Problems That Remain

Notwithstanding the great strides that have been made, foreign corruption has not been, and will not be, deterred through reliance entirely on enforcement actions by national enforcement authorities alone because many countries remain unwilling or unable to undertake all the reforms needed to deter foreign and local corruption effectively.

For example, one party to the convention, Argentina, did not adopt a law imposing liability on corporations for foreign corruption until nearly 20 years after the OECD convention obligated it to do so (OECD 2016, p. 22).

Other parties to the convention adopted laws but structured their corporate liability regimes in a way that limits their deterrent effect. Some, such as Ireland, Italy, France, Germany, Portugal, and Sweden, have limited the effectiveness of their corporate liability laws by insulating corporations for liability for bribery unless the misconduct was committed or condoned by a manager, e.g., someone considered the "directing mind" of the firm or a "responsible person" who is "acting for the management" (OECD 2016, pp. 49–51d).[4] Others reduce the deterrent effect of corporate liability by adopting corporate liability and sanctioning regimes that do not

[2]Under a DPA, the prosecutor files criminal charges but agrees not to seek conviction so long as the firm satisfies the terms of the agreement. Under an NPA, the prosecutor agrees not to charge the firm so long as it satisfies the agreement. DPAs generally require the firm to admit to a statement of facts detailing the misconduct. Both types of agreements also generally impose financial sanctions. In addition, most DPAs and some NPAs require the firm to undertake internal reforms (hereinafter mandates), which can include hiring and paying for a prosecutor-approved monitor. See Benjamin M. Greenblum, 'What Happens to a Prosecution Deferred? Judicial Oversight of Corporate Deferred Prosecution Agreements' (2005) 105 *Columbia Law Review* 1863; see also Jennifer Arlen and Marcel Kahan, 'Corporate Regulation Through Non-Prosecution' (2017) 84 *University of Chicago Law Review*, 323.

[3]See, e.g., 'The Fraud Section's Foreign Corrupt Practices Act Enforcement Plan and Guidance' (*U. S. Department of Justice – Criminal Division*, 5 April 2016) <www.justice.gov/criminal-fraud/file/838416/download>; see also 'Schedule 17 of Crime and Courts Act 2013' (*U.K. Government*, 2013) <www.legislation.gov.uk/ukpga/2013/22/schedule/17/enacted>.

[4]France, in Sapin II, has expanded its corporate liability regime to include an obligation to have an effective compliance program. Other countries, such as Chile, only hold a corporation liable if enforcement authorities can prove either that an owner or manager participated in or condoned the crime or that the crime was committed by a "person under their direction or supervision" provided that the offense also resulted from breach of an entity's supervisory function. Russia's law appears to impose broad corporate liability but courts have not yet held a corporation liable for acts by people other than a "director or founder." See, e.g., 'The Liability of Legal Persons for Foreign Bribery: A Stocktaking Report' (*OECD*, 2016) 49, 51 <www.oecd.org/daf/anti-bribery/Liability-Legal-Persons-Foreign-Bribery-Stocktaking.pdf>.

provide for any mitigation of the form of liability or the sanction in the case of companies that either self-report misconduct or fully cooperate with authorities (OECD 2016, pp. 148–154; see Arlen 2012, 2018, explaining why such mitigation is vital to effective deterrence).

Moreover, even when a country has an apparently effective corporate liability regime on the books, some in effect neutralize the deterrent effect of their own regimes. Countries can do this in a variety of ways. Some have established a maximum sanction for corruption that is sufficiently low to be unlikely to present a threat to large corporations contemplating profitable corruption.[5] Others have laws that are not enforced effectively either because enforcement officials are required to take all cases to trial, notwithstanding the resulting long delay (OECD 2016, pp. 158–164), or because government officials have consistently not pursued companies for public corruption.[6]

Deterrence of foreign corruption is also undermined by practices in developing countries that create conditions that encourage corruption through actions like underpaying government workers and failing to genuinely enforce internal laws prohibiting corruption.[7] It also is undermined by the failure of Russia and China to take the first steps toward attempting to deter foreign bribery by their companies.

These problems are not entirely surprising. Corruption is a source of enormous potential personal benefits for the elites in many developing countries. It also can be the key to obtaining enormous profits for corporations doing business in such countries. Countries with strong anticorruption enforcement risk putting their companies at a competitive disadvantage when they compete with companies from jurisdictions with either no foreign antibribery laws or little if any commitment to enforcement. While some countries, such as the United States and the United Kingdom, can mute the anticompetitive consequences through the broad jurisdiction provided by companies' desire to either access their capital markets or do business in the jurisdiction, many other countries cannot. In this situation, even when all countries would benefit if all countries could truly commit to eliminating foreign corruption, some, if not many, countries appear to have incentives to soft-pedal their own enforcement efforts. In this situation, truly effective deterrence requires the intervention of other players, with sufficient power to provide a deterrence effect and no direct ties to either the corporate bribe payers or the bribe recipients. The World Bank is ideally suited to this role.

[5]For example, ten countries have a fixed maximum sanction for corporations that is less than 1 million Euros, ibid 130.

[6]For example, France fined only one company for making payments to foreign officials between 2000 and 2016.

[7]This includes excessively low wages for government workers and a custom under which certain officials, such as police officers, must pay a form of "key money" to obtain positions in desirable locations—key money that exceeds the value of the position if no bribes are obtained.

The World Bank as an Instrument for Deterring Bribery

The World Bank is a powerful force in the developing world. In FY 2017 and FY 2016, it committed $58.8 billion and $61.3 billion, respectively, in loans, grants, equity investments, and guarantees to developing countries.[8] Access to this funding can be vitally important to many developing countries. The World Bank's successful action depends on its ability to ensure that its funds in fact go to well-constructed and effective projects that benefit the people. Corruption undermines the World Bank's efforts at their very core. Corruption dooms projects from the outset through both cost overruns and the selection of low-quality providers of goods or services. When corruption distorts development projects, loans intended to promote development may simply lead a country farther into debt without providing any much-needed economic development.

The World Bank, like other multilateral development banks, has a powerful tool—sanctions—that can be used to help ensure that its monies are used to benefit developing countries. The potential power of the World Bank sanctions regime lies in the vesting of sanctioning authority in officials who are not subject to the economic and political pressures that have led enforcement officials in the home jurisdiction of many bribe-paying individuals and entities to eschew aggressive enforcement of their own laws against foreign corruption. Those seeking to deter corruption can benefit enormously from understanding the existing structure of the World Bank sanctions regime and ways in which it could be improved through analysis of this important book.

World Bank Sanctions Regime

The World Bank sanctions regime allows the bank to exclude individuals and entities for a variety of violations—including both paying bribes and committing fraud. Rather than relying on external authorities to determine whether actionable misconduct occurred—such as local authorities in the recipient country or authorities with jurisdiction over an entity involved in corrupting or defrauding the recipient country—the World Bank regime empowers its own officials to identify and investigate misconduct *sua sponte*. In addition, and as described in detail by Manacorda and Grasso, the bank has established its own quasi-judicial process for determining whether sanctions should be imposed, complete with charges and an adjudicatory process where it is possible for both sides to present evidence to a panel of internal and external adjudicators who assess the sufficiency of the evidence that a violation occurred (Manacorda and Grasso 2018, p. [xv]).

---

[8] See 'Nearly $59 billion in World Bank Group Support to Developing Countries in Fiscal Year 2017' (*The World Bank Group*, Press Release, 18 July 2017) <www.worldbank.org/en/news/press-release/2017/07/18/nearly-59-billion-in-world-bank-group-support-to-developing-countries-in-fiscal-year-2017>.

As the authors point out, the World Bank not only employs its own processes for determining whether to sanction individuals and entities but also has adopted its own rules governing entity-level liability. Specifically, the World Bank in effect employs *respondeat superior liability* to determine whether a company is potentially eligible to be sanctioned for its employee's misconduct. Firms can usually mitigate the sanction by establishing that the employee was true "rogue employee"—a defense that is less credible to firms that did not have an adequate compliance program (Manacorda and Grasso, Sect. 4.2).

Corporations and others can take actions to mitigate the sanction imposed. Of particular importance, mitigating factors include evidence that the party "took voluntary corrective action or cooperated in the investigation or resolution of the case, including through settlement." Voluntary corrective actions may warrant the greatest sanction reduction: up to 50%. These measures include cessation of the misconduct, remedial actions against responsible individuals, voluntary reform of the entity's compliance program, and restitution of any unjust enrichment. Cooperation may entitle the party to a reduction of up to 33% (Manacorda and Grasso, Sect. 6.10).

The World Bank also has adopted a practice of employing negotiated resolution agreements. NRAs are a form of deferral agreement that freezes the proceedings for a period of time, during which the respondent is required to satisfy certain conditions. This form of agreement appears to be inspired by the deferred prosecution agreements (DPAs) used by the United States. The Bank is less transparent when entering into settlements than when entering into formal resolutions (Manacorda and Grasso, Sect. 6.15).

Finally, consistent with jurisdictions such as the United States, in 2006 the Bank adopted a voluntary disclosure program (VDP) (Manacorda and Grasso, Sect. 6.17). Under this program, the Bank offers a large reward to those who self-report before the Bank starts investigating: entities and individuals that self-report (and otherwise satisfy the requirements of the program) avoid public debarment for disclosed misconduct; their identity also remains confidential. Firms that are accepted under the voluntary disclosure program are not subject to financial sanctions. Interestingly, in recent years, the Bank has started handling self-reporting through NRAs, with conditional nondebarment as the sanction, instead of through the VDP.

Opportunities for Reform and Lessons for Others

The rich and detailed analysis of the Bank's existing system offers insights on approaches that could improve enforcement in many countries, as well as raising questions about features of the World Bank's system that could benefit from reconsideration.

The World Bank's approach to self-reporting (through either VDP or NRAs) has both characteristics. The World Bank's approach to voluntary disclosure is superior to that of many other countries—including the United States—by stating clearly up-front the benefit that a company can get from self-reporting. Questions remain about whether the difference in expected sanctions imposed on firms that do not self-report as compared to those that do self-report is sufficiently great enough to induce self-reporting. The answer may well depend on the degree to which self-reporting would be likely to subject the entity to an enforcement action by a government enforcement authority that does not provide sufficient credit for self-reporting.

In addition, the authors highlight the very important issue of transparency with respect to the outcomes of negotiated settlements. Transparency is important for several reasons. First, it helps ensure consistency in resolutions across similarly situated persons—which is important when wielding the level of threat available to the World Bank (see Arlen 2016). Second, transparency and predictable resolutions are needed to support the World Bank's effort to induce self-reporting. The World Bank must ensure that the benefits available to entities that self-report, cooperate, and remediate are sufficiently greater than those available to entities that merely cooperate and remediate, without self-reporting (see Arlen 2018).

The authors' analysis also raises interesting questions about whether the World Bank could benefit developing countries by expanding the scope of its sanctions regime. The World Bank has targeted its sanctioning policies at bribe payers. It has chosen not to sanction foreign officials who accept bribes, out of respect for the sovereignty of its members and the facts that alternative means of redress are available (Manacorda and Grasso, Sect. 4.1, 2018). Yet given the dearth of enforcement against senior foreign officials in many developing countries, and the deterrence benefits that could be obtained at targeting a powerful sanction such as exclusion directly at individual corrupt foreign officials, it would appear appropriate to reconsider whether exclusion should also be aimed at foreign officials.

Manacorda and Grasso's insightful and in-depth analysis of the existing regime provides readers with the information they need to draw their own conclusions on the merits of these and other potential reforms.

Acknowledgement
I would like to thank Howard Dean for his helpful comments.

New York University School of Law, New York, NY, USA

Program on Corporate Compliance and Enforcement, New York University, New York, NY, USA

Jennifer H. Arlen

References

Alexander, C. R., and Cohen, M. A., 'The Evolution of Corporate Criminal Settlements: An Empirical Perspective on Non-Prosecution, Deferred Prosecution, and Plea Agreements' (2015) 52 *American Criminal Law Review* 537.

Arlen, J., 'Corporate Criminal Liability: Theory and Evidence, Section 1,' in Hylton, K. and Harel, A. (eds), *Research Handbook on Criminal Law* (Edward Elgar 2012).
Arlen, J., 'Prosecuting Beyond the Rule of Law: Corporate Mandates Imposed Through Pretrial Diversion Agreements' (2016) 8 *Journal of Legal Analysis* 191.
Arlen, J. and Kahan, M., 'Corporate Regulation Through Non-Prosecution' (2017) 84 *University of Chicago Law Review* 323.
Arlen, J., 'Corporate Criminal Enforcement in the United States: Using Carrots and Sticks to Turn Corporations from Criminals into Cops,' in Manacorda, S. and Centonze, F. (eds), *Criminalità d'impresa e giustizia negoziata: esperienze a confronto* (Giuffrè 2017).
Greenblum, B. M., 'What Happens to a Prosecution Deferred? Judicial Oversight of Corporate Deferred Prosecution Agreements' (2005) 105 *Columbia Law Review* 1863.

Introduction

The World Bank Group (WBG)[9] represents one of the world's foremost international financial institutions and provides funding for several governments that are its members; it can be considered the leading multilateral development bank (MDB)[10] vastly overshadowing the others. In its fiscal year 2016, the WBG committed US$61 billion in loans, grants, equity investments, and guarantees to its members and private businesses.[11] Such an economic support allows borrowers to carry out projects, which usually involve the procurement of goods, works, and services.

This volume will focus on the sanctions process recently introduced by the World Bank (hereinafter "the Bank"). It can be described as a blacklisting mechanism intended to sanction individuals and entities concerned in the perpetration of some "sanctionable practices," which are essentially comparable to offenses like fraud, corruption, and extortion, in Bank's related projects.

This system represents a new form of sanctioning process developed at the global level in order to impose punitive measures to prevent further corruptive, fraudulent, and

---

[9]The World Bank Group is currently formed by five institutions: the International Bank for Reconstruction and Development (IBRD), the International Development Association (IDA), the International Finance Corporation (IFC), Multilateral Investment Guarantee Agency (MIGA), the International Centre for Settlement of Investment Disputes (ICSID). Strictly speaking, the term "World Bank" refers to the IBRD, which represents the original institution, that was founded on the grounds of the Articles of Agreement negotiated at Bretton Woods in 1944 and opened its doors for business on 25 June 1947. In this work, the term "World Bank" will refer to both the IBRD and the IDA as both institutions use the same procurement procedures.

[10]Multilateral development banks (MDBs) are supranational institutions set up by sovereign states, which are their shareholders. Their primary purpose is to foster economic and social progress in developing countries by financing projects, supporting investment and generating capital. See 'Multilateral Development Banks' (*The European Investment Bank*) <www.eib.org/about/partners/development_banks>.

[11]See 'The World Bank Group Support Tops $61 billion in Fiscal Year 2016' (*The World Bank Group*, Press Release, 12 July 2016) <www.worldbank.org/en/news/press-release/2016/07/12/world-bank-group-support-tops-61-billion-in-fiscal-year-2016>.

other illicit practices from dishonest individual entities. A similar regime has also been developed by the other main MDBs;[12] however, the one adopted within the World Bank's legal framework currently appears to be the most comprehensively developed one.

The World Bank conceived a quasi-judicial process for the purpose, which has currently acquired a considerable significance and represents an innovative instrument to combat corruption and other criminal phenomena at the global level. In particular, the implementation of this sanctions regime appears to be a clear expression of the supranational legal order that is the result of the impossibility of regulating a globalized world[13] relying only on domestic laws.[14]

There is no doubt that we have entered a new era of global governance, which has been fostered by globalization and free trade. As many scholars have argued, these new forms of governance, which rely on new conceptions of political community, representation, and accountability, have somehow left the nation-states behind.[15] The financial crisis of 2008 has encouraged the formulation of new proposals of global governance such as the establishment of an international bankruptcy court, a world financial organization, and an international bank charter. As expressed by Boisson de Chazournes and Fromageau:

> The profile of international organizations has significantly evolved in the last few decades. International organizations have been exposed to new demands, and in response they have developed innovative rules and mechanisms, which in turn have required specific policing measures. These functions include, *inter alia*, regulatory activities and the establishment of compliance and sanctions procedures.[16]

Although its adoption might be considered as innovatory at the international level, sanctions systems related to public procurements have been already adopted at the domestic and supranational levels since many years ago. Such administrative procedures have been developed by public administrations as the key legal tool

---

[12]Traditionally, the MDBs included the World Bank and other four less influential financial institutions operating at the regional level: the African Development Bank (AfDB), the Asian Development Bank (AsDB), the European Bank for Reconstruction and Development (EBRD), and the Inter-American Development Bank (IDB). However, two new MDBs, which are outside the sphere of influence of the WBG, have been recently established: the New Development Bank (NDB) and the Asian Infrastructure Investment Bank (AIIB). The former represents a joint venture among the BRICS countries (Brazil, Russia, India, China, and South Africa), while the latter has been initiated by China and jointly founded by fifty-seven member countries from Asia. See Hongying Wang, 'New Multilateral Development Banks: Opportunities and Challenges for Global Governance' (*Wiley Online Library*, 7 February 2017) <http://onlinelibrary.wiley.com/doi/10.1111/1758-5899.12396/full>.

[13]In this study the term "globalized" refers to the process of economic globalization by which products and capital markets have become increasingly integrated since the Second World War. See Alan Dignam and Michael Galanis, *The Globalization of Corporate Governance* (Ashgate 2009) 90.

[14]See Mireille Delmas-Marty, *Ordering Pluralism: A Conceptual Framework for Understanding the Transnational Legal World* (Naomi Norberg tr, Hart 2009) 20.

[15]See Dani Rodrik, *The Globalization Paradox* (Oxford University Press 2011) 208.

[16]See Laurence Boisson de Chazournes and Edouard Fromageau, 'Balancing the Scales: The World Bank Sanctions Process and Access to Remedies' (2012) 23(4) *European Journal of International Law* 963.

implemented in order to restrain dishonest entities from participating in public procurements and to punish them in case of violation of bids rules. Moreover, the issuance of Transparency International's 2014 volume on combating procurement corruption[17] and of the Organisation for Economic Co-operation and Development's 2016 procurement integrity handbook[18] is emblematic of the importance that, over the course of last years, fighting procurement corruption has acquired also at the international level.

This volume will offer an in-depth analysis of the sanctions system adopted by the Bank with a special focus on the level of defense's rights recognized within its procedure.

In particular, Chap. 1 will include a general introduction to the World Bank's sanctions process, which will outline its structure and the way in which it functions. This chapter will also offer a comprehensive analysis of the reasons on which the World Bank's sanctions process is founded and the multileveled approach it has developed in order to prevent and to fight corruption. Finally, it will analyze the sanctions process from a comparative perspective. In particular, having underlined the crucial role that blacklisting serves in the fight against economic offenses at both the domestic and transnational level, the chapter will present the sanctions systems developed by the other MDBs.

Chapter 2, which deals with the evolution of the World Bank's sanctions process, will provide the historical background to the introduction of the blacklisting mechanism. Then, a clear illustration of the various reforms that have been introduced since the establishment of the formal sanctions regime in 1996 will be offered.

Chapter 3 of the volume will deal with the various sources that the World Bank's judging bodies consult in deciding a case, addressing issues such as the role of internal precedents and the resolution of conflicts between the different regulatory sources. Then, the chapter will turn to a detailed examination of the various procedural phases in which the sanctions process is divided.

A detailed analysis of the various misconducts that can be sanctioned by the World Bank, the so-called sanctionable practices, will be included in Chap. 4. The same chapter will also examine the various types of possible perpetrators (i.e., individuals, firms, and corporate groups) and the criteria for attributing liability.

Chapter 5 will deal with the defense's rights and the rule of evidence. As regards the former, among other things, there will be a particular focus of interest on crucial issues such as the right to evidence disclosure and the right to a hearing. Concerning the latter, the volume will address, inter alia, legal questions like the standard of proof and the shift of the burden of proof, as well as the evidential value of party's silence and the restrictions on respondents' access to evidence.

---

[17]See 'Curbing Corruption in Public Procurement: A Practical Guide' (*Transparency International*, 24 July 2014) <www.transparency.org/whatwedo/publication/curbing_corruption_in_public_procurement_a_practical_guide>.

[18]See 'Integrity Framework for Public Investment' (*OECD*, 29 February 2016) <www.oecd.org/publications/integrity-framework-for-public-investment-9789264251762-en.htm>.

Chapter 6, after an examination of all the types of sanctions that the World Bank may impose, will address the most relevant sentencing practices such as the way in which aggravating and mitigating factors are weighed, the sentencing rationales adopted by the financial institution, and the level of consistency and predictability currently present in its sentencing practices. This chapter will also deal with the role played by corporate compliance systems and the manner in which the World Bank fosters their adoption and monitors their implementation.

The sanctions process has been developed in order to avoid the establishment of commercial relationships between the World Bank and dishonest entities. However, not any illicit conduct perpetrated by a bidder within a Bank-financed project is considered relevant. Indeed, the responsibility of a corporation, as well as of individual persons, may only derive from the perpetration of the five following specific sanctionable practices: corrupt practice, fraudulent practice, collusive practice, coercive practice, and obstructive practice.

As it will be discussed more widely in Chap. 4, these illicit conducts resemble the offenses of corruption, fraud, collusion, coercion, and obstruction of justice provided for by domestic legal orders.

The World Bank has opted to define such practices in an autonomous way, as provided by Article 1.14 of the Guidelines Procurement Under IBRD Loans and IDA Credits:

> In pursuance of this policy, the Bank defines, for the purposes of this provision, the terms set forth below as follows:
>
> (i) 'corrupt practice' is the offering, giving, receiving or soliciting, directly or indirectly, of anything of value to influence improperly the actions of another party;
>
> (ii) 'fraudulent practice' is any act or omission, including a misrepresentation, that knowingly or recklessly misleads, or attempts to mislead, a party to obtain a financial or other benefit or to avoid an obligation;
>
> (iii) 'collusive practice' is an arrangement between two or more parties designed to achieve an improper purpose, including to influence improperly the actions of another party;
>
> (iv) 'coercive practice' is impairing or harming, or threatening to impair or harm, directly or indirectly, any party or the property of the party to influence improperly the actions of a party;
>
> (v) 'obstructive practice' is
>
> (aa) deliberately destroying, falsifying, altering or concealing of evidence material to the investigation or making false statements to investigators in order to materially impede a Bank investigation into allegations of a corrupt, fraudulent, coercive or collusive practice; and/or threatening, harassing or intimidating any party to prevent it from disclosing its knowledge of matters relevant to the investigation or from pursuing the investigation, or
>
> (bb) acts intended to materially impede the exercise of the Bank's inspection and audit rights provided for under par. 1.14 (e) below.[19]

[19]See 'Guidelines Procurement Under IBRD Loans and IDA Credits' (May 2004, revised on 1 October 2006 and 1 May 2010) Article 1.14 <http://pubdocs.worldbank.org/en/828321467230376082/Procurement-GuidelinesEnglishMay2010.pdf>.

These definitions appear conceived in an extensive and unsophisticated way. This, in particular, is in relation to corruption. Indeed, the broad definition given by the WBG can cover a wide range of illicit behaviors like bribery, nepotism, the misallocation of government benefits, and other forms of bureaucratic corruption.[20]

In order to deal with individuals or legal entities involved in the commission of sanctionable practices, the World Bank has developed a substantial arsenal of sanctions, which will be examined in greater detail in Chap. 6. Suffice here to say that the entire sanctions process revolves around a blacklisting mechanism through which the sanctioned party is excluded for a given period of time from the participation in any Bank-financed project.

To this end, the Bank has conceived four types of debarment, which differ depending on the length of the period of exclusion, which can be definite or indefinite, or on the circumstance that certain conditions might be imposed so that if the sanctioned party complies with them, the blacklisting will be avoided (i.e., the conditional nondebarment) or terminated (i.e., the debarment with conditional release).

Debarment represents the main sanction of the World Bank;[21] however, the World Bank might also adopt other types of punitive actions such as a formal letter of reprimand in cases of minor misconduct. In other circumstances, the wrongdoer might be ordered to pay a sum in restitution or to provide other financial remedies to the borrower or to take other actions to remedy the harm done by its misconduct.[22]

The World Bank sanctions process may be described as a quasi-judicial blacklisting mechanism intended to sanction individuals and entities. It is possible to break such a process down into three main parts: the investigation phase, the first tier, and the second tier. Although Chap. 4 of this volume will deal with each of these parts in a detailed way, it follows an outline of the sanctions process functioning.

Where any indicator emerges that a sanctionable practice has occurred in connection with a Bank-financed project, an independent unit within the Bank, the so-called Integrity Vice Presidency (INT), is charged with investigating the related allegations. If, after the investigation, INT believes that there is sufficient evidence that the involved entities have committed a sanctionable practice, it submits a Statement of Accusations and Evidence (SAE) to the competent World Bank official, i.e., the Suspension and Debarment Officer (SDO).[23] Prior to the issuance of the latest Sanctions Procedures in 2016, the SDO was formally called the Evaluation and Suspension Officer (EO).

---

[20]See Sope Williams, 'The Debarment of Corrupt Contractors from World Bank-Financed Contracts' (2007) 36(2) *Public Contract Law Journal* 277, 286.

[21]See Laurence Folliot-Lalliot, 'Introduction to the World Bank's policies in the fight against corruption and conflict of interests in public contracts' in Jean-Bernard Auby, Emmanuel Breen and Thomas Perroud (eds), *Corruption and Conflicts of Interest* (Edward Elgar 2014) 243.

[22]See Anne-Marie Leroy and Frank Fariello, 'The World Bank Group Sanctions Process and Its Recent Reforms' (*World Bank*, 2012) 5 <http://siteresources.worldbank.org/INTLAWJUSTICE/Resources/SanctionsProcess.pdf>.

[23]ibid 4.

Over the course of the investigations, it is possible to apply a sort of precautionary measure, known as temporary suspension. Such measure, which may be requested by INT and imposed by the SDO, consists in a mechanism for suspending the investigated entities or individuals from eligibility during this phase of the process.[24]

The actual sanctions process begins with the first-tier review of the SAE by the SDO, who has to evaluate if the accusations are supported by sufficient evidence. In that case, the SDO recommends an appropriate sanction issuing a Notice of Sanctions Proceedings to the investigated party, who is formally addressed as respondent. Subsequent to the reception of the notice, the respondent may stay silent or contest the SDO's decision filing an explanation with the Bank's official. In the former case, the respondent's silence is considered as equivalent to an implicit acceptance, and consequently the recommended sanction is imposed. On the contrary, in cases where the respondent contests the SDO's determination, the second-tier review of the sanctions process is triggered.[25]

The second-tier review is the phase that more closely matches a judicial proceeding. At that stage, the case is considered *de novo* by a semi-judicial body composed of three Bank staff officers and four non-Bank staff members and chaired by a person appointed among the second group. Differently from the first phase of the proceedings, which is conducted exclusively on the basis of written pleadings, the second-tier review might include hearings.

[24]ibid.

[25]ibid.

Contents

Chapter 1
The World Bank Sanctions System: Historical Overview and Background

1.1 The Emerging Reasons for Fighting Corruption at the World Bank: Protecting Its Own Resources

The adoption of the World Bank sanctions process appears to be grounded on different reasons: the first being the specific Bank's aim of protecting its own resources from possible misuses and the second corresponding to the fight against corrupt and fraudulent activities as part of the World Bank's commitment to reduce poverty and inequality. A third factor, related to the global policy against economic crimes, has recently emerged.

As regards the necessity of protecting the Bank's resources, it is explicitly provided by the Articles of Agreement, which require the institution to make arrangements to ensure that the funds provided by the financial institution are used for their intended purposes. In particular, section 5(b) of Article III of the IBRD Articles of Agreement expressly provides:

> The Bank shall make arrangements to ensure that the proceeds of any loan are used only for the purposes for which the loan was granted, with due attention to considerations of economy and efficiency and without regard to political or other non-economic influences or considerations.[1]

This provision has to be read in conjunction with section 1(a) of the same Article, which defines what the Bank's resources have to be used for. It states that "the resources and the facilities of the Bank shall be used exclusively for the benefit of members with equitable consideration to projects for development and projects for reconstruction alike."[2]

---

[1]See 'IBRD Articles of Agreement' (*World Bank*, 27 June 2012) Article III, 5(b) <http://siteresources.worldbank.org/EXTABOUTUS/Resources/IBRDArticlesOfAgreement_links.pdf>.
[2]ibid Article III, 1(a).

S. Manacorda, C. Grasso, *Fighting Fraud and Corruption at the World Bank*,
https://doi.org/10.1007/978-3-319-73824-6_1

As a result, it is the responsibility of the Bank's staff to ensure that the loans are used only for the purposes for which they are made. The Bank has also to verify that considerations of economy and efficiency are met, but not necessarily through international competitive bidding, and that the resources are utilized without regard to political or other noneconomic influences.[3]

The circumstance that the funds provided by the Bank may be diverted from their original purpose represents a vexed question, which traditionally was related to the possible use of the Bank's resources for military purposes. In order to avoid the assets financed through the loans to be unduly diverted, legal safeguards were progressively introduced in the legal documents of each project (i.e., the Project Agreement). For instance, in some documents, various contractual provisos were included requiring legally binding commitments from the participants to prevent the misuse of assets and facilities funded by the loans.[4]

However, the legal safeguards that may be included in the agreements cannot assure *per se* an absolute protection against any possible misuse of the resources provided by the Bank.[5] As a result, the adoption of a system through which the financial institution might impose sanctions upon individuals and legal entities that use the received funds in a dishonest way, even if working *ex post*, appears to represent a necessary element in the protection of the Bank's resources. In other words, the sanctions process seems to be perfectly aligned to the necessity of making "arrangements to ensure that the proceeds of any loan are used only for the purposes for which the loan was granted," as established by section 5(b) of Article III of the IBRD Articles of Agreement.

1.2 Pursuing the Clear Business Goal

The implementation of the World Bank sanctions process appears also associated with another reason, which is the pressing necessity of fostering clear business operations at the global level. In the recent years, the increasing awareness that to counter poverty it is essential to promote good governance has made the fight against economic crime a major global priority.

Over the course of the last two decades, an essential link between good governance and poverty reduction has clearly emerged. In particular, a certain relationship has been ascertained between firms' performances and elements that may exert an influence on government efficiency such as the effectiveness of the judiciary, the presence of corruption, the quality of the bureaucracy, and tax compliance.[6]

---

[3]See Ibrahim F. I. Shihata, *The World Bank Legal Papers*, (Kluwer Law International 2000) 479.

[4]ibid 481.

[5]See Shihata, *The World Bank Legal Papers* (n 3) 481.

[6]See Rafael La Porta, Florencio Lopez-De-Silanes, Andrei Shleifer, and Robert W. Vishny, 'Trust in Large Organizations' (1996) no. w5864 *National Bureau of Economic Research* 333, 336.

In a major study undertaken by the World Bank's Development Research Group, the effects of several dimensions of governance such as political stability, absence of violence, government effectiveness, regulatory quality, rule of law, and control of corruption were monitored covering 150 countries.[7] The research highlighted the existence of an association between the abovementioned phenomena and three development outcomes: i.e., *per capita* incomes, infant mortality, and adult literacy.[8] In particular, the authors found that improvements in governance bring considerable rewards in terms of development outcomes.[9] Those kinds of researches have raised a growing awareness of the directly proportional relationship existing between weak governance and poverty. This is because the impact of poor standards of governance commonly falls most heavily on the less wealthy social groups, who are generally excluded from the participation in the policy-making process.[10] Establishing rules for sound economic management and adequate economic mechanisms is among the suggested reforms to be implemented in order to improve the quality of life of the indigent people.

The way in which the financial sector intersects with corruption at the global level, as well as the degree of responsibility, which in that regard can be attributed to international institutions such as the World Bank, is still obscure. However, what has emerged with some clarity is that the system through which international financial institutions have traditionally carried out their funding activities, especially in relation to developing countries, appears to be one of the potential problems of the spread of corruption within such communities.[11] There is no doubt that corruption remains a serious issue for the vast majority of the countries to which the Bank issues its loans. This has raised questions about whether the Bank's lending practices have fostered corrupt behaviors and require modification or even regulation.[12] Furthermore, such a situation has been aggravated by the identification of several structural constraints to the adoption of effective anticorruption efforts within the Bank: the operational model, governance structure, oversight capacity, staff and contractor incentive structure, bureaucratic norms, political motivations, and the status of the internal investigative body.[13] Moreover, as it has been argued, with the Bank having

---

[7] See Daniel Kaufmann, Aart Kraay, and Pablo Zoido-Lobatón, 'Governance Matters' (1999) no. 2196 *World Bank Policy Research Working Paper* <http://ssrn.com/abstract=188568>.

[8] ibid 12.

[9] ibid.

[10] See 'Ensuring Good Governance for Poverty Reduction' (*The Poverty Task Force*, 2002) 2 <http://siteresources.worldbank.org/INTVIETNAM/Resources/Localizing-MGDs-for-Poverty5.pdf>.

[11] See Paul Sarlo, 'The Global Financial Crisis and the Transnational Anti-Corruption Regime: A Call for Regulation of the World Bank's Lending Practices' (2014) 45(4) *Georgetown Journal of International Law* 1293, 1296.

[12] ibid 1297.

[13] See Chanda Parthapratim, 'The Effectiveness of the World Bank's Anti-Corruption Efforts: Current Legal and Structural Obstacles and Uncertainties' (2004) 32(2) *Denver Journal of International Law and Policy* 315, 339.

serious conflicts of interest in disciplining its own business activities, an effective transformation should be carried out through persuasion from external sources, like an independent international organization.[14]

In the meantime, the international community—in its effort to improve economic freedoms—has clearly recognized that corruption is no longer a local matter but a transnational criminal phenomenon that affects all societies and economies and that international cooperation to prevent and foil corrupt practices is essential. Emblematic of such an approach is the adoption of several international conventions[15] aimed at combating corrupt behaviors, including the United Nations Convention Against Corruption (UNCAC)[16] and the OECD Convention on Combating Bribery of Foreign Public Officials in International Business Transactions.[17] Similarly, a worldwide drive to combat money laundering has emerged, and the concept of a general global anti-money laundering system has been developed by the Financial Action Task Force (FATF).[18]

---

[14]See Sarlo, 'The Global Financial Crisis and the Transnational Anti-Corruption Regime' (n 11) 1318.

[15]Many multilateral instruments to prevent and combat corruption have been developed including, *inter alia*: the Inter-American Convention against Corruption, adopted by the Organization of American States on 29 March 1996; the Convention on the Fight against Corruption involving Officials of the European Communities or Officials of Member States of the European Union, adopted by the Council of the European Union on 26 May 1997; the Convention on Combating Bribery of Foreign Public Officials in International Business Transactions, adopted by the Organisation for Economic Cooperation and Development on 21 November 1997; the Criminal Law Convention on Corruption, adopted by the Committee of Ministers of the Council of Europe on 27 January 1999; the Civil Law Convention on Corruption, adopted by the Committee of Ministers of the Council of Europe on 4 November 1999; the African Union Convention on Preventing and Combating Corruption, adopted by the Heads of State and Government of the African Union on 12 July 2003.

[16]The UNCAC was adopted by resolution 58/4 of 31 October 2003 and, in accordance with article 68 (1) of resolution 58/4, it entered into force on 14 December 2005. The words that the U.N. Secretary-General Kofi A. Annan wrote about corruption in the Convention foreword appear illustrative of the above-mentioned global attitude of pressure to fight economic crimes: "Corruption is an insidious plague that has a wide range of corrosive effects on societies. It undermines democracy and the rule of law, leads to violations of human rights, distorts markets, erodes the quality of life and allows organized crime, terrorism and other threats to human security to flourish."

[17]The OECD Convention was adopted by the Negotiating Conference on 21 November 1997. It entered into force on 15 February 1999. Currently, 34 OECD member countries and six non-member countries — Argentina, Brazil, Bulgaria, Colombia, Russia, and South Africa — have endorsed it. All countries party to the Convention commit themselves to ensuring that their national parliaments approve the Convention and pass legislation necessary for its ratification and implementation into national law.

[18]This inter-governmental body, which was established in 1989, plays many important roles in the fight against money laundering such as identifying the techniques that are utilised to launder and developing methods to thwart them; setting out global standards by means of the issue of periodically revised recommendations; evaluate the effectiveness of domestic implementation of such standards through a peer review system adopted between member States. See 'The FATF Recommendations' (*FATF*, 2012) <www.fatf-gafi.org/publications/fatfrecommendations/documents/fatf-recommendations.html>.

The identification of the fight against economic crime as a major priority at the international level has made entering into agreements with unethical or otherwise corrupt parties politically unacceptable to governments and international organizations. Such a global uncompromising attitude of contrast has heightened after the recent financial crisis. Indeed, due to the crisis itself and the ensuing austerity, governments have been induced to give urgent priority to the fight against the perpetrators of financial crimes (e.g., corruption and tax evasion).

In any case, the combination of the two abovementioned factors—the awareness that good governance is a key element in reducing poverty and the emergence of a global priority of fighting against economic crime—eventually induced the Bank to work with governments, businesses, and civil society to promote ethical and transparent governmental processes, endorse public accountability, and reduce corruption.

In particular, the first general issue that the financial institution had to address was the necessity of safeguarding the integrity of its contracts. Due to the circumstance that the World Bank loans are provided through formal agreements, safeguarding contract integrity has become one of the primary objectives of the Bank. In fact, those agreements might be affected by several causes that can potentially put their integrity at risk such as the opaqueness of contract award processes and of contract implementation, the secrecy of contracts, and the inherent susceptibility to corruption of the agreements.[19] Specifically, to achieve such an aim, the Bank has developed a multileveled approach, which includes efforts to promote good governance both locally and at the global level, to enhance due diligence of project-implementing entities, and to impose sanctions against malefactors.

1.3 A Multileveled Approach in Fighting Corruption: Promoting Good Governance at the Domestic Level

As regards the promotion of accountable and transparent administrative processes and institutions, the Bank has made a firm commitment to assist governments in their efforts to improve ethical behaviors and effective service delivery. Specifically, the financial institution has focused on two main areas: on the one hand, its activities aim at strengthening public sector management systems within the executive branch, including the management of public finances and public employment; on the other, they have the purpose of improving the broader governance environment within

[19]See 'Strengthening Governance: Tackling Corruption. The World Bank Group's Updated Strategy and Implementation Plan' (*World Bank*, 6 March 2012) 50, para 132 <http://siteresources.worldbank.org/PUBLICSECTORANDGOVERNANCE/Resources/285741-1326816182754/GACStrategyImplementationPlan.pdf>.

which the public sector operates, supporting institutions such as parliaments and offices of the ombudsman for public accountability.[20]

These Bank's efforts fall within the so-called public sector management policy, which the financial institution has adopted to achieve the abovementioned purposes. It consists in improving public sector results by changing the way governments work. In other words, when the Bank arranges a lending in a country, it deliberately tries to change the structures and processes within the public sector. As a matter of fact, they define how financial and physical resources and people are deployed and accounted for.[21] In order to do so, the financial institution uses its economic leverage being by far the largest traditional provider of funds to support public sector management in certain countries.[22]

It has to be mentioned that historically the Bank has not used such an economic leverage neutrally. As a matter of fact, the main policy of the financial institution has traditionally been inspired by the objectives of the so-called Washington Consensus, under which the developed world has relentlessly pushed other countries to embrace free trade. In other words, the development assistance needed by the poor countries was provided subject to the condition that they agreed to adopt a sort of standard package of liberal economic, legal, and political reforms, which include elements like the shrinking of the state, the deregulation and privatization of the economy, and the removal of barriers to free trade.[23] Such an attitude has been criticized by many because although countries in the developed world usually engage in mutually beneficial free trade when their economies achieve similar levels of sophistication and development, where developing countries adopt such policies, they may experience extremely adverse and potentially catastrophic effects. This depends on the fact that frequently the sociopolitical, administrative, and economic structure of these countries, which are characterized by extreme inequality and poverty, is not ready to adopt free trade. Consequently, the adoption of the policies based on the Washington Consensus might cause dramatic events such as the aggravation of the resource curse phenomenon, the decimation of key sectors of the economy, the

[20]See 'Governance and Public Sector Management' (*World Bank*, Public Sector & Governance Board, Poverty Reduction and Economic Management, Data Sheet, 2013) <http://siteresources.worldbank.org/PUBLICSECTORANDGOVERNANCE/Resources/PSGDataSheet.pdf>.

[21]See 'The World Bank's Approach to Public Sector Management 2011-2020: "Better Results from Public Sector Institutions"' (*World Bank*, Public Sector & Governance Board, Poverty Reduction and Economic Management, 3 February 2012) 3 <http://siteresources.worldbank.org/PUBLICSECTORANDGOVERNANCE/Resources/285741-1287520109339/PSM-Approach.pdf>.

[22]The World Bank has a large and influential public sector lending portfolio. Since 1995, the financial institution has approved over 1,500 lending projects with significant public sector components. In FY2010 alone it committed nearly US$3.6 billion to public sector lending. See ibid 5.

[23]See Thomas Kelley, 'Beyond the Washington Consensus and New Institutionalism: What is the Future of Law and Development' (2010) 35(3) *North Carolina Journal of International Law & Commercial Regulation* 539, 542.

movement of crucial financial resources out of the country.[24] Although the financial institution has always strenuously supported its free-trade policies, it appears that it has eventually acknowledged that the growth of global free trade has not been a success for all.[25]

The public sector management reforms[26] are carried out using a new problem-solving approach, which does not rely on the mere introduction of new laws and regulations but is based on a concrete evaluation of the achieved successes demonstrated by outcomes and results.[27]

In order to promote good governance and anticorruption across countries, sectors, and regions in which the Bank carries out its activities, many Bank projects and country programs integrate political economy assessments, risk identification, mitigation measures, stronger controls, and oversight mechanisms.

In particular, one of the measures developed by the Bank is represented by the Operational Risk Management Framework (ORAF), which was introduced in all projects in 2011. It is a system designed to work at the project identification stage in order to weigh trade-offs between expected project results and related financial management risks.[28] The risk template that is prepared with the ORAF is a dynamic product. It consists in an assessment to be conducted by several teams of the Bank so as to include a wide spectrum of risk aspects.[29] Specifically, in order to assess fraud and corruption risk, which is included among the various issues that such an assessment tries to identify,[30] the system uses several indicators both at the country

---

[24]See Ziyad Motala, 'Free Trade, the Washington Consensus, and Bilateral Investment Treaties the South African Journey: A Rethink on the Rules on Foreign Investment by Developing Countries' (2016) 6(1) *American University Business Law Review* 31, 32.

[25]See Kamal Ahmed, 'World Bank admits some have lost out from free trade' (*BBC*, *Bank*, 6 October 2016) <http://www.bbc.co.uk/news/business-37580844>.

[26]See 'Governance and Public Sector Management' (*World Bank*, 2013) (n 20).

[27]In practice, under such a policy, every time the Bank is involved in a new project, its project manager assigns percentage-shares for at least one and up to five themes, which are meant to reflect the goals of Bank activities, and at least one and up to five sectors, which are used to indicate which part of the economy is supported by the Bank's intervention. A thematic classification that has been used under the public sector management policy distinguishes between the following goals: Public Expenditure, Financial Management and Procurement, Civil Service and Administrative Reform, Tax Policy and Administration, Decentralization, Anti-corruption, and Other Public Sector Governance projects. See Jürgen René Blum, 'What predicts how World Bank public sector management projects perform? A review of the World Bank's public sector management portfolio' (*World Bank*, Public Sector & Governance Board, 28 January 2014) 24 <http://siteresources.worldbank.org/PUBLICSECTORANDGOVERNANCE/Resources/285741-1287520109339/PSM-PORTFOLIO-REVIEW-WEB-VERSION-v_f.pdf>.

[28]See 'Reference Material on the Operational Risk Assessment Framework (ORAF)' (*World Bank*, Governance and Anti-Corruption, 28 January 2014) 1 <http://siteresources.worldbank.org/EXTGOVANTICORR/Resources/3035863-1285875404494/100501_QRC_ORAF_FM.pdf>.

[29]ibid.

[30]The assessment covers several types of risk: Stakeholder Risk; Country Risk; Institutional Risk; Capacity Risk; Governance Risk; Fraud & Corruption Risk; Design Risk; Safeguards Risk; Program & Donor Risk; Delivery Quality Risk; and Other Risks. See ibid 2.

and sector levels. Some examples include the repeal of major laws aimed at reducing corruption, the closure of an effective anticorruption agency, the occurrence of major incident of fraud or corruption in a specific sector.[31] Moreover, other indicators denoting corruption vulnerability (e.g., measurement of quality and quantity of outputs, cost inflation, payment delays, and so on) are used within the ORAF.[32]

The Bank also produces detailed political economy analyses for countries, sectors, projects across all regions, which are used to evaluate determined governance risks in a specified geographic area.[33]

In the last decade, the financial institution has also increasingly focused on fostering budget transparency through its lending operations. The statement made in 2011 by the World Bank President, Robert Zoellick, clearly illustrated such a policy:

> We will encourage governments to publish information, enact Freedom of Information Acts, open up their budget and procurement processes, build independent audit functions, and sponsor reforms of justice systems. We will not lend directly to finance budgets in countries that do not publish their budgets or, in exceptional cases, at least commit to publish their budgets within twelve months [. . .] Some of that may be what we think of as politics, but most of it is also what we know is good economics; most of it is what we know is good for fighting corruption; most of it is what we know is good for inclusive and sustainable development.[34]

Another instrument that was developed by the Bank to foster good governance and fight against corruption is represented by the Governance Partnership Facility (GPF), which was specifically designed to respond to the Governance and Anti-Corruption (GAC) strategy implementation plan. It was launched in December 2008 and lasted up to June 2015. The GPF specifically aimed at boosting World Bank staff capacity by funding governance specialist staff positions and providing resources to Bank staff intending to integrate governance into its operations at the country level and into sectors.[35] This policy was carried out through the implementation of several

---

[31]ibid 3.

[32]ibid 5.

[33]See for instance the study related to the "Mauritania Utility Service Reform," in which it was highlighted how the obsolete nature of the legal and regulatory framework in Mauritania was a catalyst for informal practices, corruption, and inefficiency, and that also underlined that legal and regulatory anti-corruption texts were not applied in the country because public officers were unaware of their content or implications, so that an environment that promoted impunity, irresponsibility, and generalized abuse of power had been established. See 'Mauritania: Restarting the Reform Program. Sector Policy Notes' (*World Bank*, Report no. 53241-MR, AFTP4 Africa Region, May 2010) <https://openknowledge.worldbank.org/bitstream/handle/10986/12630/532410ESW0P1180TES0EN0FINAL0July020.pdf?sequence=1&isAllowed=y>.

[34]See 'Citizen Empowerment, Governance Key for Middle East-Zoellick' (*World Bank*, Press Release, 6 April 2011) <http://www.worldbank.org/en/news/press-release/2011/04/06/citizen-empowerment-governance-key-middle-east-zoellick>.

[35]See 'Governance Partnership Facility. Final Report 2009–2015. Results, Lessons, and Legacy' (*World Bank*, GPF, 2016) 2 <http://documents.banquemondiale.org/curated/fr/575891468187475516/pdf/103852-WP-GPFAR14-FINAL-PUBLIC.pdf>.

specific projects, which focused on the governance issues of the related country. To make an example, it is possible to mention the GPF program implemented in Nigeria, with which the Bank pursued various objectives such as the enhancement of transparency and accountability in the financial and oil and gas sectors through the strengthening of the Ministry of Finance's capacity to collect and analyze the related information and the aim of increasing citizens' voice and inclusion into the decision-making process through the development of mechanisms aimed at building social capital, promoting social cohesion, inclusion, and mobilization.[36]

Finally, the Bank has developed a so-called Country Policy and Institutional Assessment (CPIA), through which the financial institution evaluates the conduciveness of a country's strategy and institutional framework to poverty reduction, sustainable growth, and the effective use of development assistance.[37] This assessment, which was initiated by the financial institution in the late 1970s, evaluates the quality of a country's present policy and institutional framework. The CPIA ratings are then used in the lending allocation process and several other Bank corporate activities. The CPIA consists of a set of criteria representing the way in which an effective poverty reduction and growth strategy may be carried out. The criteria have evolved over time, reflecting the numerous lessons learned. In 2004, the Bank appointed an external Panel to review the CPIA scores and methodology. On the basis of the Panel recommendations, some criteria were deleted and others were combined, leading to the adoption of the present 16 criteria. After a revision carried out in 2011 by the World Bank's Independent Evaluation Group,[38] it was concluded that "the CPIA is largely relevant for growth and poverty reduction."[39] The CPIA's 16 criteria are grouped into four categories: economic management, structural policies, policies for social inclusion and equity, and public sector management and institutions.[40] Among them, a specific criterion is devoted to transparency, accountability, and corruption in the public sector (see Fig. 1.1). This criterion assesses the extent to which the executive, legislators, and other high-level officials can be held accountable for their use of funds, administrative decisions, and obtained results. As it is specified in the World Bank Group's document on the CPIA Criteria of 2011:

---

[36]See 'World Bank Governance Partnership Facility Programme' (*UK Aid*, Development Tracker) <https://devtracker.dfid.gov.uk/projects/GB-1-202854>.

[37]See 'The World Bank's Country Policy and Institutional Assessment. An Evaluation' (*World Bank*, Independent Evaluation Group, 2010) xi <http://siteresources.worldbank.org/EXTCPIA/Resources/CPIA_eval.pdf>.

[38]The Independent Evaluation Group evaluates the development effectiveness of the World Bank. It is independent of the Management of the World Bank Group and reports directly to the Executive Board. See 'About IEG' (*World Bank*, Independent Evaluation Group) <http://ieg.worldbankgroup.org/about-us>.

[39]See 'The World Bank's Country Policy and Institutional Assessment' (*World Bank*, 2010) (n 37) xiv.

[40]ibid xi.

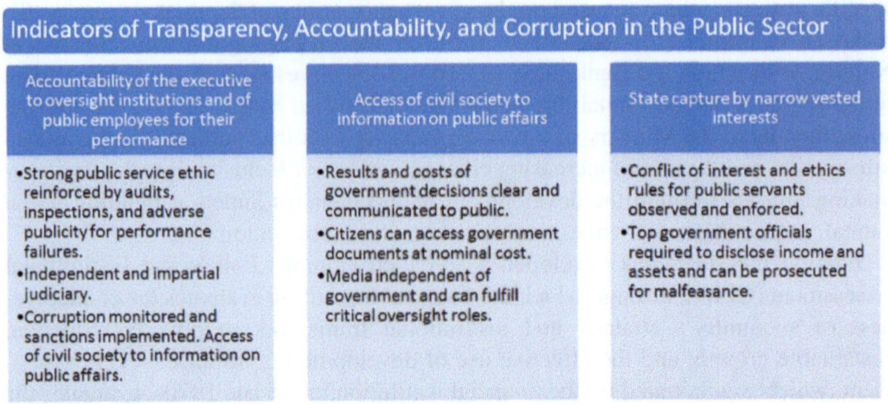

Fig. 1.1 CPIA Indicators for the Presence of Corruption in the Public Sector. *Source*: See 'The World Bank's Country Policy and Institutional Assessment. An Evaluation,' (*World Bank*, Independent Evaluation Group, 2010) 70 <http://siteresources.worldbank.org/EXTCPIA/Resources/CPIA_eval.pdf>

> Accountability is generally enhanced by transparency in decision-making, access to relevant and timely information, public and media scrutiny, and by institutional checks (e.g., inspector general, ombudsman, or independent audit) on the authority of the chief executive. The criterion covers four dimensions: (a) the accountability of the executive and other top officials to effective oversight institutions; (b) access of civil society to timely and reliable information on public affairs and public policies, including fiscal information (on public expenditures, revenues, and large contract awards); (c) state capture by narrow vested interests; and (d) integrity in the management of public resources, including aid and natural resource revenues. Each of four dimensions should be rated separately and national and sub-national government's issues appropriately discussed. For the overall rating, these four dimensions should receive equal weighting.[41]

1.4 Fostering a Collective Action on Global Governance

Another pillar of the global anticorruption strategy developed by the Bank is represented by its initiatives in support of a collective action on global governance. In particular, in December 2010, the World Bank launched the International Corruption Hunters Alliance (ICHA), which is an international initiative to tackle corruption. It is a network formed by more than 350 members of anticorruption enforcement authorities and representatives of international organizations from 130 countries.[42] The participants use this forum to share know-how and experiences

[41]See 'CPIA 2011 Criteria' (*World Bank*, IDA, 15 September 2015) 8 <http://siteresources.worldbank.org/IDA/Resources/73153-1181752621336/CPIAcriteria2011final.pdf>.

[42]See 'Impunity for Corruption. Global Knowledge for Local Impact. Third Biennial Meeting of the World Bank Group's International Corruption Hunters Alliance (ICHA)' (*World Bank*, Conference

in the fight against corruption. During the 2014 ICHA meeting, which was held in Washington, D.C., the session focused on two main objectives: "following the money" to combat the vast illicit outflows that are hampering economic development and poverty reduction and "ending impunity" for corruption through both enforcement and accountability measures.[43] Specifically, the panelists recognized the increasing trends in cross-border bribery and, in order to enhance international cooperation among national authorities, issued the following recommendations:

> Maintain active conversations and relationships with foreign counterparts. Take advantage of resources available under existing legal frameworks—including treaties, global networks, and foreign bribery enforcement actions. Use foreign anti-bribery instruments to help launch their own investigations, step up domestic prosecutions, and engage in settlement discussions or proceedings.[44]

Moreover, a key message endorsed by all the panelists focused on the need for enforcement agencies to enhance investments in prevention activities and strike a better balance with their traditional investigative role. In this regard, in 2015, the ICHA published the results of a survey on the most relevant anticorruption prevention activities that the various agencies commonly engage in (see Fig. 1.2).

The Bank has also supported international programs such as the Stolen Assets Recovery (StAR) Initiative and the Extractive Industries Transparency Initiative (EITI), among others.

The former is an initiative carried out by the Bank in partnership with the United Nations Office on Drugs and Crime (UNODC). It aims at supporting international efforts to eliminate safe havens for corrupt funds. It operates in conjunction with developing countries and financial centers to prevent the laundering of the proceeds of corruption and ease the recovery of stolen assets.[45] In particular, this program includes various activities to enhance asset recovery practices such as organizing workshops and advanced training courses; publishing policy papers, expert guides, and specialized case databases; and providing technical assistance to countries that undertake asset recovery operations.[46] The StAR initiative is based on four main elements: empowerment, partnerships, innovation, and international standards. "Empowerment" consists in assisting countries in establishing the legal tools and institutions required to recover the proceeds of corruption; "Partnerships" aims at creating a permanent forum of discussion dedicated to governments, regulatory authorities, donor agencies, financial institutions, and civil society organizations from both financial centers and developing countries; "Innovation" serves the purpose of generating knowledge on the legal and technical tools available to

---

Report, 10 December 2014) v <http://pubdocs.worldbank.org/en/438751449245488882/ICHA-2014-Report.pdf>.

[43]ibid 10.

[44]ibid 18.

[45]See 'Our-vision' (*World Bank*, Stolen Assets Recovery Initiative) <http://star.worldbank.org/star/about-us/our-vision>.

[46]ibid.

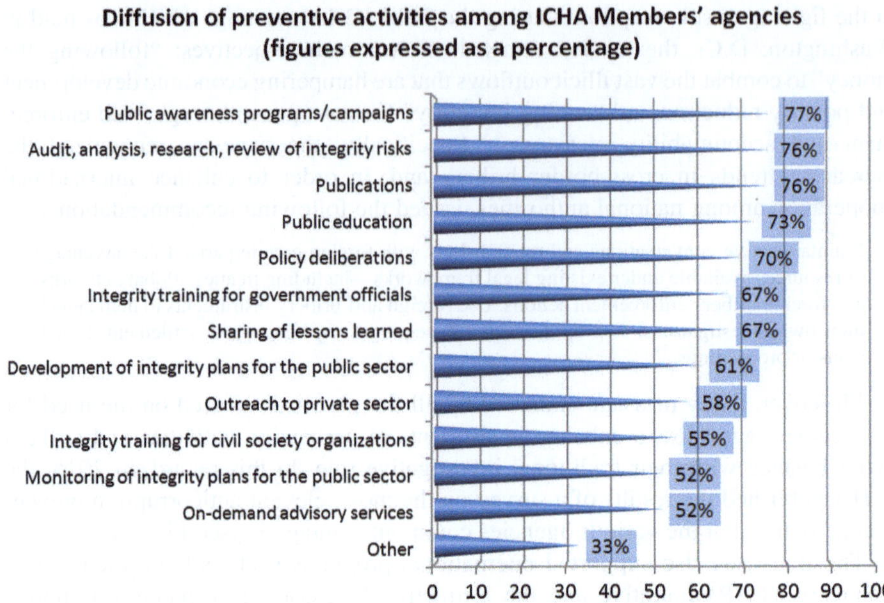

Fig. 1.2 ICHA Members' Corruption Prevention Survey (2014). *Source*: World Bank Group's International Corruption Hunters Alliance. 2015. *Ending Impunity for Corruption: Global Knowledge for Local Impact.* Conference Report of the Third Biennial Meeting of the International Corruption Hunters Alliance, World Bank, Washington, DC, December 8–10, 2014, 67 <http://pubdocs.worldbank.org/en/438751449245488882/ICHA-2014-Report.pdf>. This is an adaptation of an original work by The World Bank. Views and opinions expressed in the adaptation are the sole responsibility of the author or authors of the adaptation and are not endorsed by the World Bank

recover the proceeds of corruption and promoting the sharing of global best practices; the "International Standards" element consists in encouraging the implementation of chapter 5 of the UN Convention Against Corruption and other international standards in the area of anticorruption.[47] In order to pursue such objectives, the World Bank cooperates with other global organizations such as the Conference of States Parties to UNCAC, the G8, the G20, the Organisation for Economic Co-operation and Development (OECD), and the Financial Action Task Force (FATF).[48]

The EITI is a global standard to promote the open and accountable management of natural resources, which aims at resolving burning governance issues in the oil, gas, and mining sectors.[49] This initiative is grounded on twelve fundamental

[47]ibid.

[48]See Emile van der Does de Willebois et al., 'The Puppet Masters – How the Corrupt Use Legal Structures to Hide Stolen Assets and What to Do About It' (*World Bank*, StAR) 2 <http://star.worldbank.org/star/sites/star/files/puppetmastersv1.pdf>.

[49]See 'Who we are' (*EITI*) <https://eiti.org/about/who-we-are>.

principles, many of them aiming at fostering high standards of transparency and accountability.[50] The last EITI standards were issued on February 23, 2016. Those standards are intended to bring greater transparency and accountability to all aspects of natural resource management, including tax transparency, commodity trading, and licensing. They also include disclosure requirements on beneficial ownership, requiring the revelation of the identity of the real owners of the oil, gas, and mining companies operating in the participating countries.[51] The implementation of these standards is based on a voluntary approach encouraged by a reputational risk system. EITI compliant countries must maintain adherence to the program requirements in order to retain the so-called compliant status. The consequences of noncompliance might include suspension or delisting from the program.[52] As of 2016, 44 countries are now implementing the EITI standard and recognized as either EITI compliant or EITI candidate.[53]

1.5 Fighting Corruption Within the Bank-Financed Projects: *Ex Ante* and *Ex Post* Measures. The Sanctions System

The Bank also developed a series of measures that aim at countering corrupt activities directly within its own projects. The Bank's direct focus on corruption in its own funded projects can be traced back to the late 1990s. The circumstance that, at the annual meeting of the Bank and the International Monetary Fund of 1996, the then President of the financial institution, James D. Wolfensohn, declared "we need to deal with the cancer of corruption" is emblematic of the fact that fighting corruption had finally moved to the forefront of the Bank's political agenda.[54] This represented a decisive turnaround on the Bank's management control system policies. As a matter of fact, for a long time, the multinational development bank had turned a blind eye to corrupt practices and avoided influencing the internal affairs of a borrower country.[55] The reasons that lie behind such an abrupt change seems to be related to a growing awareness of the need to tackle corruption to foster

[50]See 'The EITI Principles' (*EITI*) <https://eiti.org/standard/principles>.

[51]See 'The EITI Standard 2016' (*EITI*, 23 February 2016) 8 <https://eiti.org/sites/default/files/documents/english-eiti-standard_0.pdf>.

[52]ibid 34.

[53]For the list of countries, see 'Countries' (*EITI*) <https://eiti.org/countries>.

[54]See Vinay Bhargava, 'Curing the Cancer of Corruption' in Vinay Bhargava (ed), *Global Issues for Global Citizens: An Introduction to Key Development Challenges* (World Bank 2006) 341 <https://openknowledge.worldbank.org/handle/10986/7194>.

[55]See Mariangela Benedetti, 'How Multilateral Development Banks invest corruption in their funded projects' in Jean-Bernard Auby, Emmanuel Breen and Thomas Perroud (eds), *Corruption and Conflicts of Interest* (Edward Elgar 2014) 222.

development. The following excerpt from an article written by Wolfensohn in 1998 supports such a proposition:

> Corruption matters. As international financial institutions, as private individuals and as representatives of the public or private sector, we need to make clear that corruption is not the grease that oils the economy, but the slippery road to cronyism and lost opportunities. Corruption creates a serious risk of marginalization in the global marketplace. It threatens to erode already waning support for development assistance to governments. It jeopardizes private sector investment. It hinders growth. And last but by no means least, it imposes a disproportionately heavy burden on the poor.[56]

In reality, it appears that the adoption of the Bank's anticorruption stance is also closely connected with the circumstance that over the course of the 1990s, globalization and its doctrine of open markets and free trade radically changed the way of conducting international business operations. The globalized economy has created an extremely competitive market environment that inherently requires a trading system characterized by honesty, transparency, and fair dealing.[57]

As the United States General Accounting Office clearly underlined in its Report to Congressional Committees of 2000, there are several reasons why the World Bank's projects expose the financial institution to considerable risks of corruption:

> Many borrowers lack well-functioning public management systems; accountable organizations; and a strong legal framework to prevent, detect, and redress corruption.[58]

The substantial corruption risk that the Bank constantly faces appears also to be connected with the information asymmetry existing between the financial institution and the countries in which its projects are implemented. Such an issue can be effectively explained in terms of corporate governance through the agency cost theory.[59] As a matter of fact, serious problems can arise where there is information asymmetry between the principal, which is the Bank, and its agents, which are the

---

[56]See James D. Wolfensohn, 'Corruption impedes development--and hurts the poor' (1998) 25 (4) *International Journal of Government Auditing* 1.

[57]See Costantino Grasso, 'The Dark Side of Power: Corruption and Bribery within the Energy Sector' in Rafael Leal-Arcas and Jan Wouters (eds), *Research Handbook on EU Energy Law and Policy* (Edward Elgar 2014) 242.

[58]See 'World Bank – Management Controls Stronger, but Challenges in Fighting Corruption Remain' (*United States General Accounting Office*, Report to Congressional Committees, April 2000) 16 <www.gao.gov/new.items/ns00073.pdf>.

[59]The agency cost theory is based on the concept of agency relationships, which may be defined as a contract under which a person (the principal) engages another person (the agent) to perform some services on his/her behalf, which involve delegating decision making authority to the agent. The cornerstone of the agency theory is the assumption that the interests of principles and agents diverge. If both parties to the relationship are utility maximizers, there is good reason to believe that the agent will not always act in the best interests of the principal. Consequently, the principal can limit divergences from his/her interest by establishing appropriate incentives for the agent and by incurring monitoring costs designed to limit the aberrant activities of the agent. The agency costs may be defined as the sum of all the costs and the residual loss due to this agency relationships. See Michael C. Jensen and William H. Meckling, 'Theory of The Firm: Managerial Behavior, Agency Costs and Ownership Structure' (1976) 3 *Journal of Financial Economics* 305.

borrowers to whom the implementation of the Bank-funded projects is delegated.[60] In other words, the Bank's attempts to curb corruption within its projects may be rendered ineffective by such an information gap. In order to solve such an issue, the Bank has recently introduced the "Project Procurement Strategy for Development," which includes a full scan of the involved countries and their entire environment (the so-called Political, Economic, Social, Technology, Legislative and Environment Analysis.)[61]

Among the anticorruption measures developed by the Bank directly within its own funded projects, it is possible to distinguish between the ones that operate *ex ante,* having a mainly preventive function, and the ones that are applied *ex post*, which are represented by the sanctions that the Bank might impose through its sanctions process.

As regards the former, the fundamental rule applicable to every project is that it is the borrower that is responsible for the procurement under a World Bank loan, not the financial institution itself. As a result, in the procurement process, the Bank plays a merely supportive role, which is performed through the issuance of its guidelines, the offering of training sessions, and the assistance that its staff provides to borrowers. This can be considered at the same time a fiduciary and a partnering role.[62]

As it has been already mentioned, such a fiduciary responsibility, which consists in ensuring that the proceeds of the World Bank financed loans are used only for their intended purposes with "due attention to economy and efficiency and without regard to political and other non-economic influences and considerations," is expressly provided by the Articles of Agreement of the International Bank for Reconstruction and Development.[63] In order to fulfill this responsibility, the financial institution supervises how the borrowers use the provided funds to procure goods, works, and services.[64] Consequently, while the responsibility for procurement remains firmly with the borrowers, the Bank's staff has only to perform a fiduciary, advisory, and supervisory role to ensure that all procurements are carried out in compliance with the Bank's policy.[65]

It is possible to mention the following list of activities carried out by the Bank to that end: assessing the borrowers and implementing agencies' procurement capacity, requiring appropriate procurement plans for each project before procurement commencement, providing guidance to borrowers to assist them in ensuring the respect

---

[60]See Haider A. Khan, 'Corporate Governance of Family Businesses in Asia: What's Right and What's Wrong?' (*Asian Development Bank*, ADBI Research Papers, 1999) 15 <https://www.adb.org/sites/default/files/publication/157212/adbi-rp3.pdf>.

[61]See *infra* notes 83–87 and accompanying text.

[62]See 'Bank-Financed Procurement Manual – July 2001 Draft – Procurement Policy and Services Group Operations Policy and Country Services VPU' (*World Bank*, 29 January 2003) <http://siteresources.worldbank.org/PROCUREMENT/Resources/pm7-3-01.pdf>.

[63]See 'IBRD Articles of Agreement' (n 1) Article III, section 5(b).

[64]See 'Bank-Financed Procurement Manual' (n 62) 1.

[65]ibid 253, para 26.3.

of its policy, and supervising project implementation by means of on-the-spot checks, prior and post reviews, and audit processes.[66]

As regards the prior and post reviews of the various procurement documents stipulated under the loan agreement, such a procedure aims at ensuring that the resources provided by the financial institution are not diverted from their intended purposes. As specified in the loan agreement, the procurement procedures have to be "followed in letter and spirit before the Bank commits funds for the relevant goods, works or services."[67] The positive outcome of the reviews leads to a "no-objection" letter issued by the Bank, as well as to the carrying out of procurement capacity assessments of the borrower and implementing agency.[68] Where a borrower is awarded a contract after the issuance of the "no-objection" letter, the Bank does not commonly declare misprocurement[69] unless the letter was issued on the basis of incomplete, inaccurate, or misleading information furnished by the borrower.[70]

The supervisory role is carried out through the monitoring of the borrower's procurement planning and implementation. In such a way, the Bank aims at ensuring and enforcing compliance with its policies and legal agreements.

There emerges an inherent tension between the Bank's dual supervisory and advisory role. As a matter of fact, these two activities might be easily inspired by completely different, if not divergent, attitudes and priorities: while in conducting the supervisory role the Bank's staff has to put under audit process the borrowers' performance, in exercising the advisory role the Bank's personnel should concentrate on assisting the borrowers.[71]

The Bank has also developed project measures specifically designed to mitigate procurement risks. Although project risk management is usually considered in geopolitical and financial terms so that it falls outside the area of procurement, it is possible to identify some specific risks, the so-called nonconventional risks, that directly affect the procurement process.[72] Such risks include potentially damaging circumstances, which can cause severe disruptions to project procurement plans determining, for instance, delays in project implementation, slower disbursements, higher commitment fees for borrowers, and a less satisfactory project performance. To make same examples, it is possible to mention the presence of ambiguities about procurement liabilities in the administration of projects, the absence of sound

---

[66] ibid 7, para 3.1.

[67] ibid 171, para 20.1.

[68] ibid 15, para 4.1.

[69] As provided by the IBRD General Conditions for Loans: "At any time, the Bank determines that the procurement of any contract [. . .] is inconsistent with the procedures set forth or referred to in the Legal Agreements [. . .] the Bank may, by notice to the Loan Parties, terminate the right of the Borrower to make withdrawals with respect to such amount. Upon the giving of such notice, such amount shall be cancelled." See 'IBRD, General Conditions for Loans' (*IBRD*, 12 March 2012) <http://siteresources.worldbank.org/INTLAWJUSTICE/Resources/IBRD_GC_English_12.pdf>.

[70] See 'Bank-Financed Procurement Manual' (n 62) 25.

[71] ibid 27.

[72] ibid 69.

procurement practices, the lack of experience or capacity in implementing agencies to handle the procurement process, and the inclination for corruption in the selection and management of contractors.[73] To minimize those "nonconventional" risks, the World Bank has developed a series of measures that include the insertion of a distinct section on procurement in the project manual, the preparation of standard bidding documents, the appointment of experienced contractors to prepare project design, the appointment of experienced procurement agents to assist the implementing agencies, the execution of robust postreview of contracts, and the arrangement of sound procurement audits.[74]

During the initial phase of the procurement process, the World Bank requires borrowers to conduct an extensive bid examination. It is an extremely delicate phase because it is at this point that the procedure can be most easily manipulated to favor a particular bidder at the expense of others in an illicit way. This also represents a neuralgic point of the entire due diligence system developed by the Bank. As it has been argued, the World Bank could minimize the misappropriation of its funds and the need for sanctions if, instead of requiring borrowing countries to perform their own due diligence, it performed by itself such fundamental activities in an autonomous and independent way.[75]

To conduct such an assessment, the borrowers must appoint a Bid Evaluation Committee, which does not need to be approved by the Bank, taking into due consideration the specificity of the procurement.[76] In particular, this examination begins during the public bid opening with a preliminary assessment of the bids. It aims at determining whether the bids meet the general procedural requirements provided by the related documents and eliminating any bid that does not meet the minimum standards of acceptability as established under the same documents.[77]

A bid can be qualified as "substantially responsive" only where it complies with the terms, conditions, and specifications in the bidding documents without material deviations, reservations, or omissions.[78]

After the preliminary phase, the "substantially responsive" bids are assessed again in order to allow the selection of the bidder that not only complies with the technical requirements in bidding documents but also offers the borrower the lowest price. During such an evaluation phase, the Bank's policies expressly require the borrower to strictly adhere to the following principles: "ensure that the bid evaluation process is strictly confidential; reject any attempts or pressure to distort the outcome of the evaluation; reject any proposed action likely to lead to fraud and

[73]ibid.

[74]ibid 70.

[75]See Sarlo, 'The Global Financial Crisis and the Transnational Anti-Corruption Regime' (n 11) 1299.

[76]See 'Bank-Financed Procurement Manual' (n 62) 133.

[77]ibid 134.

[78]ibid 135.

corruption; comply with the Bank's prior review requirements; and strictly apply only the evaluation and qualification criteria specified in the bidding documents."[79]

As regards its internal dimension, the Bank has also arranged an accreditation mechanism for its staff through which the Procurement Board certifies that a particular individual is qualified to perform the procurement functions for which he or she is being accredited. Specifically, the financial institution aims at assuring that its employees are capable of applying the Bank's rules, policies, and procedures to the full range of its procurements.[80]

The creation of an Internal Audit Department (IAD) represents another measure that the Bank has developed in order to mitigate procurement risks. It performs routine audits of its procurement activities to assess if the necessary standards and criteria given in the guidelines and procurement directives are met. This department has also to verify if the integrity of the Bank's procurement system is maintained.[81] Although the World Bank established its internal audit procedures several years ago, up to the end of 1990s such controls were criticized for being weak. Specifically, as it has been argued, the audit process was focused on administrative compliance issues rather than on determining whether the resources allocated through the projects were used for the established purposes.[82]

Since July 2016, the Bank has been implementing a new "Procurement Framework." Under such a new framework, all procurement actions are governed by a determined set of principles,[83] which include, *inter alia*, integrity:

> The principle of integrity refers to the use of funds, resources, assets, and authority according to the intended purposes and in a manner that is well informed, aligned with the public interest, and aligned with broader principles of good governance. The Bank therefore requires that all parties involved in the Procurement Process, [...] observe the highest standard of ethics during the Procurement Process of Bank-financed contracts, and refrain from fraud and corruption, as that term is defined in the Anti-Corruption Guidelines.[84]

According to the new procurement framework, the Bank's assessment will take into consideration several operational factors that may affect the procurement approach, the motivation of bidders to participate, and the success of any subsequent contracts. Among them, a special focus is given to "governance aspects," which are described as follows:

---

[79] ibid.

[80] ibid 13.

[81] ibid.

[82] See Jeffrey A. Winters, 'Criminal Debt' in Jonathan R. Pincus and Jeffrey A. Winters (eds), *Reinventing the World Bank* (Cornell University Press 2002) 124.

[83] The principles are: value for money; economy; integrity; fit for purpose; efficiency; transparency; and fairness. See 'Procurement in IPF and Other Operational Procurement Matters' (*World Bank*, Policies and Procedures, 28 June 2016) 4 <https://policies.worldbank.org/sites/ppf3/PPFDocuments/Forms/DispPage.aspx?docid=4002&ver=current>.

[84] ibid.

Fig. 1.3 PESTLE analysis—operational context factors. *Source*: 'Project Procurement Strategy for Development – Long Form Detailed Guidance' (© *World Bank*, July 2016) 12 <http://pubdocs.worldbank.org/en/847531467334322069/PPSD-Long-Form.pdf>, License: Creative Commons Attribution license (CC BY 3.0 IGO) <https://creativecommons.org/licenses/by/3.0/igo/>

> Fragile or conflict-affected situations that may raise security concerns; state involvement in the specific economic sector (such as state owned enterprises receiving government subsidies), legislative processes that may regulate the market/bidders; the overall legal framework; and disaster or emergency situations.[85]

Such assessment is carried out utilizing different methodologies and, in particular, by means of the so-called Political, Economic, Social, Technology, Legislative and Environment (PESTLE) Analysis (see Fig. 1.3). It is an examination of the borrower's operating and business environmental influences, as well as their direct and indirect effects. PESTLE aims at providing information and "intelligence" to guide the overall design of the procurement approach.[86]

As it has been illustrated, the Bank's approach to fighting corruption "combines a proactive policy of anticipating and avoiding risks in its own projects with a commitment to helping clients and stakeholders identify and combat corruption at national and international levels."[87]

Finally, the financial institution has developed specific measures that aim at countering corrupt activities within its own projects *ex post*, that means after that

---

[85]See 'Project Procurement Strategy for Development – Long Form Detailed Guidance' (*World Bank*, July 2016) 11 <http://pubdocs.worldbank.org/en/847531467334322069/PPSD-Long-Form.pdf>.

[86]See ibid Annex II, at page 113.

[87]See 'Combating Corruption' (*World Bank*, 11 May 2017) <http://www.worldbank.org/en/topic/governance/brief/anti-corruption>.

the perpetration of such illegal activities has occurred. These measures are represented by the sanctions that the Bank might impose through its sanctions process, to which this volume is mainly devoted. As a matter of fact, in the latest years, the Bank's investigating body, i.e. the Integrity Vice Presidency (INT), has specifically dedicated the vast majority of its investigative, preventive, and forensic resources to reducing the risk of corrupt and fraudulent activities in Bank-financed projects. Suffice here to say that, only in 2015, the World Bank sanctioned 71 entities, 65 of which were debarred and prevented from participating in future Bank-financed projects for periods ranging from 6 months to 13 years.[88]

In conclusion, within such a multifaceted scenario, it is possible to affirm that the Bank sanctions process represents the essential closing clause of a complex strategy that the financial institution has developed in order to fight the criminal phenomenon of corruption. The following chapters will focus on an in-depth analysis of this system.

1.6 The Other MDBs' Sanction Systems

The development of a sanction process is not a feature unique to World Bank as similar regimes have been developed by other main multilateral development banks (MDBs). Although it is beyond the scope of this volume to analyze these systems in a comprehensive way, it follows a brief description of the most relevant ones.

The European Bank for Reconstruction and Development (EBRD)[89] has developed a specific enforcement policy and a related set of procedures (EPPs) aiming at combating fraud and corruption in EBRD-financed projects and, in particular, at sanctioning individuals or entities involved in the so-called prohibited practices. The prohibited conducts are corrupt, fraudulent, coercive, collusive, obstructive practices; theft; and misuse of EBRD's resources.[90] According to the EBRD website, the financial institution has conceived its own definitions of fraud and corruption. While fraud is defined as "the deliberate use of deception to secure an advantage," the

[88]See 'The World Bank Group Integrity Vice Presidency – Annual Update – Fiscal Year 2015' (*World Bank*, Publications) 2 <http://pubdocs.worldbank.org/en/136451449168835691/INT-FY15-Annual-Update.pdf>.

[89]The European Bank for Reconstruction and Development (EBRD) was established in 1991 by an agreement signed by the participating government to create a new post-Cold War era in central and eastern Europe, furthering progress towards "market-oriented economies and the promotion of private and entrepreneurial initiative." It is currently owned by 65 countries from five continents, as well as the European Union and the European Investment Bank. See 'Who we are' (*European Bank for Reconstruction and Development*) <www.ebrd.com/who-we-are.html>.

[90]See 'Prohibited Practices Guidelines for EBRD Operations' (*European Bank for Reconstruction and Development*, Integrity and compliance, February 2016) <www.ebrd.com/integrity-and-compliance.html>.

notion of corruption "involves the abuse of public or individual office for personal profit."[91] The procedure of the EBDR's "Enforcement Proceedings" may be summarized as follows. When a suspected prohibited practice is reported, the Chief Compliance Officer (CCO) is in charge of the investigations. If the CCO determines that there is sufficient evidence to support findings that, more likely than not, the suspected prohibited practice was committed, he or she may submit a "Notice of Prohibited Practice" to the Enforcement Commissioner.[92] Consequently, the Enforcement Commissioner, who is the first-tier decision maker of enforcement proceedings,[93] may ask the CCO to supplement the draft Notice, to provide additional information and/or clarification on certain matters and/or consider other prohibited practices.[94] If the Enforcement Commissioner makes a *prima facie* determination that the evidence is not sufficient, the case is dismissed but the CCO may appeal against such determination.[95] Alternatively, if the Enforcement Commissioner considers the evidence as sufficient, he or she commences the enforcement proceedings issuing a "Notice of Prohibited Practice" to the involved party.[96] The concerned party (so-called respondent) may submit a "Response to the Notice of Prohibited Practice," which may include counterarguments and/or written evidence in response to the material provided in the Notice.[97] The procedures also provide for a CCO's "Reply,"[98] as well as the possibility for additional submissions.[99] Upon consideration of all the materials collected, which are expressly evaluated without the application of any formal rule of evidence,[100] the Enforcement Commissioner issues his or her decision.[101] Both the respondent and the CCO may present an "Appeal" against this decision, which triggers the second tier of the EBRD's sanctions process.[102] The appeal is received by the Enforcement Committee, which consists of three external and two internal members, the latter selected from among senior staff members of the Bank.[103] At any time during the course of the

[91]See 'Investigating fraud and corruption' (*European Bank for Reconstruction and Development*) <http://www.ebrd.com/who-we-are/our-values/investigating-fraud-and-corruption.html>.

[92]See 'Enforcement Policy and Procedures – The mechanism to combat fraud and corruption in EBRD projects' (*European Bank for Reconstruction and Development*, Integrity and compliance, November 2015) s 4.2 <www.ebrd.com/integrity-and-compliance.html>.

[93]ibid s 4.1.

[94]ibid s 5.1(ii).

[95]ibid s 5.1(iii).

[96]ibid s 5.1(i).

[97]ibid s 6.1.

[98]ibid s 6.2.

[99]ibid s 6.3.

[100]ibid s 6.4(iii).

[101]ibid s 6.6(i).

[102]The appeal automatically suspends the eligibility of the Respondent and any of its affiliates to become a EBRD Counterparty. See ibid s 6.8(iii).

[103]See 'Enforcement Policy and Procedures' (*European Bank for Reconstruction and Development*) (n 92) s 7.2.

appeal, the Committee may, as a matter of discretion, authorize the parties to submit additional evidence.[104] Although informal hearings might also be authorized by the Committee, the procedures expressly provide that "there shall be no live witness testimony."[105] Section 11.2 of the procedures lists all the "enforcement actions" (i.e., sanctions) that can be included in the final decision: rejection of a proposal for award of contract, cancelation of a portion of Bank finance allocated to a respondent, formal letter of censure, debarment, conditional nondebarment, debarment with conditional release, restitution.[106] The EBRD also publishes on its website a list of all the ineligible entities with the related debarment periods.[107]

Within the African Development Bank's (AfDB)[108] operations and activities, the investigations into allegations of "Sanctionable Practices" (i.e., fraud, corruption, collusion, coercion, and obstruction)[109] are carried out by the Investigation Division of the Integrity and Anti-Corruption Department (IACD).[110] The sanctions procedures establish that the IACD submits the "Findings of Sanctionable Practices" to the Sanctions Office, which represents the first tier of the sanctions procedure and is headed by a Sanctions Commissioner.[111] If the Sanctions Commissioner determines that the findings support a *prima facie* conclusion that the involved party (so-called respondent) has engaged in a sanctionable practice, a "Notice of Sanctions Proceedings" is issued to the respondent.[112] Then the respondent may, within 60 days of receipt of the Notice, submit a "Response" to the Sanctions Commissioner contesting the findings.[113] No later than 30 days after the receipt of the respondent's Response, the Sanctions Commissioner has to take a Sanctions

---

[104]ibid s 8.5.

[105]ibid s 8.6(vi).

[106]ibid s 11.2.

[107]See 'Ineligible entities' (*European Bank for Reconstruction and Development*) <www.ebrd.com/ineligible-entities.html>.

[108]The African Development Bank is a regional multilateral development bank, engaged in promoting the economic and social development of its Regional Member Countries. It was founded in 1964 and is constituted by the African Development Bank (ADB), the African Development Fund (ADF) and the Nigeria Trust Fund (NTF). Its shareholders currently include 54 African countries and 27 non-African countries. See 'Corporate Information' (*African Development Bank*) <www.afdb.org/en/about-us/corporate-information>.

[109]See 'Sanctions Procedures of the African Development Bank Group' (*African Development Bank*, 18 November 2014) Part A, s 4.2 <www.afdb.org/fileadmin/uploads/afdb/Documents/Generic-Documents/AfDB_Sanctions_Procedures_-_November_2014.pdf>.

[110]See 'Annual Report 2014 – Integrity and Anti-corruption Department' (*African Development Bank*) 4 <https://www.afdb.org/fileadmin/uploads/afdb/Documents/Generic-Documents/IACD_-_2014_Annual_Report_En.pdf>.

[111]See 'Sanctions Procedures' (*African Development Bank*) (n 109) Part A, ss 3.1 and 3.2.

[112]ibid Part A, s 5.4.

[113]ibid Part A, s 5.6. It has to be underlined that, under section 5.13 of the procedures, it is expressly provided that "where the Respondent fails to submit a Response within the deadline provided in section 5.6 of these Sanctions Procedures, the allegations in the Notice will be deemed to be uncontested. The Sanctions Commissioner then imposes a sanction from the list of sanctions."

Decision determining whether or not a preponderance of the evidence supports findings that the respondent has engaged in a sanctionable practice.[114] If new evidence emerges that IACD could not have discovered following a diligent search prior to the determination made by the Sanctions Commissioner, the investigating body can submit to the same Commissioner a request for revision, which triggers a sort of renewal of the first-tier process.[115] However, only the respondent may present, within 25 days of receipt of the Sanctions Decision, an "Appeal of the Sanctions Decision" to the Appeals Board.[116] The Board includes three members: one internal member selected from among senior staff members of the Bank and two external experts.[117] The procedures clarify that the Appeals Board shall make its "Final Decision" on the basis of the written record and that the parties have no right to an oral hearing; however, the Board might in its discretion hold hearings as it deems appropriate.[118] If the Appeals Board finds that a preponderance of the evidence supports findings that the respondent engaged in a sanctionable practice, it imposes a sanction on the respondent.[119] The sanctions procedures include the following list of sanctions: letter of reprimand, conditional nondebarment, debarment, debarment with conditional release, permanent debarment, restitution and/or remedy.[120] Moreover, it is provided that in a Sanctions Decision or a Final Decision, it is possible to impose "other Sanctions" of unspecified nature that may include, for instance, the reimbursement of the costs associated with investigations and proceedings.[121] The names of the individuals and firms sanctioned by the AfDB or by signatories to the Agreement for Mutual Enforcement of Debarment Decisions are made publically available on the Bank's website.[122]

A sanctions process has been established also by the Asian Development Bank (AsDB).[123] It is a process for dealing with allegations of "integrity violations" involving bidders, consultants, contractors, suppliers, or other third parties in AsDB-related activities.[124] In 2015, the AsDB has received 258 complaints, opened

---

[114]ibid Part A, s 5.7.

[115]ibid Part A, s 5.8.

[116]ibid Part A, s 8.1.

[117]ibid Part A, s 3.3.

[118]ibid Part A, s 8.8.

[119]ibid Part A, s 10.4.

[120]ibid Part A, s 11.2.

[121]ibid Part A, s 11.2(g).

[122]See 'Debarment and Sanctions Procedures' (*African Development Bank*) <www.afdb.org/en/projects-and-operations/procurement/debarment-and-sanctions-procedures>.

[123]The Asian Development Bank (AsDB) has been founded in 1966 and headquartered in the Philippines capital of Manila. From 31 members at its establishment, the AsDB has grown to encompass 67 countries, 48 of which are from within Asia. See 'Who we are' (*Asian Development Bank*) <www.adb.org/about/main>.

[124]See 'Anticorruption and Integrity: Investigations' (*Asian Development Bank*) <www.adb.org/site/integrity/investigations>.

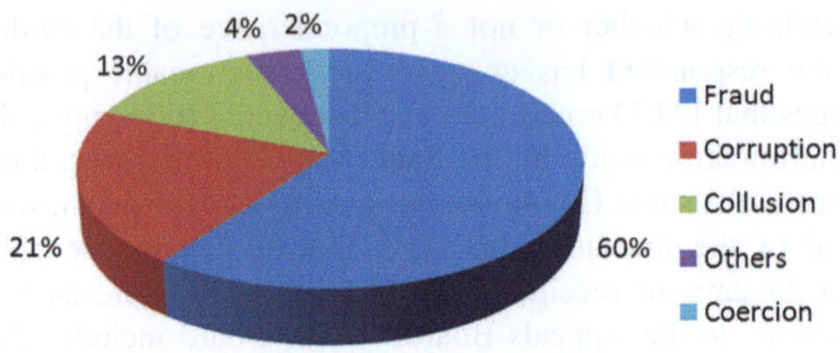

Fig. 1.4 Asian Development Bank: Types of Integrity Violations Investigated in 2015 (figures expressed in percentage). *Source*: 'Office of Anticorruption and Integrity: Annual Report 2015' (© *Asian Development Bank*) v <www.adb.org/documents/office-anticorruption-and-integrity-annual-report-2015>. License: Creative Commons Attribution license (CC BY 3.0 IGO) <https://creativecommons.org/licenses/by/3.0/igo/>. Please note that changes were made to the original image

120 investigations, and sanctioned 49 firms, as well as 40 individuals.[125] The vast majority of these cases were related to the perpetration of fraudulent practices (see Fig. 1.4). The AsDB's Office of Anticorruption and Integrity (OAI) is in charge of the investigations. Specifically, when a complaint is received, the OAI assesses it, determining whether or not it is within its mandate, credible, verifiable, and material. Only complaints that meet all four criteria are converted into full investigations.[126] The AsDB's definition of "integrity violations" involves any act that violates its anticorruption policy, including corrupt practice, fraudulent practice, coercive practice, collusive practice, abuse, conflict of interest, obstructive practice, violations of sanctions, retaliation against whistle-blowers or witnesses, and other unspecified violations of the AsDB's anticorruption policy, including failure to adhere to the highest ethical standards.[127] If the results of an investigation indicate that any party committed an integrity violation, the OAI will take all reasonable steps to present its findings to the involved party, allowing an opportunity to respond.[128] In particular, the OAI may include in the findings letters a proposed sanctions. Then the party is given a reasonable period to respond, which generally shall be no less than 30 calendar days.[129] The AsDB's sanction guidelines expressly provide that if a party fails to respond, the "OAI shall draw an adverse inference from such refusal or failure, and this refusal or failure shall be considered as an aggravating circumstance."[130] Where the party disputes the findings or proposed sanction, the OAI has to bring the

[125]ibid.

[126]ibid.

[127]See 'Integrity Violations' (*Asian Development Bank*) <www.adb.org/site/integrity/integrity-violations>.

[128]See 'Office of Anticorruption and Integrity – Integrity Principles and Guidelines (2015)' (*Asian Development Bank*) para 55 <www.adb.org/sites/default/files/institutional-document/32131/integrity-principles-guidelines.pdf>.

[129]ibid para 63.

[130]ibid para 66.

case before the Integrity Oversight Committee (IOC), which is formed by three voting members, one of whom shall be a reputable external non-AsDB staff.[131] Although the majority of IOC members are internal, the procedures try to compensate such an issue of reduced independency of the judging body by means of a quite articulated voting procedure. Specifically, it is provided that where the external member's vote is not part of the majority decision, a new meeting shall be called, involving the three members that initially discussed the case, plus an additional internal member, as well as an additional external member. At such second IOC meeting, the decision shall be by majority vote.[132] Within 90 days, the sanctioned party may propose appeal against the IOC's decision before the Sanction Appeals Committee.[133] This appellate body consists of two or three AsDB's vice presidents, depending upon the nature of the case and the length of the sanction.[134] In this case, the procedures provide that the Bank's secretariat has to ensure that the members of the Committee do not have any conflict of interest when considering the appeal.[135] The Sanction Appeals Committee should reach its decision only on the basis of a consensus of all members.[136] These decisions are considered as final, binding, and not subject to further appeal.[137] The AsDB has developed a range of sanctions that includes debarment, debarment with conditional reinstatement, conditional nondebarment, reprimand, restitution and/or remedy, and caution.[138] Although the access to the full list of entities sanctioned by the AsDB is restricted, the Bank publishes on its website a list containing only the names of entities who violated the sanctions while ineligible, who committed second and subsequent violations, or who resulted not contactable.[139]

The last blacklisting mechanism that will be examined is the one developed by the Inter-American Development Bank (IDB).[140] The IDB Group prohibits the following five "Prohibited Practices": corrupt practice, fraudulent practice, coercive

[131]ibid para 69.

[132]ibid.

[133]ibid para 96.

[134]ibid para 99.

[135]ibid.

[136]ibid para 100.

[137]ibid para 101.

[138]ibid paras 79, 86.

[139]The list includes also the names of cross-debarred entities. See 'Published List' (*Asian Development Bank*, Anticorruption and Integrity) <http://lnadbg4.adb.org/oga0009p.nsf/sancALLPublic?OpenView&count=999>.

[140]The Inter-American Development Bank (IDB), which was established in 1959 as a partnership between 19 Latin American countries and the United States, represents the leading source of development financing for Latin America and the Caribbean. Its shareholders currently include 48 member countries, 22 of which are non-regional members. See 'How Are We Organized' (*Inter-American Development Bank*) <http://www.iadb.org/en/about-us/how-the-inter-american-development-bank-is-organized,5998.html>.

practice, collusive practice, and obstructive practice.[141] The Office of Institutional Integrity (OII) is responsible for investigating allegations of prohibited practices.[142] If, as a result of an investigation, the OII believes that a preponderance of the evidence supports findings of a prohibited practice, it presents a "Statement of Charges and Evidence" to the Sanctions Officer.[143] This Bank's official reviews the statement and determines whether it supports findings that the investigated party (so-called respondent) engaged in a prohibited practice.[144] If this is the case, the Sanctions Officer sends a formal notice to the respondent, who in turn may respond submitting written materials to the Sanctions Officer within 60 days from delivery of the notice.[145] After the expiration of this 60-day period, the Sanctions Officer issues his or her decision (so-called Determination). The respondent may appeal the Sanctions Officer's Determination in writing and within 45 days from the date of the delivery of such Determination.[146] However, the procedures expressly provide that where the respondent does not submit a response to the Sanctions Officer, he or she is deemed to have admitted the allegations and as a result waived the opportunity for appeal.[147] The appeal is held by a Sanctions Committee of seven members, of whom three members are appointed from the internal Bank Group staff (i.e., "Internal Members") and four members are appointed from outside the Bank (i.e., "External Members").[148] The decision of the Sanctions Committee is final and takes effect immediately.[149] Although neither OII nor a respondent shall have a right to a hearing, the Committee may, in its discretion, hold such hearings as it deems appropriate.[150] The Sanctions Officer and the Committee may impose the following sanctions: reprimand, debarment, conditional nondebarment, debarment with conditional release, as well as other unspecified sanctions that include, but are not limited to, the restitution of funds and the imposition of fines representing reimbursement of the costs associated with investigations and proceedings.[151] The IDB publishes on its website a list of sanctioned firms and individuals.[152]

---

[141]See 'Prohibited Practices at the IDB Group' (*Inter-American Development Bank*) <www.iadb.org/en/topics/transparency/integrity-at-the-idb-group/prohibited-practices-at-the-idb,2704.html>.

[142]See 'Sanctions Procedures' (*Inter-American Development Bank*) para 3.1 <http://idbdocs.iadb.org/wsdocs/getdocument.aspx?docnum=39676437>.

[143]ibid para 3.3.

[144]ibid para 4.1.

[145]ibid para 4.7.

[146]ibid para 6.1.

[147]ibid para 4.8.

[148]ibid Annex A – Sanctions Committee Charter, at article 3(2).

[149]ibid para 7.3.

[150]ibid para 11.3.

[151]ibid para 8.2.

[152]See 'Sanctioned Firms and Individuals' (*Inter-American Development Bank*) <www.iadb.org/en/topics/transparency/integrity-at-the-idb-group/sanctioned-firms-and-individuals,1293.html>.

Although the sanctions processes adopted by the different MDBs present structural and terminological dissimilarities, it is possible to trace a common thread among them. Each system provides for two-tier assessment of the allegedly perpetrated misconducts. While, with the exception of the Asian Development Bank, the first-tier decision is taken by a single Bank official,[153] the second-tier judgment is held by a semi-judicial body whose composition includes a majority of external members.[154] The presence of the external members should guarantee a certain level of independence of the judging bodies; however, the various procedures do not establish any clear criteria for their appointment. Another common feature is that the first-tier decision is entirely based on written documents, whereas hearings might be held, in the judging bodies' discretion, during the appeal phase. Even if they are collectively called in different manners,[155] all the MDBs sanction the same illicit conducts, which include corrupt, fraudulent, coercive, collusive, obstructive practices.[156] Finally, the range of sanctions developed by the different MDBs appears to be extremely similar,[157] with the exception of the AfDB and the IDB, whose procedures allow also for the imposition of "other" unspecified sanctions representing a not predetermined open category.

1.7 Harmonization of Sanctions Procedures and Cross-Debarment Regime

On February 18, 2006, the leaders of the five major MDBs (World Bank, AfDB, EBRD, AsDB, IDB) and the International Monetary Fund (IMF)[158] established a Joint International Financial Institutions (IFI) Anti-Corruption Task Force in order to

[153]I.e. the World Bank's Evaluation and Suspension Officer; the EBRD's Enforcement Commissioner; the AfDB's Sanctions Commissioner; the IDB's Sanctions Officer.

[154]I.e. the World Bank's Sanctions Board; the EBRD's Enforcement Committee; the AfDB's Appeals Board; the IDB's Sanctions Committee.

[155]The World Bank and AfDB refer to them as "sanctionable practices," the EBRD and IBD call them "prohibited practices," the AsDB uses the term "integrity violations."

[156]Only the EBRD and the AsDB have adopted a longer list of possible violations. Specifically, besides the common ones, the EBRD's one includes also theft and misuse of EBRD's resources; whilst the AsDB list comprises also abuse, conflict of interest, retaliation against whistle-blowers or witnesses, and violations of ethical standards.

[157]See Benedetti, "How Multilateral Development Banks invest corruption in their funded projects" in *Corruption and Conflicts of Interest*, (n 55) 229.

[158]The International Monetary Fund (IMF), which was founded in 1945, represents an international organization of 189 countries, which aims at fostering global monetary cooperation, securing financial stability, facilitating international trade, promoting high employment and sustainable economic growth, and reducing poverty around the world. See 'About the IMF' (*International Monetary Fund*) <www.imf.org/external/about.htm>.

work toward a consistent and harmonized approach to combat corruption in the activities and operations of the member institutions.[159]

Moreover, the involved institutions agreed on the need to standardize their definition of the most relevant illicit practices to be sanctioned (i.e., corrupt, fraudulent, coercive, and obstructive practices). The standardization of these definitions was considered critical to the success of the harmonized approach:

- A corrupt practice is the offering, giving, receiving, or soliciting, directly or indirectly, anything of value to influence improperly the actions of another party.
- A fraudulent practice is any act or omission, including a misrepresentation, that knowingly or recklessly misleads, or attempts to mislead, a party to obtain a financial or other benefit or to avoid an obligation.
- A coercive practice is impairing or harming, or threatening to impair or harm, directly or indirectly, any party or the property of the party to influence improperly the actions of a party.
- A collusive practice is an arrangement between two or more parties designed to achieve an improper purpose, including influencing improperly the actions of another party.[160]

Furthermore, in order to promote consistency in the sanctioning practices of the member institutions, the IFI also developed common principles and guidelines for investigations. For instance, it has been established that the various investigative bodies have to maintain objectivity, impartiality, and fairness throughout the investigative process;[161] that each organization has to publish an annual report highlighting its antifraud and corruption activities;[162] and that the standard of proof that has to be used is the "more probable than not" one.[163]

As we have discussed in the previous section, each of the member institutions of the IFI Task Force has developed its own anticorruption policies. As a result, the IFI Task Force recognized that it was necessary to implement a system of mutual recognition of the various enforcement actions.[164]

Therefore, on April 9, 2010, the five MDBs signed the "Agreement on Mutual Enforcement of Debarment Decisions." The statement released by then WBG President Robert B. Zoellick on that occasion appears emblematic of this new approach:

---

[159]See 'International Financial Institutions Anti-Corruption Task Force' (*Asian Development Bank*, September 2006) <www.adb.org/publications/uniform-framework-preventing-and-combating-fraud-and-corruption>.

[160]ibid 1.

[161]ibid attachment 1, para 3.

[162]ibid para 6.

[163]ibid para 12.

[164]ibid 2.

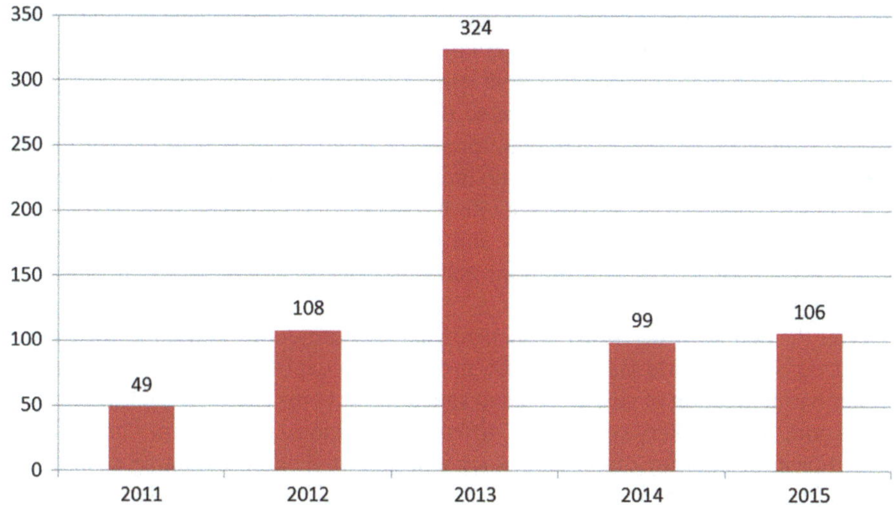

Fig. 1.5 MDBs: Cross-debarred entities (firms and individuals). *Source*: 'Annual Reports 2011–2015' (*Asian Development Bank*, Office of Anticorruption and Integrity) <www.adb.org/site/integrity/publications?page=1>

> With today's cross-debarment agreement among development banks, a clear message on anticorruption is being delivered: Steal and cheat from one, get punished by all.[165]

The MDBs developed a cross-debarment regime providing that where an individual or firm is debarred by one multilateral development bank, it is also sanctioned, for the same misconduct, by all the other MDBs participating in the regime.[166] As a result, one MDB's debarment of concerned entities also renders the same entities ineligible to participate in another participating MDB's activities (for the overall amount of cross-debarred entities, see Fig. 1.5), significantly extending the reach and impact of sanctions.[167]

In practice, the cross-debarment consists in the recognition of debarment decisions. This regime is automatically applied where the following conditions are met: the sanctioned party is debarred for one or more of the four sanctionable offenses—fraud, corruption, collusion, or coercion—defined by the Uniform Framework,[168]

[165] See 'Cross-Debarment Accord Steps Up Fight Against Corruption' (*World Bank*) <http://web.worldbank.org/WBSITE/EXTERNAL/NEWS/0,,contentMDK:22535805~pagePK:64257043~piPK:437376~theSitePK:4607,00.html>.

[166] See 'The World Bank Group: Mutual Enforcement Of Debarment Decisions Among Multilateral Development Banks' (*World Bank*, 3 March 2010) <http://siteresources.worldbank.org/INTDOII/Resources/Bank_paper_cross_debar.pdf>.

[167] See 'Report to The President – Office Of Anticorruption And Integrity – Annual Report 2011' (*Asian Development Bank*, 2012) 12 <www.adb.org/sites/default/files/institutional-document/33423/files/oai-ar-2011.pdf>.

[168] See 'International Financial Institutions Anti-Corruption Task Force' (*Asian Development Bank*) (n. 159) 1.

the period of debarment exceeds one year, the original decision to debar is made after the Cross-Debarment Agreement came into effect.[169]

The adoption of the cross-debarment regime appears to be underpinned by several rationales: avoiding the risk that, due to the participation of a sanctioned party in contracts financed by fellow MDBs, a prejudice might be caused to the borrowing clients, to donors, and to the poor (who are intended to be the ultimate beneficiaries of the work conducted by all MDBs); minimizing the reputational risks connected to the cooperation between any MDBs and entities found to have committed illicit practices by another sister institution; enhancing the deterrent effect of sanctions imposed by the MDBs.[170]

Over the course of the Third Suspension and Debarment Colloquium, which was organized by the World Bank in 2015, the panelists expressly debated the issue of further harmonization of suspension and sanctions systems at the global level. In this discussion, the speakers considered different definitions of the term "harmonization." For instance, they discussed if such a notion implies transplanting an existing system's goals and procedures into a different context or it merely involves a synthesis of different aims and ideals. The panelists also drew a distinction between harmonization in the processes for suspending or debarring entities and harmonization of the consequences (i.e., the extent to which a debarment decision of one system should be recognized and adhered to by other systems).[171] It is interesting to note that some speakers expressed a certain degree of reluctance. In particular, it was argued that conceptual definitions of suspension and debarment are not easily transferrable to other contexts and nations.[172] As regards cross-debarment and mutual recognition of debarment decisions, some panelists affirmed that, although those policies could provide more flexibility between systems, the notion of "recognition" may mean something less than automatic debarment (i.e., a trigger for further investigation) and that automatic cross-debarment may be problematic if a debarment would not have been possible in the country's own system.[173]

It has also to be highlighted that, within the World Bank's sanctions process, the circumstance that an investigated firm had been already debarred by another MDB for a different illicit conduct may be also considered as an element justifying the application of a severe aggravating factor.[174]

---

[169]See 'The World Bank Group: Mutual Enforcement Of Debarment Decisions' (*World Bank*) (n. 166) 6.

[170]ibid.

[171]See 'Third Suspension and Debarment Colloquium 2015' (*World Bank*, 16 December 2015), <www.worldbank.org/en/events/2015/11/05/third-suspension-and-debarment-colloquium-2015#5>.

[172]ibid.

[173]ibid.

[174]See *infra* note 72 and accompanying text in Chap. 6.

Chapter 2
The Evolution of the World Bank Sanctions System

2.1 Historical Background and the Adoption of the Sanctions System (1996)

The use of World Bank's funds for illicit purposes, including allocations for cronyism and politically driven investments (e.g., military spending), arose as a major problem during the last 20 years. Prior to 1997, the immediate question was whether funds that governments misappropriated constituted a breach of contract as stipulated on the grounds of the Articles of Agreement.[1] However, the World Bank officials consciously avoided any use of the word corruption. Corruption was considered an internal affair that was beyond the World Bank's mandate. Inaction was the unfortunate consequence of such a situation. This inertia was justified on the grounds of the Articles of Agreement themselves, which specifically prohibit staff members from making lending decisions on the basis of political considerations:

> The Bank and its officers shall not interfere in the political affairs of any member; nor shall they be influenced in their decisions by the political character of the member or members concerned. Only economic considerations shall be relevant to their decisions, and these considerations shall be weighed impartially to achieve the purposes stated in Article I.[2]

This nonpolitical mandate appears to be one of the most distinguishing features of the World Bank. As it has been underlined, being the borrowers also members of the financial institution, they should be allowed to maintain at least some appearance of sovereignty.

---

[1]The Article of Agreements outline the conditions of membership and the general principles of organization, management, and operations for each of the World Bank Group organizations, which operates according to the procedures established by such governing documents. See 'IBRD Articles of Agreement' (*World Bank*, amended on 16 February 1989) <http://siteresources.worldbank.org/EXTABOUTUS/Resources/ibrd-articlesofagreement.pdf>.

[2]ibid Article IV, section 10.

S. Manacorda, C. Grasso, *Fighting Fraud and Corruption at the World Bank*,
https://doi.org/10.1007/978-3-319-73824-6_2

The scope of this limitation was explained in a 1992 report where it was specified that

> the Bank cannot be influenced by the political character of a member; it cannot interfere in the partisan politics of a member; it must not act on behalf of industrial member countries to influence a borrowing member's political orientation or behaviour; it cannot be influenced in its decisions by political factors that do not have a preponderant economic effect; and its staff must not build their judgements on the possible reactions of a particular Bank member or members.[3]

However, it has been argued that this prohibition has been systematically circumvented and that the World Bank has made, on several occasions, choices grounded on political reasons. Specifically, the financial institution is well known for granting policy-linked loans and for its efforts to influence the behavior of borrowing governments.[4] In fact, since its origins, the Bank's stance on its antiinterference in the political affairs of its borrowers has often been the subject of much controversy. This is not surprising taking into consideration that for several reasons, the Bank can be defined as a political institution, not a merely economic one: its members are nation-states and, therefore, political in their very nature; its voting system is influenced by its largest shareholders, the world's most powerful nations; the circumstance that it is headquartered in Washington, D.C., and the tradition of nominating an American citizen as its president make it particularly vulnerable to interference from the US; it has historically acted as a major player in both Cold War and post-Cold War politics.[5]

Anyway, an unintended consequence of such a provision was that the World Bank would make loans to authoritarian governments whose leaders would use the financial aid to support their brutal regimes. This occurred, in particular, under Robert McNamara, who served as head of the World Bank from April 1968 to June 1981. Over the course of his presidency, the borrowing process denoted a significant degree of arbitrariness, repressiveness, and lack of popular participation.[6] The justification for granting funds to authoritarian regimes was based on an alleged difference between economic and political human rights. Though it cannot be disregarded that while the Bank stood up for the former through its antipoverty and related initiatives, it deliberately ignored the latter.[7]

In order to make few examples of such politically linked loans that were granted to authoritarian governments, it is possible to mention the close connection between

[3]See Francis Adams, *Deepening Democracy: Global Governance and Political Reform in Latin America* (Praeger 2003) 80.

[4]See Devesh Kapur, John Lewis and Richard Webb, *The World Bank: Its First Half Century*, vol 1 (Brookings 1997) 449.

[5]See Heather Marquette, 'Corruption, Democracy and the World Bank,' (2001) *Crime Law and Social Change* <www.researchgate.net/profile/Heather_Marquette/publication/226054235_Corruption_Democracy_and_the_World_Bank/links/557ac24608aee5c460448add.pdf>.

[6]See Kapur, *The World Bank: Its First Half Century*, (n 4) 476.

[7]ibid 477.

the World Bank and Haile Selassie,[8] who was Ethiopia's Emperor from 1930 to 1974.[9] Again, in the late 1960s, the Bank established an idyllic relationship with the military regime installed in Indonesia by Haji Mohammad Suharto,[10] whose government was mainly formed of generals, many of whom were corrupt.[11] A more recent example is represented by the Bank's support of the dictatorship in Turkey from 1980 to 1983,[12] which is a clear illustration of how thoroughly the World Bank's policies have traditionally been determined by geostrategic interests, particularly those of the United States. In fact, over the course of that period, the World Bank provided funds to Turkey not merely because it had been hit by a serious financial crisis but on the basis of other geopolitical reasons such as the occurrence of the Iranian revolution, the circumstance that Turkey was moving closer to the Soviet Union, and the invasion of Afghanistan.[13]

This situation persisted until in the late 1990s, when the Bank launched its own Governance and Anti-Corruption (GAC) strategy to fight against corruption in Bank-financed operations and support clients to strengthen their corruption fighting capacity (see Fig. 2.1).

The change was driven by two main circumstances: on the one hand, the global support for the removal of authoritarian governments and the spread of democracy in the Third World and, on the other, the general acceptance of the proposition that corruption has adverse effects on development.

In latest times, the fight against economic crime has come to light as a major priority at international level, and such global uncompromising attitude of contrast has heightened after the recent financial crisis. In particular, in relation to corruption, at international level it has been recognized that it is no longer a local matter but a transnational criminal phenomenon that affects all societies and economies and that international cooperation to prevent and foil it is essential. Emblematic of such an approach is the adoption of several international conventions aimed at combating

[8]After World War II, Haile Selassie established and led for forty-four years an empire that represented an ineffective and corrupt feudo-imperial regime. See Alemante G. Selassie, 'Ethiopia: Problems and Prospects for Democracy' (1992) 1(2) *William and Mary Bill of Rights Journal* 205, 208.

[9]In the autumn of 1968 Robert McNamara described itself as "an admirer of the Emperor" and after two years he openly supported the Ethiopia's necessity for an increased military spending. See Kapur, *The World Bank: Its First Half Century*, (n 4) 476.

[10]In Indonesia Suharto's government eroded civil and political liberties and turned democratic institutions into hollow shells. See Adam Schwarz, 'Indonesia After Suharto' (1992) 76(4) *Foreign Affairs* 119, 120.

[11]See Kapur, *The World Bank: Its First Half Century*, (n 4) 470.

[12]Claiming that under Turkish law it was the army that had the duty to safeguard the Republic, the military seized control of the government in a bloodless coup led by General Kenan Evren in 1980. The National Security Council was then installed to lead the new government under which the Grand National Assembly was abolished and all political parties and politicians that were active before the military coup were banned. See Nicole Pope and Hugh Pope, *Turkey unveiled: Atatürk and after* (John Murray 1997) 141.

[13]See Kapur, *The World Bank: Its First Half Century*, (n 4) 549.

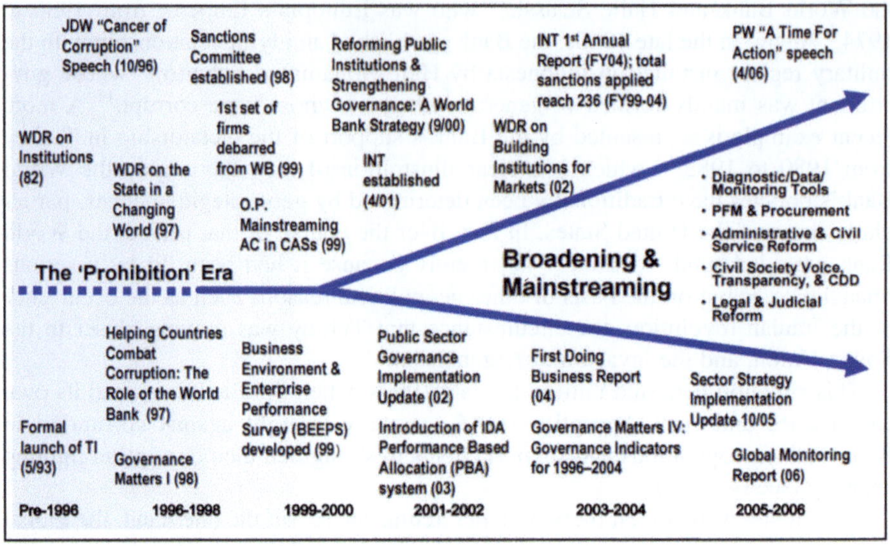

Fig. 2.1 World Bank's Milestones in Governance and Anticorruption. *Source*: 'Strengthening World Bank Group Engagement on Governance and Anticorruption' (© *World Bank*, 21 March 2007) Annex A, 39 <http://siteresources.worldbank.org/EXTGOVANTICORR/Resources/3035863-1281627136986/GACStrategyPaper.pdf>, License: Creative Commons Attribution license (CC BY 3.0 IGO) <https://creativecommons.org/licenses/by/3.0/igo/>

corrupt behaviors and, among them, the United Nations Convention Against Corruption (UNCAC) and the OECD Convention on Combating Bribery of Foreign Public Officials in International Business Transactions, which are commonly deemed to be the foremost treaties.

Such a pressure to fight economic crime has resulted in the development of related legal frameworks in domestic jurisdictions and, at international level, has led to the adoption of the sanctions systems within the MDBs.

As a matter of fact, to address fraud and corruption in Bank-financed projects, the World Bank has established an independent sanctions system, which consists in gathering and assessing evidence of potential misconducts in Bank-financed operations and applying its sanctions where the alleged conducts are ascertained.

The World Bank has originally adopted its sanctions regime in 1996. Specifically, it was first formulated in a paper presented to the Executive Directors in July 1996 and then implemented in the January 1998 Operational Memorandum.

Since then, a pressing and constant necessity of reforming has been recognized. There are several reasons behind such need: the degree of complexity of the cases has constantly increased, the practitioners working within the sanctions process have adopted a progressively more sophisticated legal thinking; respondents and their legal counsel have adopted a more and more aggressive legal approach.[14]

Such a situation has originated a sharp contrast between, on the one hand, a marked tendency to be guided by both the formal and procedural principles of the rule of law and, on the other, the keenness to keep the sanctioning proceedings summary and free form formality.

It does not surprise that, for many years, the Bank's sanctions system, which was traditionally administered by bank personnel, has been criticized because of its lack of independence and accountability.

Indeed, although the importance of assuring the basic requirements of due process is now recognized by the World Bank, it appears that the complex and costly procedural system that more stringent guarantees would require is still considered as a serious cause for concern.

The opinion expressed by the Bank's judging body in one of its decisions in order to dismiss the arguments of a respondent based on the alleged inconsistency of the sanctioning procedure with minimum standards of fairness and due process is emblematic of such an approach: "The Sanctions Board is not a jury. The present proceedings are administrative in nature, without formal rules of evidence."[15]

However, notwithstanding the marked reluctance showed by the World Bank officials, in the latest years several important reforms have been adopted and others are planned to be implemented in the near future.

2.2 The Establishment of the Sanctions Board (2004)

Among the most relevant reforms, the change in the composition of the main judging body can be seen as particularly significant. In fact, the original process was managed by a Sanctions Committee composed of senior Bank staff members.[16] That body gave rise to several issues such as perceived conflicts of interest, potential external pressures, and lack of independence from the Bank.[17]

---

[14]See Anne-Marie Leroy and Frank Fariello, 'The World Bank Group Sanctions Process and Its Recent Reforms' (*World Bank*, 2012) 6 <http://siteresources.worldbank.org/INTLAWJUSTICE/Resources/SanctionsProcess.pdf>.

[15]See, among others, *World Bank v Anonymized Respondent*, [2013] Sanctions Board 55, para 42.

[16]The Sanctions Committee was established in November 1998 in order to review allegations of fraud or corruption and to recommend the sanctions to be imposed on those firms or individuals found to have engaged in fraudulent or corrupt activities. The Committee's membership consisted of the Managing Director overseeing Operations (Chair), the Senior Vice President and General Counsel, and two other senior members of the staff selected thanks to their operational experience (one Regional Vice President and the Vice President of Human Resources). See 'Reform of the World Bank's Sanctions Process' (*World Bank*, Board Papers R2004-0025/1, Report Number 29527) 1 <http://documents.worldbank.org/curated/en/921411468779446341/pdf/295270rev.pdf>.

[17]ibid 4.

As a result, in 2004, the Bank's judging body was replaced with the current Sanctions Board, which, including a majority of external members, appears to be more independent and enhance the credibility of the process, helping insulate it from political pressures.[18] The management believed that such a new mixed composition would benefit the process by providing the Board with a combination of more independence and continued operational expertise in the procedures and guidelines associated with Bank-financed projects.[19] Such a significant enhancement has eventually transformed the World Bank's sanctions process in what can be defined as a quasi-judicial model.[20]

The 2004 reform also included the expansion of the list of the applicable sanctions. As a matter of fact, up to 2004, the Bank had the possibility to impose only a limited number of punitive measures: i.e., a period of ineligibility from Bank-financed contracts (limited or indefinite), a letter of reprimand, and the setting up by the respondent of training and integrity programs for its workers.[21]

2.3 The Implementation of More Effective Measures Against Fraud and Corruption (2006)

In 2006, the Bank embarked on a series of reforms aimed at making the sanctions process a more successful instrument in the fight against fraud and corruption. In particular, the World Bank's officials recognized that the way in which fraudulent and corrupt practices were perpetrated was more complicated than they had at first realized and that the mere focus on the Bank-financed procurement was inadequate. Experience had shown that those criminal activities could also occur outside procurement.[22] For instance, a financial intermediary could avoid sanction if it made false representations to the borrower and the Bank in order to persuade them that the entity satisfied requirements for participating in the project.[23]

As a result, the Multilateral Development Bank adopted some specific improvements to enhance the sanctions regime. Specifically, the regime was expanded beyond procurement to cover all fraud and corruption that may occur in connection

[18]Three different options were evaluated to amend the composition of the Board: a committee composed entirely of Bank staff such as the current Sanctions Committee; a committee composed entirely of members from outside the Bank; and a committee composed of a mix of Bank staff and members from outside the Bank. The latter option eventually prevailed. See ibid.

[19]ibid.

[20]See Laurence Folliot-Lalliot, 'Introduction to the World Bank's policies in the fight against corruption and conflict of interests in public contracts' in Jean-Bernard Auby, Emmanuel Breen and Thomas Perroud (eds), *Corruption and Conflicts of Interest* (Edward Elgar 2014) 238.

[21]See 'Reform of the World Bank's Sanctions Process' (*World Bank*) (n 16) 11.

[22]See Leroy, 'The World Bank Group Sanctions Process' (*World Bank*) (n 14) 11.

[23]See 'The World Bank's Anti-Corruption Guidelines and Sanctions Reform – A User's Guide' (*World Bank*) 5 <http://siteresources.worldbank.org/PROJECTS/Resources/40940-1173795340221/RevisedPMNDFinaluserGuideline031607.pdf>.

with the use of funds made available by the Bank. In practice, from the definitions of all the sanctionable practices, the words "in order to influence a procurement process or the execution of a contract" were removed, and, as a consequence, their purpose was delinked from procurement context.[24]

Furthermore, through the 2006 reform, the Bank adopted an autonomous definition of "obstructive practice" as a specific sanctionable offense consisting in deliberately destroying, falsifying, altering or concealing of evidence material to the investigation, or making false statements to investigators in order to materially impede a World Bank investigation.[25] Before this enhancement, it had been possible for a firm to escape sanction even though it obstructed an investigation to the point that the Bank could not gather sufficient evidence to prove the allegation of fraud and corruption.[26]

2.4 The Introduction of the "Early Temporary Suspension" and Cross-Debarment Regime (2009–2010)

Over the course of 2009 and 2010, several other enhancements of the sanctions process were put in place. These reforms included the introduction of the so-called early temporary suspension, which is a suspension prior to the commencement of the sanctions procedure. Moreover, the World Bank adopted the debarment with conditional release as its "baseline" sanction and established the related Integrity Compliance Office (ICO). A formal mechanism for the settlement of sanctions cases was also introduced, and an enhanced guidance on the treatment of corporate groups was developed.[27] During this period, following a recommendation issued by a panel led by Paul Volcker, the Sanctions Board presidency transitioned from an internal to an external person.[28]

---

[24]See 'Cover Note to Borrowers on Sanctions Reform' (*World Bank*, 2006) <http://siteresources.worldbank.org/PROJECTS/Resources/40940-1173795340221/CoverNoteInfoBorrowers.pdf>.

[25]See 'Anti-Corruption Guidelines' (*World Bank*) (n 23) 8.

[26]ibid 4.

[27]See 'The Review of the World Bank Group Sanctions System' (*World Bank*, Report Number 76282, 26 March 2013) 2 <http://documents.worldbank.org/curated/en/546411468331022285/pdf/762820WP0Box370ctions0Review0final.pdf>.

[28]On the 16th of February 2007, the President of the World Bank Group, in consultation with the Board of Executive Directors, appointed the Volcker panel to review the Integrity Vice-Presidency's work and to find more systematic ways to integrate it into Bank Group operations. In particular, in its recommendation no. 12, the panel observed that "to enhance the effectiveness and perceived independence of the new sanctions process, the Bank should require that the Chair of the Sanctions Board and of any Panel thereof be one of the outside members of the Board." See 'Implementing the Recommendations of the Independent Panel Review of the World Bank Group's Department of Institutional Integrity (INT)' (*World Bank*, Operations Policy and Country Service, 15 January 2008) 22 <http://documents.worldbank.org/curated/en/310211468153542519/pdf/421800SecM200810013.pdf>.

In particular, the Volcker panel underlined how

> Real change will only happen if staff across the Bank are fully committed to fighting fraud and corruption and collaborate effectively across the institution towards this end. For this to occur, Bank Group leadership must continue to articulate a clear policy framework, with defined responsibilities and accountabilities, operational systems and processes which send clear signals to staff and to partner countries.[29]

Finally, in April 2010, the Bank entered into an agreement for the mutual recognition of their debarment decisions with four other multilateral development banks (MDBs): the African Development Bank (AfDB), the Asian Development Bank (AsDB), the European Bank for Reconstruction and Development (EBRD), and the Inter-American Development Bank (IDB).[30] In practice, the agreement allows the cross-debarment of firms and individuals found to have engaged in wrongdoing within MDB-financed development projects.[31]

All the abovementioned reforms were definitively incorporated into the sanctions process through the issuance of new Sanctions Procedures and related internal guidance in January 2011.[32] It has to be mentioned that, as of June 2016, the sanctions process is governed by the latest version of the Sanctions Procedures.[33]

2.5 Reaching a Higher Level of Accountability and Transparency (2011)

Another crucial issue that had to be addressed was represented by the degree of transparency of the sanctions process. In fact, for many years, the documents related to the sanctioning proceedings were treated as having a classified nature, establishing what has been defined as a "black box" system.[34]

---

[29]ibid 2.

[30]For an analysis of the harmonization of the MDBs' Sanctions procedures see *supra* notes 158–174 and accompanying text in Chap. 1.

[31]See 'Cross-Debarment Accord Steps Up Fight Against Corruption' (*The World Bank*, News and Broadcast, 9 April 2010) <http://web.worldbank.org/WBSITE/EXTERNAL/NEWS/0,,contentMDK:22544921~pagePK:64257043~piPK:437376~theSitePK:4607,00.html>.

[32]See 'World Bank Sanctions Procedures: as adopted by the World Bank as of January 1, 2011' (*World Bank*, 2011) <http://siteresources.worldbank.org/EXTOFFEVASUS/Resources/WBGSanctionsProceduresJan2011.pdf>.

[33]See 'Bank Procedure: Sanctions Proceedings and Settlements in Bank Financed Projects' (*World Bank*, 28 June 2016) <http://siteresources.worldbank.org/EXTOFFEVASUS/Resources/3601045-1377105390925/Procedure_Bank_Procedure_Sanctions_Proceedings_and_Settlements_in_Bank_Financed_Projects(6.28.2016).pdf>.

[34]See Elizabeth Lin Forde, 'The World Bank's Sanction System As An Example' (2012) 106 *Proceedings of the Annual Meeting (American Society of International Law)* 122, 124.

This issue was already examined in the External Communications Strategy Report of 3 June 2004. In the report, it was clearly highlighted that the World Bank's communication strategy had to pursue the following goals:

> Affirm the Bank's recognition and endorsement of the fundamental importance of accountability and transparency in the development process; Prevent and deter incidents of fraud and corruption related to Bank-financed projects;
>
> Contribute to knowledge and understanding of the nature of fraudulent and corrupt activities;
>
> Promote broader awareness of the Bank's strong commitment to the fight against corruption. [35]

The same report specified that, although the World Bank occupied a leading position among international organizations in relation to investigations and sanctions, much of what it was doing was not known, and the impact was not leveraged by increased public awareness and understanding.[36]

The following main concerns and constraints were identified behind the limited approach to communications adopted by the Bank:

> (a) that publicity related to fraud and corruption in any Bank project could make it appear that the Bank has acted negligently in its supervision of projects and impede the good work of many;
>
> (b) that disclosing more detailed information could provide a basis for litigation or other challenges;
>
> (c) that the current World Bank disclosure policy does not provide for: expanded disclosures of information related to sanctions, confirmation of ongoing Bank investigations, disclosure of the closing of prior Bank investigations of fraud and corruption, or confirmation of a Bank report to a member state relating to an investigation.[37]

Therefore, the original reluctance to publish the Sanctions Board's decisions and opinions appeared to reflect primarily the intent to avoid a mechanism for accountability.

It was not until 2011 that the World Bank finally adopted a policy of transparency. Such an innovative approach was originally carried out by means of the issuance of a Law Digest in December 2011, which contained short and anonymized summaries of 20 decisions. Finally, as of May 2012, the World Bank has begun to publish all the decisions of the Sanctions Board on its external website.

Such new level of transparency, which gives a wide publicity to the Sanctions Procedures, undoubtedly exposes both the Bank and the respondents to an increased reputational risk. Indeed, thanks to the publication regime currently adopted, if the

---

[35]See 'External Communications Strategy Related to Investigations and Sanctioning of Fraud and Corruption in World Bank-Financed Projects' (*World Bank*, Department of Institutional Integrity, Report Number 29855, 3 June 2004) 1 <http://siteresources.worldbank.org/INTDOII/Resources/Ext_Comm_Strategy29855.pdf>.

[36]ibid 3.

[37]ibid.

Sanctions Board takes a questionable decision, the latter will be publicly known and judged. Moreover, the publication of the Sanctions Board's decisions may potentially expose respondents sanctioned as a result of a weak case to an unfair reputational risk.

Notwithstanding these potential drawbacks, transparency has to be regarded as a virtue itself and has to be extremely welcomed. Indeed, it enhances legal certainty developing a fundamental body of jurisprudence, acts as an inherent safeguard against arbitrary decisions, and increases the deterrent value of the sanctions imposed by the World Bank.[38]

In any case, it is necessary to point out that the level of transparency adopted by the Bank, although significant, cannot be considered entirely adequate. In fact, evidence and other considerations underlying the sanctions are not yet published on the World Bank's website. Moreover, the Bank has not published the Sanctions Board's pronouncements previous to Decision 46 of 2012, this even if the Board commonly makes express references to interpretative principles included in such earlier judgments.

2.6 The First Phase of the Sanctions Regime General Review (2013)

Until recently, no general review of the sanctions regime as a whole had been conducted. However, while the sanctions regime has not been operational for very long, at the request of the Audit Committee, the Bank's management recently agreed to undertake such a review that was conducted in two different phases.

The first phase started in July 2011 and ended in July 2013. It represented an assessment part and focused on the evaluation of the system as so far implemented and its various reforms over the years, with a view to identifying possible entry points for making improvements. In order to go forward with the implementation, efficiency, and effectiveness of the sanctions system and to identify possible areas for making improvements, the Legal Vice Presidency of the World Bank Group conducted consultations with external stakeholders.[39] Specifically, this part of the

[38]See Leroy, 'The World Bank Group Sanctions Process' (*World Bank*) (n 14) 25.

[39]The World Bank has identified various potential stakeholders connected with the sanctions process: "Those external parties who have engaged in the system in the past, in particular former Respondents and their legal counsel; private sector actors, in particular contractors and consultants who participate in Bank Group supported projects, which may engage in the system or are impacted by it; country officials that have been involved in (i) the implementation of projects affected by corruption or Bank sanctions and/or (ii) anti-corruption or debarment matters; other international organizations with sanctions systems, in particular other MDBs; civil society organizations with a stake in the fight against corruption; and academics whose studies focus on governance and anti-corruption, public procurement and/or development effectiveness." See 'Review of the World Bank Group Sanctions System: Consultation Plan' (*World Bank*, Sanctions System Stocktaking, 5 September 2013) 2 <http://

review also assessed the impact of the regime on World Bank operations and the legal adequacy of the system in the light of current developments in national and international law.[40]

A preliminary report was discussed with the Audit Committee on the 22nd of March 2013. The overall assessment of the sanctions system that emerged from the first phase of the review underlined that

> after a slow first few years, the system as a whole has been heading in a positive direction since early 2010; this trend has accelerated since early 2011. The picture is one of steady improvement in processing times, coupled with increasing output in terms of sanctions imposed. Notwithstanding this overall positive picture, the review team recommended steps to further improve the overall performance of the system, including: acceleration of the rollout of an system-wide automated case management system; a study of quality controls across the system; the adoption of performance standards; possible use of panels by the Sanctions Board (SB) rather than plenary sessions for cases that do not pose novel issues; expansion of SB membership to include additional alternates to facilitate quorums; and a resequencing of the first tier of sanctions proceedings before the Evaluation and Suspension Officer (EO) [currently known as Suspension and Debarment Officer (SDO)].[41]

The results of the feedback received in the first phase of this review offered interesting insights into the sanctions regime adopted by the World Bank. In particular, stakeholders had the possibility to underline the deficiencies of the sanctions process related to due process, transparency, and independence.

For instance, it was highlighted that, since the Sanctions Board normally held its sessions at the principal office of the Bank in Washington, D.C., travel costs and other associated hurdles represent an insurmountable geographic barrier for certain types of respondents, so it was suggested that the World Bank should hold sessions in the country offices in order to give equal opportunities to all respondents, including those with limited means.[42]

Furthermore, the fact emerged that, due to the absence of sufficient clarity about the practical implications of conditions for release, the imposition of conditions in case of conditional debarment, including a corporate compliance program, may pose issues of proportionality and may potentially have the effect of turning conditional debarment into indefinite debarment, especially concerning low-capacity respondents.[43]

---

consultations.worldbank.org/Data/hub/files/consultation-template/consultation-review-world-bank-group-sanctions-systemopenconsultationtemplate/materials/sanctionsreview_consultationplan.pdf>.

[40]See ‘Consultation on Review of the World Bank Group Sanctions System’ (*World Bank*, Consultations) <http://consultations.worldbank.org/consultation/sanctions-reviews>.

[41]See ‘The Review of the World Bank Group Sanctions System’ (*World Bank*) (n 39) 1.

[42]See ‘Review of the World Bank Group Sanctions System – Global Multi-Stakeholder Consultations, Phase I: July-October 2013, Feedback Summary’ (*World Bank*) 5 <http://siteresources.worldbank.org/INTLAWJUSTICE/Resources/FeedbackSummaryPhaseI.pdf>.

[43]ibid 8.

Finally, it was also argued that the criteria used by the Integrity Vice Presidency (INT) to select cases to be investigated presented a serious lack of transparency.[44]

In its official comments issued on October 31, 2013, the U.S. Defense Bar clearly disagreed with the Bank's opinion that the current sanctions system had reached an appropriate degree of balance between due process and efficiency. In fact, the U.S. Defense Bar affirmed:

> We believe, in fact, that there is much more the Bank can and should do. As the impact of sanctions has grown, in terms of the number of cases, the nature of sanctions, the targets of sanctions, and the effect of sanctions (through crossdebarment and other collateral effects), the importance of a transparent and balanced process for investigation and sanctions which meets due process standards for those adversely affected also grows.[45]

As clearly pointed out in a paper released by the law firm Freshfields Bruckhaus Deringer in connection with the abovementioned external consultation phase of the review of the World Bank Group's sanctions system, today's sanctions system carries greater risks and consequences for contractors than ever before. This represents the effect of a plurality of elements: the increased financial and human resources available to the Bank's investigators, the recent enhanced focus of the Bank's officials on larger and multinational corporate contractors, the imposition of debarment to affiliates within corporate groups, the establishment and related application of cross-debarment, the increase in referrals to national authorities for local enforcement.[46]

Therefore, the international law firm affirmed:

> Without further reforms to ensure due process, there is a risk that the system will make resources unavailable to member countries that need them, by unnecessarily debarring contractors. Unduly aggressive debarment can reduce competition, in turn reducing options for development and increasing the costs of goods and services for Bank-financed projects.[47]

The second phase, which is not yet started, will evaluate the overall efficiency and effectiveness of the sanctions process assessing whether or not the system as a whole is meeting its objectives of excluding corrupt actors and deterring fraud and corruption in World Bank Group operations at an appropriate cost to the World Bank Group. The timing of this second part of the review is yet to be determined.

---

[44]ibid 2.

[45]See 'Comments of the U.S. Defense Bar as coordinated by the Co-Chair of the ABA Section of International Law, Anti-Corruption Committee' (*World Bank*, Consultation on Review of the World Bank Group Sanctions System, Comments Received, 31 October 2013) 2 <https://consultations.worldbank.org/consultation/sanctions-reviews>.

[46]See 'Freshfields Bruckhaus Deringer LLP' (*World Bank*, Consultation on Review of the World Bank Group Sanctions System, Comments Received, 31 October 2013) 3 <https://consultations.worldbank.org/consultation/sanctions-reviews>.

[47]ibid.

Chapter 3
Framing the World Bank's Sanction Power: Sources and Procedure

3.1 Sources of the Sanctions System and the Rule of Law: General Remarks

The first section of this chapter will be devoted to an analysis of the various legal sources governing the sanctions process. Moreover, it will be offered an evaluation of the extent to which the legal framework created by the World Bank is respectful of the principle of the rule of law. However, before conducting such an assessment, it is necessary to verify if the rule of law can, in principle, be considered as applicable to the Bank's sanctions process.

The origins of the concept of the rule of law go back to ancient Greece[1] and, specifically, to democratic Athens of the classical period.[2] The Athenian conception of rule of law was then inherited by Republican Rome, which similarly subscribed to the idea that laws should be applied equally to all citizens. It is emblematic that Marcus Tullius Cicero, who was a Roman politician and lawyer, condemned the king who does not abide by the law as a horrible and dangerous despot.[3] During the Middle Ages, philosophers and religious scholars also referenced principles of universal law, where application of a single law should be made to both king and subjects.[4]

[1]For an overview of the Athenian legal system and a catalogue of Athenian evidence for the relationship between the rule of law and equality. See Paul Gowder, 'Democracy, Solidarity, and the Rule of Law: Lessons from Athens' (2014) 62(1) *Buffalo Law Review*, 1.

[2]Fundamental to the idea of Athenian democracy was the concept of "isonomia," (i.e., political equality through legal equality). The literal sense of the term *isonomia* can be deemed to be "equality of law" meaning "equality before the law." See Gregory Vlastos, 'Isonomia' (1953) 74 (4) *The American Journal of Philology* 337, 350.

[3]See Brian Z. Tamanaha, *On the Rule of Law: History, Politics, Theory* (Cambridge University Press 2000) 11.

[4]ibid.

S. Manacorda, C. Grasso, *Fighting Fraud and Corruption at the World Bank*,
https://doi.org/10.1007/978-3-319-73824-6_3

Notwithstanding its ancient roots and the fact that rule of law principles underlie the structures of many governments, the modern notion of the rule of law, whose central tenet is that the state should be governed in accordance with the law and not arbitrarily,[5] is traditionally associated with the development of the English legal system. From this perspective, its origins may be traced back to the early seventeenth century, when the judiciary informed King James that

> The King in his own person cannot adjudge any case, either criminal or betwixt party and party; but it ought to be determined and adjudged in some Court of Justice, according to the law and custom of England.[6]

A contemporary restatement of the principle requires that the rules have to be "accessible, and so far as possible intelligible, clear and predictable."[7] In other words, the rule of law, which marks a fundamental move away from what can be defined "the rule of men,"[8] requires that laws be publicly known prior to their enforcement so that individuals can comply with them and can identify potential abuses of authority by those in power.

In the context of the Council of Europe, the principle of the rule of law has found supranational recognition in the European Convention of Human Rights. In that regard, the European Court of Human Rights had the opportunity to explain the scope of its notion in order to clarify the meaning of the term "prescribed by law," which is used in some articles of the Convention.[9] In particular, in a landmark case, the Court affirmed:

> The law must be adequately accessible: the citizen must be able to have an indication that is adequate in the circumstances of the legal rules applicable to a given case. Secondly, a norm cannot be regarded as a "law" unless it is formulated with sufficient precision to enable the citizen to regulate his conduct: he must be able [. . .] to foresee, to a degree that is reasonable in the circumstances, the consequences which a given action may entail.[10]

[5]See 'Rule of Law' in Daniel Greenberg (ed), *Jowitt's Dictionary of English Law* (Sweet & Maxwell 2015).

[6]See *Prohibitions del Roy*, 77 ER 1342, 12 Co. Rep. 64.

[7]See Lord Bingham, 'The Rule of Law'(2007) 66(1) *The Cambridge Law Journal* 66, 67.

[8]This term was used by the US Supreme Court in the landmark case *Marbury v. Madison*, where it stated: "The Government of the United States has been emphatically termed a government of laws, and not of men. It will certainly cease to deserve this high appellation if the laws furnish no remedy for the violation of a vested legal right." See *Marbury v. Madison*, 5 U.S. 1 Cranch 137 (1803), para 163.

[9]The term "prescribed by law" is used in Articles 5(1), 9(2), 10(2), 11(2), and in Protocol 7 at Article 2(2). See Convention for the Protection of Human Rights and Fundamental Freedoms [1950].

[10]See *The Sunday Times v. the United Kingdom* (1979) ECHR 1, para 49.

Still at the regional level, the rule of law has been formally recognized by the European Court of Justice way back in 1986, when it affirmed that "the European Economic Community is a community based on the rule of law."[11] Under the Treaty of Amsterdam, the principle has acquired renewed importance where it has been established that "The Union is founded on the principles of liberty, democracy, respect for human rights and fundamental freedoms, and the rule of law, principles which are common to the Member States."[12] Finally, the Lisbon Treaty has reiterated this concept providing that

> The Union is founded on the values of respect for human dignity, freedom, democracy, equality, the rule of law and respect for human rights, including the rights of persons belonging to minorities. These values are common to the Member States in a society in which pluralism, non-discrimination, tolerance, justice, solidarity and equality between women and men prevail.[13]

Therefore, in the European Union's constitutional framework, the rule of law does not represent only a common foundational value, but it has also acquired an external dimension as an instrument to assess the actions of candidate countries and as a transversal foreign policy objective.[14]

Notwithstanding that, the rule of law is traditionally considered inherently related to state power. In other words, it commonly characterizes domestic legal systems structured in both "horizontal" and "vertical" ways (i.e., where citizens are at the same time associated with one another and are subject to an office of authority). Consequently, from a political realist perspective, such a principle cannot be applied *per se* at the international level. This is because, under the typical conditions of international power, the rule of law cannot be realized in the absence of proper authorities that make and enforce the rules.[15]

However, there are convincing reasons to believe that the principle of the rule of law should be respected also by nonstate actors operating at the international level.

[11] See Case 294/83 *Les Verts v Parliament* [1986] ECR I-1339, para 23.

[12] See Treaty of Amsterdam Amending the Treaty on European Union, the Treaties Establishing the European Communities and Certain Related Acts [1997] OJ C340, Article 1(8).

[13] At the present time, this provision is enshrined in Article 2 of the Consolidated versions of the Treaty on European Union and the Treaty on the Functioning of the European Union. See Treaty of Lisbon Amending the Treaty on European Union and the Treaty Establishing the European Community [2007] OJ C306/01, Article 1(3).

[14] See Laurent Pech, 'Rule of law as a guiding principle of the European Union's external action' (2011) *CLEER Working Papers* 1, 10.

[15] See Terry Nardin, 'Theorising the International Rule of Law' (2008) 34(3) *Review of International Studies* 385, 391.

Firstly, although it is characterized by fragmentation,[16] asynchrony,[17] and polychrony,[18] it is possible to support the proposition that a global order exists. The creation of the current supranational legal order may be traced back to the establishment of the United Nations in June 1945 and the adoption of the Universal Declaration of Human Rights in 1948.[19]

Moreover, the rule of law being a fundamental principle of justice, it has to be considered as a moral concept, which implies limits on the means by which authorities, entities, and individuals pursue their goals. If this is true, it should not be considered as a synonym for state law, nor should its applicability be limited to national legal frameworks. Like any other existing legal order, the international legal system is an ambiguous mixture of instrumental and noninstrumental regulations.[20]

Consequently, it is possible to assert that the principle of the rule of law is applicable to the current global legal system.[21] This especially taking into consideration that, within such a scenario, the existing regional and international organizations, such as multilateral development banks and the International Monetary Fund, are increasingly playing a role comparable to the one served by national authorities. As a matter of fact, the circumstance that individual human beings and legal entities have rights and duties unmediated by domestic authorities, and that they can be subject to sanctions in case of misconducts, not only makes their processes similar to the ones utilized in the traditional vertical justice systems but also creates the compelling need for them to establish an independent legal framework that guarantees equality before the rules and executives that are fully subject to the same set of regulations.

[16]Without an universally applicable international legal framework the global legal space appears open to a generalized fragmentation. For instance, even the Universal Declaration of Human Rights, which can be considered a milestone document in the history of human rights that is supposed to have universal value, has been affected by fragmentation where its regional instruments where not ratified by certain states or where, in certain areas of the world, its application seems to be totally absent. See Mireille Delmas-Marty, *Ordering Pluralism: A Conceptual Framework for Understanding the Transnational Legal World* (Naomi Norberg tr, Hart 2009) 99.

[17]The development of the supranational legal order appears to be subject to significant variations in speed from one area to another. For instance, while the internationalization of the law on bribery, which stemmed from the adoption of the U.S. Foreign Corrupt Practices Act of 1977, took more than 30 years to occur, the dramatic terrorist attacks of 11 September 2001 led to an extraordinarily rapid adoption of international legal instruments against terrorism. See ibid 119.

[18]Even within the same area of law, the global legal framework is applied in a different way to different international actors. For instance, the U.N. Framework Convention on Climate Change has provided for "common but differentiated responsibilities" depending on the level of countries' development. See ibid 133.

[19]ibid 97.

[20]See Nardin, 'Theorising the International Rule of Law' (n 15) 397.

[21]ibid 399.

3.2 Applicable World Bank's Texts

The legal framework regulating the Bank's debarment procedure appears fragmented[22] and inevitably lacunose. The Sanctions Board recognized such a situation observing that

> No statutory or procedural framework can be expected to anticipate and comprehensively address all conceivable scenarios or issues that may arise. To the contrary, as the Statute recognizes, lacunae are inevitable; and the Sanctions Board may assert authority, consistent with Article XI of the Statute and the instructions of the Sanctions Board Chair, to fill procedural gaps.[23]

As a matter of fact, section 11 of the Sanctions Board Statute provides:

> In all matters not addressed in the WBG Sanctions Framework, the Sanctions Board shall follow the instructions of the Sanctions Board Chair for the operation of the Sanctions Board.[24]

The issue was considered also in the Advisory Opinion requested in 2010 by the Bank's Integrity Vice Presidency in order to be provided with advice on a series of fundamental legal questions that have arisen in connection with the sanctions process.[25] In the opinion, it was clearly affirmed that "perhaps the most fundamental issue that arises in sanctions cases is what 'law' applies to the case."[26] In particular, the Bank's General Counsel affirmed:

> Given that the formal legal framework for the Ban's sanctions regime is rather 'thin' and the main legal standards to be applied to sanctions cases, the various definitions of Sanctionable Practices, are notoriously broad, it has always been recognized that they would require interpretation over time.[27]

As a mere example of a crucial matter not directly addressed within the Bank's legal framework, it is possible to mention the absence of any rule on the possibility of reconsidering a case under exceptional circumstances. To override the principle of finality, the Sanctions Board had to resort to general principles of law.[28]

---

[22]It is emblematic that the very definition of the sanctionable practices changes with the type of contract used for the Bank-financed project. See *infra* note 69 and accompanying text in Chap. 4.

[23]See *World Bank v De Lorenzo of America Corp. S.A. de C.V.*, [2013] Sanctions Board 57, para 6.

[24]See 'WBG Policy: Statute of the Sanctions Board' (*World Bank*, 18 October 2016) s III(A) (11) <http://siteresources.worldbank.org/EXTOFFEVASUS/Resources/3601045-1377105390925/WBG_Policy_Statute_of_the_Sanctions_Board_(10.18.2016).pdf>.

[25]From time to time, the Bank's General Counsel may issue Advisory Opinions, either at the request of the Integrity Vice Presidency, the Office of Suspension and Debarment or the Sanctions Board, or of his or her own accord, on general principles of law applicable to the sanctions regime. See 'Advisory Opinion on Certain Issues Arising in Connection with Recent Sanctions Cases' (*World Bank*, 15 November 2010) <http://siteresources.worldbank.org/INTLAWJUSTICE/214574-1300377840517/23440937/AdvisoryOpinion.pdf>.

[26]ibid 1, para 3.

[27]ibid 4, para 13.

[28]See infra notes 97–101 and accompanying text in Chap. 5.

Although it is rarely mentioned in the Sanctions Board decisions, the underlying legal basis for the sanctions regime is provided by the Articles of Agreement, which assume a sort of "constitutional" relevance within the sanctions regime framework.[29] Furthermore, other sources such as the Thornburgh Reports[30] and the 2004 Sanctions Reform Board Paper,[31] which are considered as constituting the "policy framework and legislative history" of the Bank's sanctions process, have only marginal effects on the disposition of individual sanctions cases.[32]

The actual legal framework for the sanctions regime, which governs every sanctions case, includes the sources regulating the Bank-financed contracts in connection with which the alleged sanctionable practices took place.[33] As a matter of fact, those documents not only set up the scope of the Bank's jurisdiction but also incorporate the relevant definitions of sanctionable practices to be used in each individual case.[34] The identification of such sources, which is not always straightforward, is made by the Sanctions Board and illustrated in its decisions. As a matter of fact, each Board's judgment contains a part entitled "Applicable Standards of Review," in which it clarifies what is the source that governs the alleged sanctionable practice in the specific case.[35]

In any case, it is possible to affirm that in the sanctions process, the primary source is represented by the Bank's Sanctions Procedures, the latest version of which has been issued on June 28, 2016.[36] They are a sort of procedural code setting out introductory provisions, definitions, rules for interpretations, as well as the fundamental procedural framework.

On the contrary, a homogenous corpus of substantive rules does not exist, and this currently seems to be the most serious lacuna of the entire sanctions system. Such rules, where present, are laid down by several different documents. For instance, various definitions of sanctionable practices are contained in different sources such as the Guidelines Procurement Under IBRD Loans and IDA Credits, the Anti-Corruption Guidelines, and the Consultant Guidelines.[37] Other relevant sources of regulation are the World Bank Sanctioning Guidelines and the World Bank General

[29]See 'Advisory Opinion' (*World Bank*) (n 25) 1, para 4.

[30]See Dick Thornburgh, Ronald L. Gainer and Cuyler H. Walker, 'Report Concerning the Debarment Process of the World Bank' (*World Bank*, 14 August 2002) <http://siteresources.worldbank.org/INTDOII/Resources/thornburghreport.pdf>.

[31]See supra notes 16–21 and accompanying text in Chap. 2.

[32]See 'Advisory Opinion' (*World Bank*) (n 25) 2, para 5.

[33]ibid 2, para 8.

[34]ibid.

[35]The most common examples of such sources are the various versions of the Procurement Guidelines, Consultant Guidelines of Anti-Corruption Guidelines.

[36]For the latest version of the procedures See 'Bank Procedure: Sanctions Proceedings and Settlements in Bank Financed Projects' (*World Bank*, 28 June 2016) <http://siteresources.worldbank.org/EXTOFFEVASUS/Resources/3601045-1377105390925/Procedure_Bank_Procedure_Sanctions_Proceedings_and_Settlements_in_Bank_Financed_Projects(6.28.2016).pdf>.

[37]See *infra* note 69 and accompanying text in Chap. 4.

Principles and Guidelines for Sanctions, the Sanctions Board Statute, and the Code of Conduct.

In truth, it is extremely complicated to compile a comprehensive list of all the applicable sources because the Sanctions Board, in order to adopt its decisions, can apply provisions contained in many documents issued by the Bank and also refer to principles of law developed by "external jurisdictions."

3.3 General Principles of Law and National Law

While it is not possible to find within the Bank's legal framework any rule that explicitly recognizes general principles as a source of law for the sanctions regime, no provision forecloses their use. In this regard, the Bank's General Counsel openly supported their utilization because of the incompleteness of the Bank's legal framework and the fact that those principles are widely used at the international and domestic levels to resolve legal issues not clearly addressed within the related legal system.[38] The issue concerning the identification of the general principles of law has traditionally represented a vexed question. In particular, the use of the term "general" raised the question on the degree of generality that is necessary in order to define a principle as falling within such a category. From the General Counsel's perspective, in order to identify a general principle of law, it suffices that the "legal theory in question is supported by leading jurisdictions in both civil and common law systems."[39] Such an approach, which can be appreciated because of its pragmatism, generates, however, some concerns due to the fact that it *de facto* aligns the general principle of law utilizable in the sanctions process with the common value of the West, whereas such a view has been fiercely criticized by scholars from other parts of the world. Specifically, socialist scholars highlighted that the principles of Western capitalism are so different from those of Marxism-Leninism, which inspire their systems; Muslim scholars tend to accept only those principles that are compatible with Islam, and scholars from developing countries reject such a perspective *a priori* because it represents a product of Western systems that have long dominated many developing nations through colonialism.[40] Such a theoretical issue has not to be underestimated, also taking into consideration that the vast majority of the Bank-financed projects are carried out within the jurisdiction of developing countries.

The situation is further complicated by the fact that, on some occasions, the Sanctions Board justified its decisions also according to principles of law deriving from national jurisdictions. The Bank's General Counsel clarified that, although national law is not binding on the Bank and it cannot be used to supersede the Bank's

[38] See 'Advisory Opinion' (*World Bank*) (n 25) 5, para 18.

[39] ibid 5, para 19.

[40] See M. Cherif Bassiouni, 'A Functional Approach to General Principles of International Law' (1990) 11/3 *Michigan Journal of International Law* 768, 782.

own legal framework, it can provide a useful point of reference to solve difficult legal issues for which the Bank's own framework provides no clear answer.[41]

For instance, in *World Bank v ASDECON Corporation Company Limited*,[42] the Bank's judging body reached its decision concerning the evidential value of party's silence[43] using legal sources related to different domestic jurisdictions. Specifically, the Sanctions Board referred, at the same time, to a reasoning made by the French Supreme Court on May 24, 2005,[44] and to the criterion offered in the volume Weinstein's Evidence, which is a commentary on rules of evidence for the United States courts and magistrates.[45]

From such a complex reference, it is possible to make some deductions about the rule of law applied by the Sanctions Board. Firstly, it appears that the Board feels free to identify and choose legal principles that are conceived not only under common law but also under other legal systems, such as the civil law jurisdictions. Moreover, it seems that the Board could combine them in order to extrapolate new, more complex, legal tenets suitable for its decisions. In other words, although the Bank is trying to establish an independent and self-ruling sanctioning system, the Sanctions Board's decisions represent evidence suggesting that this system is not self-sufficient. Indeed, it is possible to distinguish between two different kinds of sources of the Sanctions Board's decisions: "Internal sources," which are represented by the various documents issued by the Bank in order to discipline its

---

[41] See 'Advisory Opinion' (*World Bank*) (n 25) 6, para 24.

[42] This case involved ASDECON Corporation Company Limited ("Respondent") and arose in the context of the Thailand Highways Management Project by which the Kingdom of Thailand sought to enhance the efficiency, productive use and management of its road network. In December 2003 the International Bank for Reconstruction and Development (IBRD) and the Kingdom of Thailand entered into a loan agreement for the Project. In November 2004, the Kingdom of Thailand's implementing agency for the Project issued a request for proposals to provide consulting services for the development and implementation of a central roads database system, bridge management system, and road maintenance management system. In December 2004, a Consortium consisting of Respondent, two other partners (TIS Consultants Company Limited and Supachai Prechaterasat) and a third firm submitted a proposal to which the Implementing Agency gave the highest technical score of all bidders. In October 2005, the Implementing Agency recommended the Contract's award to the Consortium. Shortly before the signing date, however, the third firm asked to postpone the signing. In July 2006, it informed the Implementing Agency that it would not proceed with the contract. ASDECON Corporation Company Limited, as well as the other two partners, were accused of engaging in corrupt practices offering (and agreeing) to pay Implementing Agency officials seventeen percent of the total contract price (THB 10 million, approximately US$ 320,000) to influence the Consortium's technical score; and soliciting (although not convincing) the third firm also to participate in such corrupt payment. At the end of the proceeding the Respondent was sentenced for a debarment with conditional release with a minimum period of ineligibility of five years. See *World Bank v ASDECON Corporation Company Limited*, [2012] Sanctions Board 50.

[43] ibid para 2.14.

[44] See Cour de Cassation (France), 1st Civ. Chamber, 24 May 2005, Bull. Civ. no. 233, Appeal no. 02-15188 (finding that while silence does not in itself amount to acceptance, other circumstances may permit giving it the meaning of an acceptance).

[45] "In all cases . . . the burden is on the proponent to convince the judge that in the circumstances of the case a failure to respond is so unnatural that it supports the inference that the party acquiesced in the statement." See Weinstein's Evidence ¶ 801(d)(2)(B)[01], at 801-202 n.15.

proceedings (e.g., the Sanctions Procedures, Consultant Guidelines, etc.), and "external sources," which are represented by legal rules developed in various national legal systems (e.g., legal tenets, statutes, judicial decisions, etc.) or in other international contexts (e.g., international conventions).[46] The former could be considered the principal sources of the Sanctions Board's decisions. An entire section of each decision, called "Applicable Standards of Review," is dedicated to identifying the internal rules relevant in the specific case. The latter are used in a less formal way to support the reasoning of the judging body. These external sources are indicated only parenthetically by means of footnotes, and sometimes their use is even implicit. Notwithstanding that the system was conceived as self-determining, the use of "external sources" appears to be unavoidable for several reasons.

Firstly, despite the issuance of many documents disciplining in detail the sanctioning system, inevitably the internal sources cannot currently represent a sufficient instrument to solve the cases. Moreover, the same circumstance that the sanctionable practices substantially refer to criminal conducts that constitute specific offenses in the various domestic legal systems implies that the Sanctions Board is naturally induced to use the notion, interpretation, and legal theories nationally developed in relation to such offenses. Finally, the reference to external sources could offer additional authoritativeness to the Sanctions Board's decisions.

Although the circumstances that the Sanctions Board does not refer to a sole legal system might be welcomed as a way of guaranteeing the necessary pluralism required in an international context, the absence of predetermined criteria on the rule of law applicable in the course of sanctioning procedures could cause serious concerns in relation to the lack of definitiveness that could undermine respondents' right to defense.

3.4 Role of Precedents

Notwithstanding the recent implementation of the sanctions process and the relatively exiguous amount of decisions taken by the Sanctions Board, it is already possible to observe a quite relevant referral to "internal" precedents. The importance of the Sanctions Board's decisions as a source of interpretation on which the financial institution deeply relies has been stressed by the Bank's General Counsel, who at the same time highlighted its limits. As a matter of fact, in the Advisory Opinion of 2010, the General Counsel asserted:

> *First*, in practical terms, it will take some considerable time for the Board to develop sufficient jurisprudence on a range of legal issues, so issues of first impression are likely to arise for the foreseeable future. *Second*, the Sanctions Board was not established as a policy-making body, so certain issues, in particular as to the proper interpretation of the Ban's legal and policy framework, lie outside its purview.[47]

---

[46]For an example, see *infra* note 76 and accompanying text in Chap. 4.

[47]See 'Advisory Opinion' (*World Bank*) (n 25) 4, para 15.

The General Counsel also specified:

> Interpretation [. . .] must be carried out according to general principles of legal interpretation, first and foremost that any interpretation must flow logically from the intended meaning of the text. Interpretation, even of texts as broadly stated as the definitions, must not slip into a disguised form of amendment—which would amount to a retroactive application of norms.[48]

The importance of the Sanctions Board's precedents as a source of interpretation has clearly emerged in *World Bank v Income Electrix Limited*,[49] where the judging body expressly referred to its previous decisions three times:

1) in setting the criteria to assert the liability of the legal person, as abovementioned;
2) in determining the sanctions, where it stated: "As reflected in Sanctions Board precedent, the Sanctions Board considers the totality of the circumstances and all potential aggravating and mitigating factors to determine an appropriate sanction";[50]
3) in considering the passage of significant time from the World Bank's awareness of the conduct to the final decision as a mitigating factor.[51]

Although at the moment it is not clear to what extent the further pronouncements of the Sanctions Board will adhere to earlier decisions and if the judging body will consider itself in a sense bound to follow previous judgments similarly to what happens under the common law doctrine of precedent, there are no doubts that its earlier pronouncements have already obtained the role of a persuasive authority in the decision process of the judging body.

---

[48]ibid 4, para 17.

[49]The case arose in the context of the Nigerian National Energy Development Project. On 15 July 2005, the World Bank's fund for the poorest, International Development Association ("IDA") and the Federal Republic of Nigeria entered into a Development Credit Agreement to provide US$172 million equivalent in financing for the project. The project sought to "facilitate a smooth transition to the new market and to increase efficiency in the power sector." IDA signed a Project Agreement with the National Electric Power Authority, later known as the Power Holding Company of Nigeria Plc ("PHCN"). On 30 January 2007, the Respondent submitted to PHCN a bid for a contract for the "Supply and Installation of Pre-Paid Meters in Abuja." The bid, signed by a manager of the Respondent, purported to be on behalf of a joint venture ("JV") between the Respondent and another partner firm. The Bidding Documents required joint ventures to include a copy of the JV agreement and a signed and notarized power of attorney in their bids. The Respondent submitted these documents with its bid, each with the Proposed JV Partner's purported signature. When the bids were opened, PHCN noted the Proposed JV Partner was named as a JV partner in two different bids: one for Respondent and one for a consortium with three other firms. Upon PHCN's inquiries, the Proposed JV Partner confirmed it had entered into a JV with the latter consortium only, and its purported signatures on the JV documents in Respondent's bid were false. PHCN rejected Respondent's bid due to the misrepresentations in its JV documentation. On those grounds INT alleged the JV agreement and power of attorney submitted with Respondent's bid were fraudulently signed in the Proposed JV Partner's name by Respondent, in violation of the May 2004 Procurement Guidelines. Eventually, the Respondent was sentenced to a fixed-term debarment of six months. See *World Bank v Income Electrix Limited*, [2012] Sanctions Board 46.

[50]ibid para 32.

[51]ibid para 43.

3.5 Resolution of Conflicts Between Internal Regulatory Sources

The incompleteness and fragmentation of the legal framework developed by the Bank inevitably generate potential conflicts between the various applicable sources. It is emblematic what occurred in *World Bank v Ultra Computers Company*,[52] where a conflict arose as to which version of the Procurement Guidelines was to be applied. Indeed, the Financing Agreement that the International Development Association (IDA) and the Republic of Azerbaijan entered into in 2008 provided that the October 2006 Procurement Guidelines (May 2004, revised October 2006) would govern the project's procurement. The bidding documents, however, remanded to the "May 2010 Procurement Guidelines." In order to solve this conflict, the Sanctions Board decided that in accordance with considerations of equity, the applicable standards in the event of such conflicts shall be those agreed between the member country and the World Bank.[53] On that occasion, the Sanctions Board identified the May 2010 Procurement Guidelines as the source governing the case.

The criterion utilized by the Sanctions Board in order to solve such a conflict between internal regulatory sources gives rise to some matters of concern. Indeed, the general reference to considerations of equity appears to be a too vague basis to ground a decision on the applicable source. An approach adhering to the key tenets related to the principle of legality should rather refer to more certain and preestablished criteria. In the Advisory Opinion of 2010, the Bank's General Counsel offered some insights into this complex issue asserting that

> Any conflict among sources of law should be settled through the application of the foregoing hierarchy. 'Constitutional' issues arising under the Articles of Agreement, for example, supersede all other considerations. Likewise, considerations of policy purposes may

[52]The case involved Ultra Computers Company ("Respondent"), one of the Azerbaijan leading IT companies, and arose in the context of the Azerbaijan Social Protection Development Project, which sought to improve the delivery of labour market and social protection interventions in Azerbaijan through strengthened institutions, enhanced institutional and human resources capacity, and improved targeting of social safety net programs. In November 2008, the International Development Association ("IDA") and the Republic of Azerbaijan entered into a Financing Agreement. In March 2011, the Ministry of Labour and Social Protection of the Population of the Republic of Azerbaijan issued bidding documents for the procurement of computer hardware and office equipment under the project. Where a bidder did not manufacture the required goods, the bidding documents required the bidder to submit manufacturers' authorization forms to demonstrate that the relevant manufacturer had authorized the bid's submission and guaranteed the goods. In April 2011, the Respondent submitted a bid for the contract, appending 10 manufacturers' authorization forms purportedly issued by manufacturers to authorize the bid's submission with full guarantees of the manufacturers' goods as offered. Because of one of the manufacturers' authorization forms was a scanned copy, the ostensible issuer was asked about the authenticity of the manufacturers' authorization form and he denied the form was authentic. Consequently, INT accused the Respondent of engagement in fraudulent practices by submitting forged certificates. See *World Bank v Ultra Computers Company*, [2013] Sanctions Board 61.

[53]ibid para 10.

> supersede the literal meaning of the definitions of Sanctionable Practices, the Bank's own legal framework supersedes general principles of law, and so on...[54]

However, as the same Counsel admitted, a thornier issue arises when equivalent sources of law, such as different versions of the legal framework, conflict.[55] In such cases, no other solution is offered than to resort to the abovementioned considerations of equity.[56]

3.6 Variation Between Earlier and Later Versions of the Bank's Sources

A critical issue has emerged in relation to the sequence of regulations within the Bank's legal framework. In particular, it occurs where there is a variation between an earlier and a later version of some Bank's documents governing the sanctions regime. For instance, this issue became relevant on some occasions where, on the one hand, the Bank updated the definitions of the sanctionable practices in the Procurement Guidelines but, on the other, the loan agreement between the Bank and the investigated party included only the earlier versions of such definitions. In this case, INT has always supported the idea that the new definitions should apply, *ipso facto*, to new sanctions cases or, at least, to alleged misconducts that occur after their adoption.[57] In the Advisory Opinion of 2010, the Bank's General Counsel expressed the opposite view. Specifically, in the document, it was clarified that, due to the fact that the sanctions regime is based on a quasi-contractual model accomplished by agreements concluded between the Bank and the relevant borrower, these legal agreements specify what particular version of the various Guidelines has to be applied to the loan and project for their overall duration.[58] However, the General Counsel also specified that, although not recommended, the opposite solution could be based on the "fiduciary duty" that the Bank has under the Articles of Agreement, which theoretically gives the financial institution the "inherent authority" to impose sanctions based on the latest versions of its documents.[59]

In *World Bank v Concept Pharmaceuticals Limited*,[60] the Sanctions Board had the opportunity to address the abovementioned issue related to sequence of

---

[54]See 'Advisory Opinion' (*World Bank*) (n 25) 7, para 27.

[55]ibid 7, para 28.

[56]ibid 10, para 41.

[57]ibid 3, para 11.

[58]ibid.

[59]ibid 3, para 12.

[60]The case involved Concept Pharmaceuticals Limited ("Respondent"), an Indian privately held pharmaceutical company possessing 5 manufacturing plants and 17 branch offices, and arose in the context of the India Tuberculosis Control Projects financed by a Development Credit Agreement ("DCA") entered into between the Republic of India and the International Development Association

regulations. Specifically, in reviewing the merits of INT's allegations against the respondent, the Sanctions Board considered whether the submission of the bidding documents might constitute fraudulent practices as defined by the applicable Procurement Guidelines.

The respondent submitted bids to supply antituberculosis pharmaceuticals both in 2000 and in 2007. As a consequence, it was necessary to verify the legislative history of the definition of fraudulent practice. Pursuant to the August 1996 Procurement Guidelines, paragraph 1.15(a)(ii), a fraudulent practice consists in "a misrepresentation of facts in order to influence a procurement process or the execution of a contract to the detriment of the Borrower." Instead, according to paragraph 1.14(a)(ii) of May 2004 Procurement Guidelines, a fraudulent practice is defined in different and broader terms as "a misrepresentation or omission of facts in order to influence a procurement process or the execution of a contract."

Therefore, under the August 1996 Procurement Guidelines, it is a required proof of detriment to the borrower, while under the May 2004 Procurement Guidelines this element is no longer required. The older, more stringent definition of "fraudulent practices" in the August 1996 Procurement Guidelines was, of course, more favorable to the respondent because it placed a wider burden of proof on INT.

Consequently, the parties argued for establishing which provision was applicable to the bid submitted in 2007. In particular, INT asserted that the respondent's conduct under the bid done in 2007 was legally governed by the May 2004 definition. Contrariwise, the respondent objected that the contract which it entered into, although signed after the issuance of the 2004 Procurement Guidelines, referred to the 1996 definition, so its conduct was legally governed by the August 1996 definition.

The Sanctions Board failed to offer a formal solution in relation to this issue, holding simplistically that the respondent's conduct under both bids in fact violated the more stringent August 1996 definition so that it was unnecessary to determine whether the allegations were governed by the August 1996 definition or the May 2004 provision.

Therefore, the Sanctions Board lost an important opportunity to clarify which is the rule of law governing the issue of sequence of regulations. In particular, the judging body did not make it clear which provision prevails where the contract that the respondent enters into refers to a rule that is different from the one subsequently adopted. In other words, this is an issue of prevalence between the obligations arising from the contract and the general rules provided by the guidelines published by the World Bank. Indeed, depending on the solution given to such an issue,

("IDA"). The Respondent submitted bids to supply antituberculosis pharmaceuticals in tenders both in 2000 and in 2007. The combined value of the contracts awarded to Respondent was approximately US$ 4.9 million. Concept Pharmaceuticals Ltd. was accused of engaging in fraudulent practices by intentionally or recklessly submitting at least eighteen forged or otherwise deceptive performance certificates and orders in support of its bids under the project. See *World Bank v Concept Pharmaceuticals Limited*, [2012] Sanctions Board 47.

important hints may be gathered on the same nature (contractual or public) of the sanctioning proceedings.

3.7 Procedure and Due Process in the Sanctions System: General Remarks

The ensuing parts of this volume will offer an analysis of the most relevant procedural rules of the sanctions process. Such an examination will be conducted in the light of the principles of due process. However, before carrying out this analysis, it is necessary to verify whether and to what extent such principles can be considered applicable to the Bank's sanctions process. In particular, we have to address two fundamental questions that appear strictly connected to one another: the first being whether or not the principles of due process, which have historically been developed at the domestic level, can be applied at the global level and the second being whether or not those safeguards, which have traditionally characterized criminal cases, should be considered also applicable to procedures that have administrative nature.

Similarly to the concept of the rule of law, also the notion of due process appears historically linked to the development of the English legal system. The English idea of due process was first embodied in chapter 39 of Magna Carta,[61] which provides:

> No free man shall be seized or imprisoned, or stripped of his rights or possessions, or outlawed or exiled, or deprived of his standing in any other way, nor will we proceed with force against him, or send others to do so, except by the lawful judgement of his equals or by the law of the land.[62]

It is necessary to clarify that for the purposes of this analysis, we will focus on the notion of procedural due process as distinct from the substantial one.[63] The former, which concerns whether the government has followed adequate procedures in taking away a person's fundamental rights, includes forms of protections such as rules on administering trials, hearings for denying government benefits, and generally ensuring the proper administration of justice and reducing the arbitrary use of power. On the contrary, the latter aims at striking down laws that, although enacted following

---

[61]Magna Carta, meaning 'the Great Charter,' is the famous document issued by King John of England in 1215. It established for the first time the principle that everybody, including the king, was subject to the law. It can be still considered as a cornerstone of the British constitution. See Claire Breay and Julian Harrison, 'Magna Carta: an introduction' (*The British Library*, 28 July 2014) <www.bl.uk/magna-carta/articles/magna-carta-an-introduction>.

[62]See 'Magna Carta 1215' (*The British Library*) <www.bl.uk/collection-items/magna-carta-1215>.

[63]For a more detailed examination of the distinction between procedural and substantive due process see Nathan s Chapman and Michael W. Mcconnell, 'Due Process as Separation of Powers' (2011) 121(7) *The Yale Law Journal* 1672.

the democratic rules, are considered as unacceptable according to broader principles of fairness, justice, and individual rights.[64]

Although the legal safeguards connected to the notion of due process characterize many civil-law-based jurisdictions[65] and can also be found enshrined in some areas of Islamic law,[66] they may be considered a firm foundation of the common law legal systems. In the United States, basic safeguards of due process are expressly provided by the Fifth and Fourteenth Amendments to the US Constitution. Under the former, due process of the law requires the government to observe proper and traditional methods in depriving one of an important right:

> No person shall be [...] compelled in any criminal case to be a witness against himself, nor be deprived of life, liberty, or property, without due process of law.[67]

Due process guarantees are then strengthened by the provision of the Fourteenth Amendment, which has had great constitutional relevance since the Supreme Court has used it to apply most of the Bill of Rights to the states:

> [...] Nor shall any State deprive any person of life, liberty, or property, without due process of law; nor deny to any person within its jurisdiction the equal protection of the laws.[68]

As Laylin and Tuttle excellently clarified as long ago as 1922, in its deepest sense, due process entails the protection of both individuals and legal entities from the unjust deprivation of an important right. They also clarified that the term right has to be interpreted broadly in this context, including not only pecuniary fines but also "less usual expedients" that apparently have a mere administrative nature such as forfeiture of office:

> Punishment we understand as including any restraint or infliction so consequentially imposed upon being, or any pecuniary mulct so exacted from a human being a corporation, the amount of which bears no relation to any possible valuation of actual or theoretical injury suffered: it may include less usual expedients, such as outlawry, civil death, disfranchisement, forfeiture of office, or even mere official degradation censure-that is, the word is used in its broadest sense.[69]

---

[64]See Erwin Chemerinsky, 'Procedural Due Process Claims' (2000) 16(3) *Touro Law Review*, 871.

[65]For instance, the German constitution, *Grundgesetz* (i.e. Basic Law), which was adopted on 23 May 1949, includes the right to judicial review of administrative actions (Art. 19 IV GG), rules regarding the independence of the judiciary (Art. 97 GG), and in the right to be heard before a court (Art. 103 I GG). See 'Basic Law for the Federal Republic of Germany,' (*Deutscher Bundestag*) <https://www.btg-bestellservice.de/pdf/80201000.pdf>.

[66]For instance, although few of these appear to be followed in the actual legal practice of Islamic law, rules and principles of due process are present within the traditional sources of Islamic criminal law: the *Quran*, the *Sunna*, and classical jurisprudence. See Sadiq Reza, 'Due Process in Islamic Criminal Law' (2014) 46 *The George Washington International Law Review* 1.

[67]See 'Constitution of the United States – Amendment V (1791)' (*United States Senate*) <www.senate.gov/civics/constitution_item/constitution.htm#amdt_5_1791>.

[68]See 'Constitution of the United States – Amendment XIV (1868)' (*United States Senate*) <www.senate.gov/civics/constitution_item/constitution.htm#amdt_5_1791>.

[69]See Clarence E. Laylin and Alonzo H. Tuttle, 'Due Process and Punishment' (1922) 20(6) *Michigan Law Review* 614, 615.

If this is true, it is not surprising that by tradition, procedural due process safeguards have been deemed as applicable mainly to criminal cases. As a matter of fact, historically the deprivation of an important right represented a consequence that followed a conviction for an offense. However, although these were the origins of the safeguards, claiming that their application has to be limited to criminal trials seems to be an arbitrary choice in the light of the evolution of the law. There are several reasons why such a choice appears at the present time hard to justify.

Traditionally, criminal law has played the role of creating or defining a range of public wrongs that concern the whole community, and the criminal trial has represented the process through which members of the community have been called to answer for their alleged perpetrations of such misconducts.[70] As a result, the relationship between criminal law and due process stemmed from the severity of the punishment applicable within domestic jurisdictions for breaking these rules.

However, the further development of legal systems has added over time a degree of complexity that, requiring more often the adoption of a multidisciplinary approach, makes it impossible to follow a legal reasoning rigidly compartmentalized into the different areas of the law. This has become particularly true in relation to the blurring of the boundaries between criminal and administrative law, which is a direct consequence of the fact that administrative procedures and bodies, rather than criminal trials and courts, have been increasingly used to sanction illicit behaviors.

The following words from Hannis Taylor are emblematic of the fact that as early as the late twentieth century, the rise of the administrative state created major complexities for the procedural due process doctrine:

> Due process of law stands as the anti-pole of what French jurists call *droit administratif*, which rests upon the assumption that the government and each of its servants possesses a body of special rights and privileges as against private citizens to be fixed on principles different from those defining the legal rights and duties of one citizen toward another.[71]

For many years, the application of due process proved to be a dark conundrum for newer forms of administrative activities carried out by governments, like benefits programs, licensing, employment, education, and corrections, and common law courts held for a long time that the due process clause did not apply.[72] However, with the increasing intrusiveness of the administrative action with respect to the private sphere, such a position became eventually untenable. Similarly to what we have already argued in relation to the rule of law, due process is a fundamental principle of justice that has to be considered as a moral concept. It implies limits on the individual discretion of state agents that otherwise may lead to tyranny. Such a

[70]See R. Antony Duff, *Punishment, Communication and Community* (Oxford University Press 2001) 75.

[71]See Hannis Taylor, 'Due Process of Law' (1915) 24(5) *The Yale Law Journal* 353.

[72]The rationale for this was the right-privilege distinction under which only the fundamental rights of liberty and property received procedural due process protection against government deprivation. See Edward L. Rubin, 'Due Process and the Administrative State' (1984) 72(6) *California Law Review* 1044, 1051.

risk, which is inherently present where there is a one-to-one interaction between a state agent and an individual or entity,[73] is dramatically increased where the administrative rules provide for the imposition of a sanction on the private subject. Finally, the process of "decriminalization" carried out over the course of the last three decades in many domestic jurisdictions, by which petty offenses are attracted in the administrative sphere and as such are no longer under the control of criminal courts, has sharpened this problem even more.

Consequently, the intimate relationship between due process and criminal trials, which has its roots in the way in which the states exercised their power until the twenty-first century, cannot be used to limit the scope of due process to criminal trials. This is particularly true at the present time, where most adjudications are carried out by administrative bodies, which have the power to impose sanctions. Rubin expressed such a concept affirming that the due process safeguards provided by the US Constitution are supposed to operate also in relation to administrative decisions:

> The adoption of the fifth and fourteenth amendments preceded the development of the administrative state. When these amendments were drafted, adjudications by states – to which due process clearly applied – were carried out almost exclusively by courts. The words 'life, liberty, or property' were sufficient to include the entire range of issues that courts adjudicated; their effect, therefore, was to describe, not to exclude [. . .] Consequently, a strong argument can be made to preserve that inclusive effect. Instead of reading 'life, liberty, or property' as referring to a particular group of interests, it could be read as referring to the entire, now-expanded range of government adjudications.[74]

In the context of the Council of Europe, due process has found supranational recognition in the European Convention of Human Rights. In particular, it is enshrined in Article 6, which provides the fundamental right to a fair trial and enumerates a series of minimum rights that have to be guaranteed to everyone charged with a criminal offense.[75] In that regard, the European Court of Human Rights had more than one occasion to explain that due process safeguards have to be applied irrespective of the way in which a certain conduct is qualified within a domestic jurisdiction. In other words, formally labeling an illicit conduct as an administrative misconduct rather than a criminal offense does not constitute in the Court's opinion a justification for not applying the due process safeguards provided by the Convention where the applicable sanctions can still be considered as criminal in character taking into consideration their "punitive nature":

> [. . .] In removing "regulatory offences" from the criminal law the German legislature had introduced a simplified procedure of prosecution and punishment conducted before administrative authorities.[76]

---

[73]ibid 1103.

[74]ibid 1094.

[75]See Convention for the Protection of Human Rights and Fundamental Freedoms [1950], Article 6.

[76]See *Öztürk v Germany* (1984) Series A no 85, para 52.

> [. . .] Whilst the [administrative] penalty appears less burdensome in some respects than [the criminal ones], it has nonetheless retained a punitive character, which is the customary distinguishing feature of criminal penalties.[77]
>
> [. . .] It would be contrary to the object and purpose of Article 6 (art. 6), which guarantees to "everyone charged with a criminal offence" the right to a court and to a fair trial, if the State were allowed to remove from the scope of this Article (art. 6) a whole category of offences merely on the ground of regarding them as petty.[78]
>
> [. . .] Conferring the prosecution and punishment of minor offences on administrative authorities is not inconsistent with the Convention provided that the person concerned is enabled to take any decision thus made against him before a tribunal that does offer the guarantees of Article 6.[79]

Such an emphasis on the "punitive nature" of a sanction appears to perfectly capture the true spirit of due process as a means of avoiding arbitrary and unjust sanctioning decisions irrespective of their formal label. The European Court of Human Rights reaffirmed such an approach in *Welch v The United Kingdom*, where it stated that, taking into consideration the "punitive elements" that characterized a confiscation order, the latter amounted in reality to a penalty rather than an administrative measure.[80] In particular, the Court considered as decisive the following elements: the fact that the confiscation order was issued regarding proceeds of crime; the possibility for the trial judge to discretionally take into consideration, in determining the amount of the confiscated sum, the degree of culpability of the accused; the possibility of imprisonment in default of payment by the offender.[81]

Due process safeguards have also obtained supranational recognition within the Charter of Fundamental Rights of the European Union, which has become legally binding as of the entry into force of the Lisbon Treaty on December 1, 2009. Specifically, Article 41, which is entitled "Right to good administration," enshrines the principle in relation to the administrative procedures carried out by the EU institutions and the Member States:

> 1. Every person has the right to have his or her affairs handled impartially, fairly and within a reasonable time by the institutions, bodies, offices and agencies of the Union.
>
> 2. This right includes:
>
> (a) the right of every person to be heard, before any individual measure which would affect him or her adversely is taken;
>
> (b) the right of every person to have access to his or her file, while respecting the legitimate interests of confidentiality and of professional and business secrecy;
>
> (c) the obligation of the administration to give reasons for its decisions.

---

[77]ibid para 53.

[78]ibid.

[79]ibid para 56.

[80]See *Welch v The United Kingdom* (1995) Series A no 307-A, para 35.

[81]ibid para 33.

> 3. Every person has the right to have the Union make good any damage caused by its institutions or by its servants in the performance of their duties, in accordance with the general principles common to the laws of the Member States.
>
> 4. Every person may write to the institutions of the Union in one of the languages of the Treaties and must have an answer in the same language.[82]

A concrete application of such a principle can be found within the European Union antitrust context. As the Director General of the Directorate General for Competition of the European Commission clarified, due process has to be guaranteed also in antitrust proceedings notwithstanding their administrative nature. In particular, defendants should benefit from a series of rights such as the following:

- The right to receive a reasoned Statement of Objections giving companies the opportunity to respond, including any expert opinion they may want to put forward.
- The right to access the case file
- The right to an oral hearing.[83]

Again, at supranational level, serious problems have arisen in relation to due process by the sanctions introduced by the UN Security Council in the context of counterterrorism measures, which consist in a blacklisting mechanism that requires all UN members to impose travel bans, an assets freeze, and an arms embargo on the listed individuals or entities.[84] At the present time, the UN blacklisting framework does not respect the traditional pattern of due process safeguards. For instance, there is no international legal mechanism for checking or reviewing the accuracy of the information forming the basis of a sanctions committee blacklisting or the necessity for, and proportionality of, measures adopted. In truth, to ensure that fair and clear procedures exist for placing individuals and entities on sanctions lists and for removing them, the UN Security Council, on December 19, 2006, adopted Resolution 1730 (2006), by which a focal point to receive delisting requests was established. However, such an intervention cannot be considered as an adequate legal mechanism because, after the submission of a delisting request from a petitioner, it follows an intergovernmental procedure carried out not in the presence of the opposing party and without giving to the petitioner any possibility of being heard.[85] Moreover, the listed subjects have no right of access to a court or a quasi-judicial body at the UN level.[86] As Professor Iain Cameron convincingly explained

---

[82]See the Charter of Fundamental Rights of the European Union [2012] OJ C326/391, Article 41.

[83]See 'Safeguarding due process in antitrust proceedings' (*The European Commission*, Fordham Competition Law Institute, Annual Conference on International Antitrust Law and Policy, 23 September 2010) 8 <http://ec.europa.eu/competition/speeches/text/sp2010_06_en.pdf>.

[84]See 'Sanctions' (*The United Nations*) <www.un.org/sc/suborg/en/sanctions/information>.

[85]See 'Focal Point For De-Listing' (*The United Nations*, Sanctions) <www.un.org/sc/suborg/en/sanctions/delisting>.

[86]See Iain Cameron, 'The European Convention on Human Rights, Due Process and United Nations Security Council Counter-Terrorism Sanctions' (*Statewatch*, Council of Europe, 6 February 2006) 2 <www.statewatch.org/terrorlists/docs/Cameron-06.pdf>.

in a study focused on the relationship between the UN blacklisting measures and the due process safeguards provided by the European Convention of Human Rights:

> The effects of blacklisting may be sufficiently serious to be the 'determination of a criminal charge,' triggering the application of Article 6 [of the ECHR] in its entirety [. . .] There are corresponding provisions on due process in the UN Universal Declaration of Human Rights (UDHR) and the Covenant on Civil and Political Rights (ICCPR), and it is submitted that the ECtHR case law to a large extent expresses general principles of due process [. . .] The rights to an effective remedy, to access to court/fair trial, to fair trial in criminal matters, to reputation, to freedom of movement and to property are all contained in the UDHR (Articles 8, 10, 11, 12, 13 and 17 respectively). The ICCPR contains the right of freedom of movement (Article 12). Article 14 sets out rights and obligations in a suit at law and Article 17 protects against interferences in a person's 'privacy, honour and reputation'. There is no protection of property rights as such. However, Article 14 ICCPR requires access to court to determine a person's 'rights and obligations at a suit at law'. Disputes over the right to dispose of possessions, bank accounts etc. undoubtedly concern rights or obligations at a suit of law.[87]

The controversy and transnational debate surrounding due process reflect that the UN decision-making process is emerging as a new tier of governance applicable and accountable to a complex, hybrid, global constituency.[88] Contexts in which international organizations, such as the United Nations and the World Bank, have assumed decision-making authority affecting individuals are exemplars of the emergence of such a global system of governance. The development of a procedural framework characterized by fairness and justice for this new tier of governance "represents a far greater theoretical and practical challenge for the international legal order than has so far been acknowledged."[89]

Having illustrated how there are strong arguments for supporting the idea that due process safeguards should be applied in their entirety to any sanctioning systems irrespective of their nature at both the domestic and supranational levels, we have now to consider if such fundamental safeguards should be deemed as applicable also to the World Bank's sanctions process.

There are at least three compelling reasons for believing that the answer is a resounding affirmative.

Firstly, as we have argued so far, the fact that the sanctions process is labeled as an administrative procedure cannot be considered a decisive element for this purpose. It appears evident that the Bank, in an attempt to avoid the introduction of full due process safeguards, has always placed great stress on the purported administrative nature of the debarment procedure.[90] The following statement is emblematic of such an approach:

---

[87] ibid 2 and 21.

[88] See Devika Hovell, 'Due Process in the United Nations,' (2016) 110(1) *The American Journal of International Law* 1, 2.

[89] ibid 48.

[90] For instance, in *World Bank v E.C. De Luna Construction Corp. and Mr. Eduardo C. De Luna* the Sanctions Board justified its denial of the retroactive application of "beneficial rules," *inter alia*, affirming that materials cited by the Respondents concerned criminal and disciplinary proceedings,

> The WBG's investigative process and sanctions system are not criminal procedure mechanisms, but rather internal administrative mechanisms set up to ensure the funds entrusted to the WBG are used for their intended purposes.[91]

However, notwithstanding such continuous attempts, the evident punitive nature of the sanctions that the Bank might impose clearly suggests that due process safeguards cannot be watered down.

Secondly, the sanctionable practices (i.e., the conducts punishable by the Bank) resemble serious offenses at the domestic level: "Corrupt practice" corresponds to bribery, "fraudulent practice" to fraud, "coercive practice" to coercion, "collusive practice" to collusion, and "obstructive practice" to obstruction of justice. As a result, a decision about guilt would be as stigmatizing as a criminal conviction, this without taking into consideration that the Bank's investigative body sends referral reports to relevant national authorities if evidence indicates that the laws of a member country may have been violated.[92] For instance, in 2016, the Bank made 30 different referrals to national prosecuting authorities.[93] From a domestic criminal procedure law perspective, the submission of such evidentiary materials gathered without the application of full due process safeguards might also cause serious issues of constitutional relevance in relation to the violation of fundamental defense rights. Such a proposition is supported also by the fact that a respondent might be subject to national criminal proceedings for the perpetration of the same facts for which it is under investigations in the Bank's sanctions process.[94]

The seriousness of the problems that the submission of the Bank's evidentiary materials to national authorities might generate strongly emerged from the Bank's investigations on corrupt practices allegedly perpetrated by some employees of SNC-Lavalin.[95] In the case at issue, the Bank shared some documents with the Royal Canadian Mounted Police. They basically consisted in a series of emails from

---

where instead sanctions proceedings are administrative in nature. *World Bank v E.C. De Luna Construction Corp. and Mr. Eduardo C. De Luna*, [2016] Sanctions Board 89.

[91]See 'World Bank Group Settlements: How Negotiated Resolution Agreements Fit Within the World Bank Group's Sanctions System' (*World Bank*, Sanctions & Compliance) 1 <http://pubdocs.worldbank.org/en/415101449169634523/Settlement-Process-Note.pdf>.

[92]Such referral reports are based on the "Final Investigation Report" that the World Bank investigative department issues where it finds sufficient evidence to conclude that it is more likely than not that a sanctionable practice occurred. See 'The World Bank Group Integrity Vice Presidency – Annual Update – Fiscal Year 2016' (World Bank, Publications) 24 <http://pubdocs.worldbank.org/en/118471475857477799/INT-FY16-Annual-Update-web.pdf>.

[93]ibid 40.

[94]See *infra* notes 86–94 and accompanying text in Chap. 5.

[95]In 2011, the World Bank, which had provided more than $1 billion in financing for the construction of a bridge over the Padma River, learned that representatives of SNC-Lavalin, a Canadian leading engineering and construction group, planned to bribe government officials in Bangladesh to obtain the related contract. See ibid 12.

tipsters suggesting that there was corruption involving SNC-Lavalin employees in the process for awarding the supervision contract and in some investigative reports.[96] Consequently, the Canadian authorities, largely relying on the information the Bank shared, sought and obtained authorizations to intercept private communications, as well as a search warrant to collect direct evidence of the criminal activities. As a result, the Crown charged four individuals under the Corruption of Foreign Public Officials Act and joined the proceedings by direct indictment intending to present intercepted communications at trial.[97] In order to defend themselves, the accused sought an order requiring the production of certain investigation records of the Bank, as well as the validation of two subpoenas issued to the investigators of the financial institution. The Bank resisted on the following grounds:

> The Articles of Agreement of the IBRD and the IDA provide that their archives shall be inviolable. In addition, the Articles of Agreement provide that all officers and employees shall be immune from legal process with respect to acts performed by them in their official capacity, except when the IBRD or the IDA waives this immunity. These immunities have been implemented in Canadian law by two Orders in Council, and the Articles of Agreement of the IBRD and the IDA have been approved by Parliament in their entirety through the Bretton Woods and Related Agreements Act.[98]

The judge of first instance stated that, although these immunities were *prima facie* applicable to the archives and personnel of INT, the Bank had waived these immunities by participating in the Canadian domestic investigation. Accordingly, he ordered that the documents be produced for review by the court.[99] However, the Supreme Court of Canada held that the immunity shields the entire collection of stored documents of the IBRD and the IDA from both search and seizure and from compelled production. It also affirmed that partial voluntary disclosure of some documents by the Bank does not amount to a waiver of this immunity. Consequently, the Court set aside the production order.[100] Such a decision raises grave concerns because it theoretically allows the Bank's investigative body to conduct cherry-picking decisions not submitting evidence that could lead to a more complete picture and that could also be favorable to the accused.[101] In other words, it may adversely affect the principle of "equality of arms" in criminal trials allowing, on the one hand, the Bank to exert a potentially undue influence on domestic criminal investigations and, on the other, depriving the accused of the right to access the evidentiary material gathered by the financial institution in its entirety.

---

[96]See *World Bank Group v. Wallace*, 2016 SCC 15, [2016] 1 S.C.R. 207.

[97]ibid.

[98]ibid.

[99]ibid.

[100]ibid.

[101]A viable solution could consist in extending to the referral process the application of the rule that, under the Sanctions Procedures, obliges INT to present all relevant evidence in its possession that would reasonably tend to exculpate the Respondent or mitigate the Respondent's culpability to the SDO. See *infra* note 125 and accompanying text.

Moreover, the circumstance that the Bank adopted, in order to structure the Sanctions Board's sentencing practice, a solution very similar to the one followed in the US and in the UK for criminal offenses clearly supports the present proposition.[102]

Finally, the sanctions process clearly represents an instrument of global governance, and, as such, it has its Achilles' heel in the inherent lack of accountability that characterizes its structure. In fact, like the other global organizations, the World Bank does not get its mandate from the electorate, which at the domestic level embodies, through the elective process, the ultimate vehicle for accountability.[103] Consequently, in order to compensate for such a lack of democratic legitimacy in the imposition of severe sanctions on individuals and legal entities that do not have any chance to influence the way in which the sanctions process is structured, the Bank should adopt due process safeguards in their entirety avoiding convenient shortcuts. As Joshua Cohen and Charles Sabel have persuasively argued, accountable behaviors in this setting is no longer a matter of compliance with a rule set down by the same organization that is supposed to apply it but rather the provision of "good explanations" for the actions that the supranational organization decides to perform.[104]

Unfortunately, the financial institution has demonstrated so far considerable opposition to provide investigated parties with full due process safeguards, preferring to apply only some of these guarantees. It is emblematic that in its information note, the Bank affirms that the process is intended to provide the accused party only with "basic due process" before any decision is made.[105] The adoption of such a minimalist approach to the rights of due process appears to be based on the anxiety over the possibility that otherwise the procedural issues raised by the defense could get the sanctions system stuck in gridlock. Regrettably, in its report of February 2014, the Independent Advisory Board (IAB), which was established in 2008 to foster the independence of the Bank's investigations, supported this limited approach affirming that

> IAB has been particularly concerned that the sanctions system not be vested with excessive 'legalism' and 'procedural requirements' which will delay effective action. The IAB has consistently recommended that the Bank remember that it is a lending institution not a judicial body. It does not have the powers of a judicial body nor does INT have the powers of a criminal investigator.[106]

---

[102]See *infra* note 53 and accompanying text in Chap. 6.

[103]See Dani Rodrik, *The Globalization Paradox* (Oxford University Press 2011) 212.

[104]Joshua Cohen and Charles F. Sabel, 'Global Democracy?' (2004) 37 *New York University Journal of International Law and Politics* 763, 778.

[105]See 'World Bank Group's Sanctions Regime: Information Note' (*World Bank*) 3 <http://siteresources.worldbank.org/EXTOFFEVASUS/Resources/The_World_Bank_Group_Sanctions_Regime.pdf>.

[106]See 'Independent Advisory Board (IAB) 2013 Annual Report' (*World Bank*, February 2014) 15 <http://siteresources.worldbank.org/PROJECTS/Resources/40940-1244163232994/IAB-2013-ANNUAL_REPORT-FINAL-28FEB14.pdf>.

It is important to point out that, over the course of the last 15 years, the debarment procedures have been reformed several times[107] and that the Bank is moving in the right direction on this issue recognizing from time to time additional due process safeguards to respondents. For instance, the Bank has recently made it clearer the provision related to the right to a hearing.[108] However, much is still to be done as the present system has not yet introduced full due process safeguards for the involved parties. This part of the work deals with the procedure as it is currently applied by the Bank as of June 28, 2016.[109]

3.8 Complaint Intake

All allegations of sanctionable practices in Bank-financed projects are referred to the Integrity Vice Presidency (INT). This body was instituted in 2001 in order to conduct investigations into allegations of fraud and corruption in Bank-financed projects and of possible staff misconducts. As an investigative unit, INT includes a staff of attorneys, accountants, and development specialists.

The Integrity Vice Presidency might receive complaints from all over the world. It is possible to distinguish between three general sources of complaints: Bank staff; non-Bank sources (e.g., contractors or other bidders, government officials, concerned citizens, employees of NGOs, the media, and other multilateral development banks), and anonymous sources. In 2016, 37% of complaints received came from the Bank's staff, and 63% originated from non-Bank sources.[110] Starting from 2014, the percentage of the complaints deriving from anonymous sources has no more been disclosed in the annual reports released by the investigative body (see Fig. 3.1).

After receiving such information, INT undertakes a preliminary screening in order to determine the pertinence of the complaints. In particular, INT verifies if they pertain to one or more sanctionable practices and involve a Bank-supported activity. If a complaint meets both criteria, INT opens an "information item."[111]

However, INT does not investigate every information item. To determine whether to move from a preliminary inquiry to a full investigation, INT conducts further assessments of the allegations taking into consideration several other elements such as the credibility of the complaint, the amount of funds involved, the quality of the information or evidence, the potential impact of the case, the ability to investigate,

---

[107] For a detailed illustration of the various reforms see Chap. 2.

[108] See *infra* note 33 and accompanying text in Chap. 5.

[109] For the latest version of the procedures see 'Sanctions Procedures' (*World Bank*) (n 36).

[110] See 'INT Annual Update 2016' (*World Bank*) (n 92) 21.

[111] See 'The World Bank Group Integrity Vice Presidency – Annual Update – Fiscal Year 2012' (*World Bank*, Publications) 32 <http://documents.worldbank.org/curated/en/722001468154785173/pdf/731010AR0Box370C0disclosed010050120.pdf>.

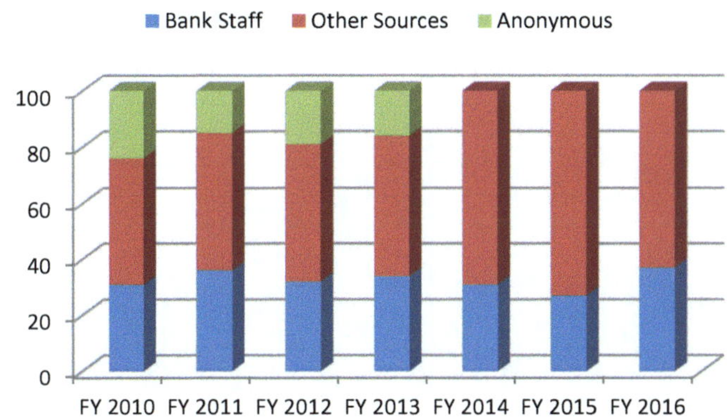

Fig. 3.1 Complaint Sources of INT External Investigations 2010–2016 (figures expressed in percentage). *Source*: 'The World Bank Group Integrity Vice Presidency – Annual Update – Fiscal Years 2010–2016' (*World Bank*, Publications) <www.worldbank.org/en/about/unit/integrity-vice-presidency>

the possible reputational risk to the Bank, and whether the matter is of sufficient gravity to warrant an investigation.[112] The absence of a mandatory nature of the investigative action, as well as of any order of priority of the abovementioned criteria, might generate a too broad discretionary power, which in turn could lead to arbitrary and obscure decisions as to the investigations to be pursued. To avoid such a risk, INT should adopt a more transparent regime under which it should declare which investigations were not conducted and for what reasons. According to INT's reports, the overall amount of complaints received by the Bank has decreased over the course of the latest 4 years reaching the minimum level of 279 during the fiscal year 2016 (see Fig. 3.2).

3.9 Investigations: The Integrity Office

It is possible to distinguish between two kinds of investigations: internal and external. Internal investigation involve World Bank staff members and focus on allegations of significant fraud and corruption occurring in Bank-financed projects or supported activities (i.e., operational fraud and corruption) or affecting the Bank's administrative budgets (i.e., corporate fraud and corruption).[113] Due to their inherent internal nature, those cases fall beyond the scope of the present volume. External

[112]When an information item involving Bank-Group activities is not opened for a full investigation, INT works with operational staff or other interlocutors to address the issues raised and undertake any action useful to minimize the potential risks that may have formed the basis of a complaint. See ibid.

[113]See 'INT Annual Update 2016' (*World Bank*) (n 92) 21.

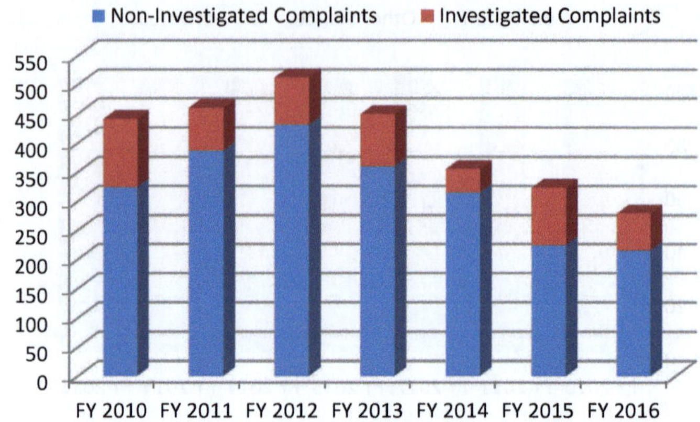

Fig. 3.2 Complaints Received—Full Investigation Ratio 2010–2016 (figures expressed in no. of cases). *Source*: 'The World Bank Group Integrity Vice Presidency – Annual Update – Fiscal Years 2010–2016' (*World Bank*, Publications) <www.worldbank.org/en/about/unit/integrity-vice-presidency>

investigations deal with allegations of the five sanctionable practices for which the Bank may impose sanctions on individuals and/or entities doing business with the Bank: fraud, corruption, collusion, coercion, and obstruction.[114]

The duty of the Bank's investigative body is to ascertain whether the involved natural or legal persons have engaged in one (or more) of such practices. The outcomes of external investigations can be various. A case is considered "substantiated" if INT finds sufficient evidence to conclude that it is more likely than not that a sanctionable conduct occurred (see Fig. 3.3). On the contrary, the allegation is considered "unsubstantiated" if INT believes that there is insufficient evidence to prove or disprove it and "unfounded" if the allegation has no basis in fact, and, consequently, it may be concluded that no sanctionable practice was perpetrated.[115]

In the event that INT substantiates a case, it also issues a Final Investigation Report (FIR), which is sent to regional management for comment before being finalized and then provided to the Bank's President.[116] FIRs also form the basis for two other important documents issued by INT: referral reports and redacted reports. The former are accounts that INT sends to relevant national authorities if evidence indicates that the laws of a member country may have been violated, while the latter are provided to the Bank's Board of Executive Directors for information,

[114]ibid.

[115]ibid 27.

[116]In some cases, a FIR is produced even if there is not reasonably sufficient evidence to substantiate a complaint; for instance, if INT believes that the investigation unearthed important lessons that should be shared with colleagues in the Bank Group and with client governments of the World Bank. See 'The World Bank Group Integrity Vice Presidency – Annual Update – Fiscal Year 2010' (*World Bank*, Publications) 27 <http://pubdocs.worldbank.org/en/233801449168548992/INT-FY10-Annual-Report.pdf>.

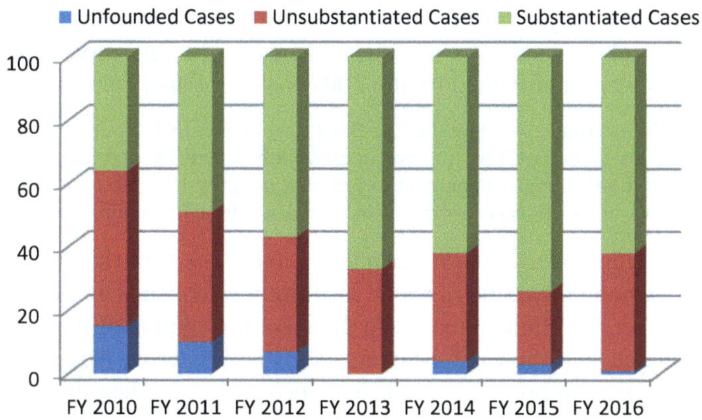

Fig. 3.3 INT's Substantiation Rate (figures expressed in percentage of cases). *Source*: 'The World Bank Group Integrity Vice Presidency – Annual Update – Fiscal Years 2010–2016' (*World Bank*, Publications) <www.worldbank.org/en/about/unit/integrity-vice-presidency>

and after the completion of all related sanctions proceedings, they are made publicly available.[117]

The average duration of the investigations that INT completed in 2016 was 12 months. Since 2010, INT has been putting a great deal of effort to close cases within 12–18 months, depending on their complexity, as it was recommended by the Volcker Panel in 2007.[118]

In its annual report for the fiscal year 2017, INT has clarified what the areas are on which the investigative body will concentrate its efforts to maximize its ability to fight against corruption and support the Bank's goals of eradicating extreme poverty and enhancing shared prosperity. Among those areas, a special focus on complex cases involving multiple perpetrators and jurisdictions is included. From INT's perspective, these cases often uncover widespread schemes, have more funds at risk, and can negatively impact development activities across a whole sector.[119] Furthermore, INT is aiming at enhancing its cooperation with national authorities. In particular, it is planning to renew its program of interim referrals and explore new ways to work with national authorities as early as feasible in the investigative cycle.[120]

---

[117]See 'INT Annual Update 2016' (*World Bank*) (n 92) 21.

[118]The Panel recommended that: "Despite the need for some investigations to extend longer than anticipated [...] INT should strive to complete its external investigations and reports within one year for noncomplex matters and within 18 months for complex matters." See 'Independent Panel Review of the World Bank Group Department of Institutional Integrity' (*World Bank*, 13 September 2007) para 94 <http://siteresources.worldbank.org/NEWS/Resources/Volcker_Report_Sept._12,_for_website_FINAL.pdf>.

[119]See 'INT Annual Update 2016' (*World Bank*) (n 92) 19.

[120]ibid.

Historically, the way in which INT was organized within the Bank structure caused concerns about its degree of independency of the operational management. Those concerns were highlighted by the 2007 Volcker Panel, which clarified:

> Within any administrative structure that the Bank may create, INT should be nurtured and maintained as an exemplary investigative organization staffed by experienced, respected professionals, with a strong commitment to program integrity [...] Because of the importance of the work of INT [it is necessary] its independence from operational management.[121]

Consequently, to enhance its independency, the Bank implemented some structural reforms. Among them, the financial institution established an Advisory Board. As a matter of fact, the Bank agreed with the recommendation of the Volcker Panel and acknowledged that the establishment of a small external Advisory Oversight Board was necessary to protect the independence and strengthen the accountability of INT.[122] As a result, the Bank created the Independent Advisory Board (IAB) and appointed its members on September 18, 2008, one year after the Volcker Panel made its recommendation. The IAB advised on both INT's relations with the Bank and the applicable policies and procedures.[123] The IAB operated from autumn 2008 to summer 2014 issuing an annual report at the end of each year. It issued its last report in February 2014.

3.10 First Tier of the Sanctions Process: The Suspension and Debarment Officer

At the end of the investigation, if INT believes that there is sufficient evidence that a firm or individual, formally called "respondent," has engaged in a sanctionable practice, it launches a sanctions case by submitting a Statement of Accusations and Evidence to a Suspension and Debarment Officer (SDO).[124] Under the Sanctions Procedures, in submitting a SAE to the SDO, INT has to present all relevant evidence in its possession that would reasonably tend to exculpate the respondent or mitigate the respondent's culpability.[125]

Indeed, in the first tier of the sanctions process, the parajudicial authority is vested in the SDO, who is a Bank official. The SDO not only performs control functions on

[121] See 'Independent Panel Review' (*World Bank*) (n 118) para 31.

[122] See 'Implementing the Recommendations of The Independent Panel Review of the World Bank Group's Department of Institutional Integrity – Report of the Working Group' (*World Bank*, 23 January 2008) 5, <http://siteresources.worldbank.org/NEWS/Resources/volcker_report_response.pdf>.

[123] See 'Independent Advisory Board (IAB) 2009 Annual Report' (*World Bank*, December 2009) 1 <http://documents.worldbank.org/curated/en/623111468154789920/pdf/562890AR0SecM21C0disclosed081241101.pdf>.

[124] See 'Sanctions Procedures' (*World Bank*) (n 36), Part A, s 3.01(b).

[125] ibid Part A, s 3.02.

the Integrity Vice Presidency, acting as a gatekeeper and legal advisor to the investigative body,[126] but also exercises a relevant power in the process as it is specified in the Terms of Reference of the Bank:

> The World Bank Evaluation and Suspension Officer [currently known as Suspension and Debarment Officer] is a critical component in ensuring an efficient, effective and fair sanctions process. The initial review of sanctions cases by the Evaluation Officer allows for their early disposition without the necessity of full sanctions proceedings in every case.[127]

Taking into consideration the SDO's considerable power within the sanctions process, the circumstance that the officer, being a Bank's employee,[128] does not enjoy sufficient independency from the financial institution represents a matter of concern. The provision of the Terms of Reference under which the SDO "shall recuse him or herself in cases where he or she may have an actual or perceived [an unspecified] conflict of interest"[129] does not appear to guarantee in a sufficient way his or her judicial impartiality. Such an issue appears even more relevant taking into consideration the *quantum* of evidence that must be presented by INT before the SDO in order to obtain a temporary suspension or the recommendation of a sanction.[130] However, although the SDO is appointed directly by the President of the Bank, the fact that the financial institution has developed a wide range of selection criteria that have to be met in order to appoint an SDO can be viewed in positive terms. Among them, it is provided that the SDO must have a minimum of 10 years of relevant experience and an advanced degree in law or other related field; have knowledge of and experience in the conduct of investigations; and be of proven competence, independence and integrity.[131]

3.11 Temporary Suspension

In submitting a Statement of Accusations and Evidence, INT may request the Suspension and Debarment Officer (SDO) to apply a "Temporary Suspension," also called "Early Temporary Suspension" (ETS). It is a recent addition to the Bank's sanctions process and consists in a mechanism for suspending firms and

---

[126]See Todd J. Canni 'Debarment is no longer private World Bank business: an examination of the Bank's distinct debarment procedures used for corporate procurements and financed projects' (2010) 40/1 *Public Contract Law Journal* 147, 155.

[127]See 'Terms of Reference of the World Bank (IBRD/IDA) Evaluation Officer' (*World Bank*) 1, <http://siteresources.worldbank.org/EXTOFFEVASUS/Resources/EO_Terms_of_Reference.pdf>.

[128]The Evaluation Officer is appointed by the President of the Bank and reports budgetarily and managerially to the Office of the President. See ibid.

[129]ibid.

[130]See *infra* notes 51–53 and accompanying text in Chap. 5.

[131]See 'Terms of Reference of the World Bank Evaluation Officer' (*World Bank*) (n 127) 2.

individuals from eligibility during the investigation phase. Therefore, if the Bank's official considers that there is sufficient evidence to demonstrate that the respondent has engaged in a sanctionable practice and believes that he or she would recommend, as an appropriate sanction for such a conduct, a debarment for a minimum period of 2 years, the SDO shall issue a "Notice of Temporary Suspension" to the respondent.[132] The notice has the same effect of a temporary debarment. The Sanctions Procedures expressly provide that "Upon issuance of the Notice of Temporary Suspension by the SDO, the Respondent shall be temporarily suspended from eligibility, with the same effect as if it had been debarred."[133]

In its report of February 2014, the Independent Advisory Board (IAB) specified that "the delicacy of the matter is that the Bank should not allow bidders under serious suspicion to continue to submit proposals for contracts." At the same time, the panel expressed the following opinion:

> The sanction procedures need to ensure that an ETS does not require the same (or even higher) standard as for a statement of accusation and evidence (SAE), let alone for a decision by the Sanctions Board (SB).[134]

In the absence of specific criteria of evaluation and minimum guarantees, the tendency to reduce the standard of proof for the adoption of a temporary suspension can cause serious concerns in terms of due process. The same IAB recognized that "an ETS prejudges the position of the bidder and can be highly damaging commercially" and, consequently, recommended that when an ETS is applied, "the sanctions system needs to be mindful, however, that the case is concluded within a reasonable time-frame."[135] However, until 2016, the sanctions process did not provide more stringent time limits for concluding cases where an ETS had been applied. The situation was complicated by the circumstance that the Sanctions Board *de facto* denied its competence to lift the temporary suspension issued by the SDO. In *Information Computer Systems*, the Sanctions Board stated:

> In its submission of September 9, 2013, the Respondent requested that the Sanctions Board lift the Respondent's temporary suspension in light of INT's "obstruction and delay tactics," as well as the length of the Respondent's temporary suspension to date. The Sanctions Procedures provide that a temporary suspension imposed by the EO [now known as SDO] shall remain in effect pending the final outcome of sanctions proceedings, unless the EO decides to terminate the suspension upon review of a Respondent's Explanation.[136]

With the adoption of the new Sanctions Procedures of June 28, 2016, the Bank has eventually adopted some procedural rules that govern the matter in a way that appears respectful of fundamental due process safeguards. In particular, they provide:

---

[132]See 'Sanctions Procedures' (*World Bank*) (n 36), Part A, s 2.01(c).

[133]ibid Part A, s 2.02.

[134]See 'IAB 2013 Annual Report' (*World Bank*) (n 106), 11.

[135]ibid 12.

[136]See *World Bank v Information Computer Systems* [2014] Sanctions Board 71, para 60.

> If, before INT concludes an investigation, the Integrity Vice President believes that there is sufficient evidence to support a finding of a Sanctionable Practice against a Respondent and that it is highly likely that the investigation will be successfully concluded and a Statement of Accusations and Evidence will be presented to the SDO within a maximum period of one year, INT may present to the SDO a Request for Temporary Suspension [...] INT shall accompany any such Request for Temporary Suspension with a description of the current progress of the ongoing investigation, including any evidence that remains to be gathered, together with a good faith estimate of the time required to complete its investigation [...] may not exceed one year.[137]

The new version of the Sanctions Procedures also provides for the duration of the temporary suspension. Specifically, they establish that a temporary suspension shall have an initial duration of 6 months, and not later than 5 months after the commencement of the temporary suspension, INT may request an extension for a further period not exceeding 6 months.[138] Moreover, the procedures provide that if a Statement of Accusations and Evidence is not submitted to the SDO prior to the end of the period of temporary suspension, the suspension shall automatically expire.[139]

3.12 Notice of Sanctions Proceedings

After examining the case, the SDO makes a first-tier review of the Statement of Accusations and Evidence in order to verify the sufficiency of the evidence. If the SDO finds that the accusations are supported by "sufficient evidence," he or she issues a "Notice of Sanctions Proceedings" to the respondent, appending the Statement of Accusations and Evidence.[140]

Upon the issuance of the Notice, the SDO shall recommend an appropriate sanction selected from the range of possible sanctions identified in the Sanctions Procedures to be imposed on each respondent.[141]

Within 30 days after delivery of the Notice, the respondent may file an "Explanation" with the SDO seeking either dismissal of the case or a reduction in the recommended sanction. The procedural rules limit this opportunity of offering explanations providing that they have to be included in a document not exceeding 20 single-sided pages, unless the SDO approves a longer submission.[142]

Although such a limitation is not absolute, it appears to be unfair, especially taking into consideration the extreme complexity of many cases investigated by the Bank and the circumstance that the SDO's decisions tend to become final. The

[137] See 'Sanctions Procedures' (*World Bank*) (n 36), Part A, s 2.01(a).

[138] ibid Part A, s 2.04(a).

[139] ibid Part A, s 2.04(c).

[140] ibid Part A, s 4.01(a).

[141] ibid Part A, s 4.01(c).

[142] ibid Part A, s 4.02(b).

Sanctions Procedures expressly provide that if the respondent does not contest the SDO's determination within 90 days, the recommended sanction "shall enter immediately into force"[143] upon issuance of a Notice of Uncontested Sanctions Proceedings.[144]

Another important effect related to the issuance of the Notice is that if the SDO recommends a sanction including a minimum period of debarment exceeding 6 months, the respondent will automatically be suspended from eligibility, with the same effect as if it had been debarred, from the date of issuance of the Notice until the date of the final outcome of the sanctions proceedings.[145] Some concerns arise from the circumstance that in such a case, the Sanctions Procedures do not provide any limit to the duration of the temporary suspension.

3.13 Second Tier of the Sanctions Process: The Sanctions Board

Within 90 days after the Notice of Sanctions Proceedings has been delivered, the respondent may contest the case by submitting a "Response" to the Sanctions Board,[146] which is a parajudicial body composed of four non-Bank staff and three Bank staff, and chaired by one of its non-Bank staff members. The presence of a number of external members higher than those of internal should assure a certain level of independence and impartiality. It could be considered as the final arbiter of whether an entity should be sanctioned.[147]

The first impression of this review system is that it could amount to a judicial appeal. In truth, after a deeper analysis, the Sanctions Board's review seems to possess particular features that make it different from what could be considered a common appeal. Indeed, the Sanctions Board cannot be considered as a forum in which the parties can appeal against decisions made by SDOs. The choice taken by SDOs during the first phase of the proceedings is defined by section 4.01(c) of the Sanctions Procedures as a mere "recommendation of appropriate sanction" and not as a formal decision of the case.[148] Such a recommendation could only potentially

[143] ibid Part A, s 4.04.

[144] As an example, see the notice issued in May 2016 to Consorcio Ocongate. See 'Notice of Uncontested Sanctions Proceedings' (*World Bank*, Sanctions Case no. 366, IBRD Loan Number 7643-PE, 24 May 2016) <http://siteresources.worldbank.org/EXTOFFEVASUS/Resources/3601045-1371577728750/Notice_of_Uncontested_Sanctions_Proceedings_Case_366(ConsorcioOcongate)(5.24.2016).pdf>.

[145] ibid s 4.02(a).

[146] ibid s 5.01(a).

[147] See Canni 'Debarment is no longer private World Bank business' (n 126) 155.

[148] Section 4.01(c) provides that "The SDO shall recommend in the Notice an appropriate sanction to be imposed on each Respondent [. . .]" See 'Sanctions Procedures' (*World Bank*) (n 36), Part A, s 4.01(c).

become a definitive decision, and in order to acquire such a quality it requires the acquiescence of respondents.[149]

On the contrary, where a respondent submits a written Response to the Sanctions Board, it summons into the ongoing proceedings the intervention of this body in order to obtain a more impartial judgment. In such a case, the decision taken by the Sanctions Board represents the sole formal judgment of the proceedings.[150] It follows from the same hybrid nature of the Sanctions Board's review that it is characterized by the two ensuing features.

Firstly, the Sanctions Board, considering *de novo* the case, is absolutely not bound by the recommendation previously issued by the SDO.[151] This conclusion is supported by the same wording of the Sanctions Procedures:

> if the Sanctions Board determines that it is more likely than not that the Respondent engaged in one or more Sanctionable Practices, it shall impose an appropriate sanction [. . .] In determining the appropriate sanction(s), the Sanctions Board shall not be bound by the recommendation of the SDO.[152]

Therefore, as a direct consequence, the Sanctions Board may impose a more severe sentence than the one recommended by the Suspension and Debarment Officer.

The second feature of Sanctions Board's review is represented by the circumstance that its scope cannot be limited by the arguments or the requests presented in the respondents' Response or INT's Reply. Indeed, the judging body has made it clear that in reaching its determinations, it needs to consider a full record, including all relevant evidence available in the case, whether inculpatory or exculpatory, aggravating or mitigating, to carry out its responsibilities.[153] In order to support this assertion, the Sanctions Board cited section 8.01 of the Sanctions Procedures, which lastly provides:

> [. . .] the Sanctions Board shall issue a written decision setting forth a recitation of the relevant facts, its determination as to the culpability of the Respondent, any sanction to be imposed on the Respondent and its Affiliates and the reasons therefor.[154]

---

[149]Section 4.04 provides that "If the Respondent does not contest the accusations or the sanction recommended by the SDO in the Notice within ninety (90) days [. . .] the sanction(s) recommended by the SDO in the Notice shall enter immediately into force." See ibid s 4.04.

[150]It is emblematic that section 8.03 defines Sanctions Board judgments in a sharpen way, providing that: "The decision of the Sanctions Board shall be final and without appeal, and shall be binding on the parties to the proceedings. The decision shall take effect immediately, without prejudice to any action taken by any government under its applicable law." See ibid s 8.03.

[151]As the same World Bank studies clearly explain: "the Sanctions Board then considers the case *de novo* and takes the final decision on the sanction to be imposed, if any." See Anne-Marie Leroy and Frank Fariello, 'The World Bank Group Sanctions Process and Its Recent Reforms' (*World Bank*, 2012) 3 <http://siteresources.worldbank.org/INTLAWJUSTICE/Resources/SanctionsProcess.pdf>.

[152]See 'Sanctions Procedures' (*World Bank*) (n 36), Part A, s 8.01(ii).

[153]See *World Bank v GHD Pty Ltd*, [2013] Sanctions Board 56, para 39. For a description of the case see note 11 in Chap. 5.

[154]See 'Sanctions Procedures' (*World Bank*) (n 36), Part A, s 8.01.

Therefore, from the Sanctions Board's point of view, this provision allows the judging body to take into consideration all evidence in the record in order to assess the underlying proof of misconduct that would demonstrate respondent's relative degree of culpability and "the full range of potentially aggravating or mitigating factors relevant to the choice of sanctions."[155]

In any case, the role of the Sanctions Board is particularly important in relation to the transparency of the procedure. Indeed, after several years during which the documents related to the sanctioning proceedings had been treated as having a classified nature, the World Bank has finally adopted a policy of transparency.[156] Such an innovative approach has been carried out by means of the issuance of a law digest in December 2011, setting out detailed information about the Sanctions Board's caseload and decisions, and subsequently through the publication of the Sanctions Board's judgments.

The next chapter will be devoted to an analysis of the potential respondents in order to verify which kind of natural and legal persons might be investigated and sanctioned by the Bank. Moreover, the five fundamental sanctionable practices, the perpetration of which may be punished through the sanctions process, will be thoroughly examined.

---

[155] See *World Bank v GHD Pty Ltd*, [2013] Sanctions Board 56, para 39.

[156] For a more detailed analysis of this reform see Chap. 2.

Chapter 4
Respondents, Sanctionable Practices, and Attribution of Liability

4.1 Respondents: Firms and Individuals, Borrowers and Consultants

As a general rule, both individuals and firms may be subject to sanction. In order to verify which kind of persons might be investigated and sanctioned, it is necessary to refer to the particular Guidelines under which the case in question is being brought.

In particular, it is possible to distinguish between three different scenarios:

- The Procurement Guidelines[1] expressly provide:

  > The principles, rules, and procedures outlined in these Guidelines apply to all contracts for goods, works, and non-consulting services financed in whole or in part from Bank loans.[2]

  They also state:

  > It is the Bank's policy to require that Borrowers (including beneficiaries of Bank loans), bidders, suppliers, contractors and their agents (whether declared or not), subcontractors, sub-consultants, service providers or suppliers, and any personnel thereof, observe the highest standard of ethics during the procurement and execution of Bank-financed contracts.[3]

[1]See 'Guidelines: Procurement of Goods, Works, and Non-Consulting Services under IBRD Loans and IDA Credits & Grants' (*World Bank*, January 2011, Revised July 2014) 1.16(d) <http://pubdocs.worldbank.org/en/492221459454433323/Procurement-GuidelinesEnglishJuly12014.pdf>.

[2]ibid para 1.5.

[3]ibid para 1.16.

S. Manacorda, C. Grasso, *Fighting Fraud and Corruption at the World Bank*,
https://doi.org/10.1007/978-3-319-73824-6_4

It is clear from this expansive formulation that the jurisdiction of the Bank's sanctions regime essentially includes any and all actors involved in Bank-financed procurements other than the borrower itself.[4]

- The relevant provisions of the Consultant Guidelines[5] parallel those of the Procurement Guidelines, and the jurisdictional analysis of cases brought under the Consultant Guidelines run along the same lines.[6]
- Under the Anti-Corruption Guidelines,[7] it is provided that

> These Guidelines apply to the Borrower and all other persons or entities which either receive Loan proceeds for their own use (e.g., "end users"), persons or entities such as fiscal agents which are responsible for the deposit or transfer of Loan proceeds (whether or not they are beneficiaries of such proceeds), and persons or entities which take or influence decisions regarding the use of Loan proceeds. All such persons and entities are referred to in these Guidelines as "recipients of Loan proceeds," whether or not they are in physical possession of such proceeds.[8]

The Anti-Corruption Guidelines specifically exclude from the Bank's ability to sanction governments and government officials. As a matter of fact, the Guidelines establish:

> The Bank will have the right to sanction in accordance with prevailing Bank's sanctions policies and procedures, any individual or entity other than the Member Country.[9]

The same Guidelines include in the concept of Member Country:

> Officials and employees of the national government or of any of its political or administrative subdivisions, and government owned enterprises and agencies that are not eligible to: bid [. . .] or participate [. . .].[10]

It has to be highlighted that, being this exemption linked to the functional nature of the service carried out by the official, it does not operate where a government official engages in a sanctionable practice in his or her private capacity.[11]

Even if neither the Procurement nor Consultant Guidelines expressly provide for this exclusion, it nevertheless has been the Bank's long-standing policy not to

---

[4]See 'World Bank Group's Sanctions Regime: Information Note' (*World Bank*) 18 <http://siteresources.worldbank.org/EXTOFFEVASUS/Resources/The_World_Bank_Group_Sanctions_Regime.pdf>.

[5]See 'Guidelines: selection and employment of consultants under IBRD loans and IDA credits' (*World Bank*, January 2011, revised July 2014) <http://documents.worldbank.org/curated/en/796061468126898713/pdf/956640PUB0Box3010Revised0July102014.pdf>.

[6]ibid para 1.23.

[7]See 'Guidelines on preventing and combating fraud and corruption in projects financed by IBRD loans and IDA credits' (*World Bank*, October 2006, revised January 2011) <http://documents.worldbank.org/curated/en/551241468161367060/pdf/611090BR0SecM21Disclosed04113120111.pdf>.

[8]ibid para 5.

[9]ibid para 11.

[10]ibid para 11, fn 17.

[11]See 'Sanctions Regime: Information Note' (*World Bank*) (n 4) 19.

sanction governments or government officials. The cooperative structure of the Bank, the respect for the sovereignty of its Members, and the fact that alternative means are available to address these cases are the rationales behind such a policy.[12]

4.2 Criteria for the Attribution of Liability to Legal Entities

The selection of the criteria to attribute liability to legal entities for an offense perpetrated by one of their members has always represented a burning issue within the various domestic jurisdictions. Although corporate liability either has existed for some time or has been introduced in most jurisdictions enabling courts to sanction corporate entities for their criminal acts, it is not possible to identify a widely accepted theory of corporate blameworthiness to justify the imposition of criminal penalties on companies.[13] Corporate criminal responsibility can be based on transferring the corporate officer's responsibility to the corporation or, alternatively, on finding fault with the legal person's internal organization. However, even if the latter is more widely accepted in terms of general principles of criminal law, neither approach is uncontroversial. The main reason behind these difficulties is represented by the circumstance that the entire criminal law system has been traditionally conceived to punish natural persons, not legal ones. As a result, many of its rules and supporting theories are inherently inadequate to punish an entity that has "no soul to damn" and "no body to kick."[14]

Within the common law countries, which first adopted the concept of corporate criminal responsibility and which are still at the forefront of this particular area of law, it is possible to identify two different tendencies as to the criteria to attribute liability to legal entities.

In the United Kingdom, it has been adopted a criterion that has historically provided legal entities with full guarantees. Specifically, in the English legal system, vicarious liability has been avoided as a criterion to impute corporate criminal liability.[15] As excellently expressed by Lord Morris in a landmark decision:

> It is here that it is important to remember that it is the criminal liability of the company itself that is being considered. In general criminal liability only results from personal fault. We do

---

[12]ibid.

[13]See Amanda Pinto and Martin Evans, *Corporate Criminal Liability* (3rd edn, Sweet & Maxwell 2013) 1.

[14]For an analysis of these crucial issues as they emerged over the course of 1980s within the common law legal systems see John C. Coffee, '"No Soul to Damn: No Body to Kick": An Unscandalized Inquiry into the Problem of Corporate Punishment' (1981) 79(3) *Michigan Law Review* 386.

[15]The doctrine of "vicarious liability" represents a mechanism by which the law attributes blame on a person for the conducts of another. Therefore, such a doctrine might inherently lead to unfair and disproportionate decisions and is kept within strict limits. See David Ormerod, *Smith and Hogans's Criminal Law* (13th edn, Oxford University Press 2011), 273.

> not punish people in criminal courts for the misdeeds of others. The principle of *respondeat superior* is applicable in our civil courts but not generally in our criminal courts.[16]

Consequently, the identification doctrine was developed in its place. Under such a criterion, corporations are liable only where the offense is committed by a natural person who is the directing mind or will of the organization.[17] Although this criterion appears to be designed to closely simulate the typical mental mechanism of humans, its narrow approach to the notion of identification and the difficulties of providing evidence for the subjective element made it highly inefficient for the purpose of prosecuting corporations. As a result, prosecutions against companies in the United Kingdom have faced major, and in many cases insurmountable, obstacles.[18] In order to ease the prosecution of corporations, a new criterion has been developed by section 7 of the Bribery Act 2010. It is conceived as a new form of corporate liability for omission that does not require knowledge, intention, or recklessness and occurs when a legal entity has failed to prevent conducts that would amount to the commission of bribery under the same statute.[19] However, this criterion is currently applicable only in relation to the few offenses, whereas in relation to almost all the other offenses the identification doctrine remains the only way to attribute criminal liability to legal entities in the English legal system.[20]

Contrariwise, in the United States, a more flexible criterion has been developed. In fact, criminal and civil corporate liability can be imposed under the legal theory of *respondeat superior*, which is a form of vicarious liability. According to this theory, "where the relationship of employer and employee exists, the employer is liable for the acts of the employee committed in the course of his employment."[21] Consequently, under such a theory, a corporation is liable for the conduct of employees who are acting within the scope of their employment, including low-level employees. The notion was clarified in several judicial decisions. Specifically, in *In re Hellenic Inc*, it was stated:

> An agent's knowledge is imputed to the corporation where the agent is acting within the scope of his authority and where the knowledge relates to matters within the scope of that authority.[22]

---

[16]See *Tesco Supermarkets Ltd. Appellants v Nattrass Respondent*, [1972] A.C. 153.

[17]See Costantino Grasso, 'Peaks and troughs of the English deferred prosecution agreement: the lesson learned from the DPA between the SFO and ICBC SB Plc' (2016) 5 *Journal of Business Law* 388, 390.

[18]See Peter Alldridge, 'The U.K. Bribery Act: "The Caffeinated Younger Sibling of the FCPA' (2012) 73 *Ohio State Law Journal* 1181, 1200.

[19]See Grasso, 'Peaks and troughs of the English deferred prosecution agreement' (n 17) 391.

[20]It is possible to identify a current trend consisting in making it easier to prosecute legal entities by means of the adoption of additional failure to prevent offenses. For instance, in September 2017, a new corporate offense of failure to prevent the criminal facilitation of tax evasion entered into force in the jurisdiction of England and Wales.

[21]See 'Respondeat Superior' in Mick Woodley (ed), *Osborn's Concise Law Dictionary* (12th edn, Sweet & Maxwell 2013).

[22]See *In re Hellenic Inc.*, 252 F.3d 391, 395 & n. 20 (5th Cir.2001).

Moreover, in other decisions, the judges affirmed that acting within the scope of employment means also "with intent to benefit the employer."[23] Both these requirements have been construed extensively by the judiciary. In relation to the requisite of acting within the scope of the employment, even the case where the employee has an apparent authority to engage in the act in question has been regarded as sufficient. Likewise, the requirement that an employee act has to benefit the company has been relaxed by a permissive interpretation because the courts have recognized that many employees act primarily for their own personal gain.[24] As a result, the adoption of the *respondeat superior* doctrine has caused in the United States an opposite effect than the one that occurred in the United Kingdom; namely, it has generated the overcriminalization of corporate conducts in the American legal system.[25]

The Sanctions Board had the opportunity to address the crucial issue related to the criteria to attribute liability to legal entities within the sanctions system in *World Bank v Income Electrix Limited.*[26] In particular, having determined that the conduct of the company's Logistics Officer constituted a "fraudulent practice," the judging body had to come to a decision about the criteria applicable to impute such a conduct to Income Electrix Limited. In doing so, the Board expressly referred to the doctrine of *respondeat superior*. Such criterion of imputation was already used in several previous decisions of the Sanctions Board. In such cases, the judging body placed particular emphasis on whether the record included evidence showing that the employer at any time implemented any controls reasonably sufficient to prevent or detect the fraudulent practices. Although the Sanctions Board has selected the criterion that offers less safeguards to respondents, the fact that it has been interpreting it in a less permissive way has to be welcomed. Specifically, as stated by the Sanctions Board in the abovementioned decision:

> Where an employer asserted it simply relied upon the honesty of its employees, and failed to implement any controls such as 'a basic four-eye-principle (i.e., a review by someone other than the individual who forged each Authorization),' for example, and the Sanctions Board found no evidence supporting a 'rogue employee' defence or any other defence, it ultimately found the employer should be held responsible for the actions of its employees acting on its behalf.[27]

Eventually, the Sanctions Board concluded that the respondent had to be held liable for the acts of the Logistics Officer in submitting a bid with fraudulent signatures for the following reasons:

1) The record showed that the Logistics Officer acted on behalf of the firm.

---

[23]See *D & S Auto Parts, Inc. v. Schwartz*, 838 F.2d 964, 967 (7th Cir.1988).

[24]See Andrew Weissmann and David Newman, 'Rethinking Criminal Corporate Liability' (2007) 82(2) *Indiana Law Journal* 411, 422.

[25]See Carlos G. Diez, 'Corporate Culpability as a Limit to the Overcriminalization of Corporate Criminal Liability: The Interplay between Self-Regulation, Corporate Compliance, and Corporate Citizenship' (2011) 14(1) *New Criminal Law Review* 78.

[26]See *World Bank v Income Electrix Limited*, [2012] Sanctions Board 46.

[27]ibid para 27.

2) The Logistics Officer was apparently motivated, at least in part, by a purpose to serve the company.
3) The Logistics Officer's actions were closely aligned to the functions that respondent had charged him to perform.
4) There was a lack of adequate supervision from respondent, whose Manager failed to take appropriate measures in the critical time period to communicate with and redirect the Logistics Officer so as to prevent an improper submission.
5) Respondent failed to show that it had controls in place at the time to address or prevent this type of misconduct.[28]

In the Advisory Opinion of 2010, the Bank's General Counsel supported such an interpretation affirming:

> We support the notion that firms should be sanctioned as Respondents for the acts of their employees for or on behalf of the firm. [. . .] The practice of sanctioning of firms for the acts of employees, to our knowledge, has been routinely followed in the jurisprudence of both the Sanctions Committee and the Sanctions Board over the years.[29]

From the abovementioned opinion, it clearly emerges the Bank's willingness to ease in the broadest way the possibility of attributing liability to legal entities. Specifically, the General Counsel asserted that "requiring a showing that a particular employee was specifically authorized to commit the Sanctionable Practice would place an unacceptable evidentiary burden on INT."[30] Consequently, from the Counsel's perspective, it should be sufficient that the employee acted on behalf of the firm to establish a *prima facie* case, and then the burden of proof should shift so that the firm would need to rebut through the interposition of an affirmative "rogue employee" defense.[31]

In *World Bank v Karl Storz GmbH & Co. KG*, the Sanctions Board had the opportunity to deal with this particular defense. Specifically, the respondent submitted a rogue employee defense with respect to the former Executive Director, who allegedly bribed the Bank's Procurement Advisor, arguing that the Director deliberately concealed the consultant's role at the Bank from its senior management.[32] In this regard, the Board affirmed that the relevant question in determining employer liability is whether the employee's misconduct was "a mode, albeit an improper mode" of carrying out an assigned duty.[33] Moreover, the Board stated:

---

[28]ibid para 29.

[29]See 'Advisory Opinion on Certain Issues Arising in Connection with Recent Sanctions Cases' 18, para 72 (*World Bank*, 15 November 2010) <http://siteresources.worldbank.org/INTLAWJUSTICE/214574-1300377840517/23440937/AdvisoryOpinion.pdf>.

[30]ibid 19, para 73.

[31]ibid.

[32]See *World Bank v Karl Storz GmbH & Co. KG*, [2017] Sanctions Board 95, para 33. For a description of the case see note 24 in Chap. 5.

[33]ibid.

> With regard to the scope and adequacy of its controls, the record does not support a finding that, at the time of the corrupt practice, the Respondent had adequate corporate policies and controls in place, which the Former Executive Director circumvented or wilfully ignored.[34]

This decision appears extremely relevant because it shows that from the Sanctions Board's perspective, the implementation of an adequate and effective antifinancial crime compliance program represents an implicit requirement for raising a rogue employee defense in a successful way.

4.3 Corporate Groups: Controlled and Controlling Entities

The Sanctions Procedures provide that also affiliates of respondents[35] may be sanctioned and that sanctions may be applied to the successors and assigns of sanctioned parties.

In particular, in determining the scope of sanctions, the procedures establish:

> When a sanction is imposed on a Respondent, appropriate sanctions may also be imposed on any Affiliate of the Respondent [. . .] Such Affiliate(s) shall have procedural rights hereunder equivalent to those of the Respondent, except that any Preliminary Explanation, Explanation, Response or other formal submission shall be consolidated with that of the Respondent unless the SDO or the Sanctions Board, as the case may be, determines, as a matter of discretion, to permit an independent submission.[36]

Some clarification of the way in which corporate groups are dealt with by the Bank has been offered by the Sanctions Process Information Note. The document confirms that the Bank has adopted a flexible approach to such an issue specifying that "flexible principles help guide the application of sanctions to affiliates of the Respondent(s) and successors and assigns."[37] It also specifies that "the Sanctions Procedures afford parent and/or other affiliated entities due process, so they may defend themselves against charges of culpability or responsibility for the Respondent's wrongdoing, with substantially the same procedural rights as Respondents themselves."[38]

---

[34]ibid.

[35]As provided by the Sanctions Procedures "Affiliate" means "any legal or natural person that controls, is controlled by, or is under common control with, the Respondent, as determined by the Bank." See 'Bank Procedure: Sanctions Proceedings and Settlements in Bank Financed Projects' (*World Bank*, 28 June 2016) II(a) <http://siteresources.worldbank.org/EXTOFFEVASUS/Resources/3601045-1377105390925/Procedure_Bank_Procedure_Sanctions_Proceedings_and_Settlements_in_Bank_Financed_Projects(6.28.2016).pdf>.

[36]ibid Part A, 9.04(b).

[37]See 'Sanctions Regime: Information Note' (*World Bank*) (n 4) 9.

[38]ibid.

As regards the criteria to impute liability to the affiliates,[39] the Bank differentiates between affiliates controlled by sanctioned parties and affiliates that control[40] respondents. While normal criteria are used for the former, in relation to the latter, the Bank has adopted a sort of corporate liability for omission that occurs where, although the controlling entity is not directly involved in the sanctionable practice, it has failed to prevent its perpetration "due to a failure to supervise or to maintain adequate controls or an ethical culture within the corporate group."[41] Such a choice, which facilitates the attribution of responsibility to corporate groups and indirectly fosters the adoption of sound antifinancial crime compliance programs, resembles the one that has been taken at the domestic level within the jurisdiction of England and Wales through section 7 of the Bribery Act 2010.[42]

However, as it has been specified by the same information note, where a controlling entity is considered as liable for the application of such a criterion, the related sentence should be more lenient:

> Responsibility does not normally lead to debarment, but rather to conditional nondebarment, or to a letter of reprimand in cases involving an isolated incident of a failure to supervise, although egregious forms of responsibility (including 'wilful blindness' to sanctionable practices) may lead to sanctions of a severity comparable to those imposed for culpability [. . .] The choice and level of sanctions applied to affiliates, however, are ultimately decided by the EO [currently known as SDO] or the Sanctions Board, in their discretion, on the merits of each case, to ensure that the sanction is commensurate with the degree of culpability or responsibility of those sanctioned and to prevent evasion of the sanctions.[43]

In particular, as it has been underlined in the overview issued by the Bank,[44] a sanction that can be considered appropriate in these cases is represented by conditional nondebarment.[45]

---

[39]The information note specifies that "An entity is an 'affiliate' of another entity if: (i) either entity controls or has the power to control the other, or (ii) a third party controls or has the power to control both entities. The definition covers entities organized after the sanction but with the same or similar management, ownership or principal employees as the sanctioned entity" See ibid 22.

[40]The information note specifies that "'Control' means the ability to direct or to cause the direction of the policies or operations of another entity, whether through the ownership of voting securities, by contract or otherwise. Indicia of control include, but are not limited to, interlocking management or ownership, identity of interests among family members, shared facilities and equipment, common use of employees, or a business entity organized following the imposition of a sanction that has the same or similar management, ownership, or principal employees as the person that was suspended or debarred." See ibid.

[41]ibid 20.

[42]See *supra* note 19 and accompanying text.

[43]See 'Sanctions Regime: Information Note' (*World Bank*) (n 4) 20.

[44]See 'World Bank Group Sanctions Regime: An Overview' (*World Bank*, 8 October 2010) <http://siteresources.worldbank.org/EXTOFFEVASUS/Resources/Overview-SecM2010-0543.pdf>.

[45]See *infra* notes 27–30 and accompanying text in Chap. 6.

On September 10, 2012, the five major MDBs (World Bank, AfDB, EBRD, AsDB, IDB) adopted harmonized principles on the treatment of corporate groups.[46] Under those principles, it is specified that sanctions will generally be applied to all entities controlled by the respondent.[47] In other words, the MDBs have opted for an automatism instead of developing proper criteria for the attribution of corporate liability to controlled entities. The principles specify that in order to avoid the liability, the respondent has to demonstrate

> *inter alia* to the satisfaction of the Institution that such entities are free from responsibility for the prohibited practice, and the application to the entities would be disproportionate, and application is not reasonably necessary to prevent evasion.[48]

This rule is certainly a matter of concern. It not only imposes on the defendant the burden of proof, but the way in which it has been structured might easily result in a *probatio diabolica* for the respondent. Suffice here to say that the inclusion of the words "inter alia" implies that the already difficult requirements expressly provided could not be sufficient to avoid the imposition of sanctions. Moreover, the principles assume that the holding should be the one to demonstrate that its controlled entities are free from responsibility. Such choice is based on the undemonstrated assumption that the interests of the holding and all its controlled entities are always aligned. In practice, the MDBs have implicitly decided to regulate corporate groups as single entities leaving the fate of subsidiary company in the hands of someone other than their direct management and directors. If it is true that some legal systems regulate corporate group as a single entity,[49] such an option does not seem always appropriate[50] and this especially in relation to the sanctions process. In fact, this rule results in a sort of vicarious liability for the perpetration of illicit conducts resembling from all points of view criminal offenses. It is not a case that, in the English legal system,

---

[46]For an analysis of the harmonization of the MDBs' Sanctions procedures see *supra* notes 158–174 and accompanying text in Chap. 1.

[47]See 'MDB Harmonized Principles on Treatment of Corporate Groups' (*Asian Development Bank*, 10 September 2012) para 3 <http://lnadbg4.adb.org/oai001p.nsf/0/A7912C61C52A85AD48257ACC002DB7EE/$FILE/MDB%20Harmonized%20Principles%20on%20Treatment%20of%20Corporate%20Groups.pdf>.

[48]ibid.

[49]Such an approach is commonly adopted in cases of insolvency or violation of antitrust regulations. For instance, in an antitrust trial an American Court stated: "[A] parent and a wholly owned subsidiary always have a unity of purpose or a common design. They share a common purpose whether or not the parent keeps a tight rein over the subsidiary." See *Copperweld Corp. v. Independence Tube Corp.*, 467 U.S. 752, 777 (1984).

[50]A more reasonable approach to this issue is to decide case by case when the whole enterprise should be responsible, because its formally separate parts are collectively conducting a single integrated enterprise under the parent's control. See Kurt A. Strasser, 'Piercing the Veil in Corporate Groups' (2005) 37(3) *Connecticut Law Review* 637, 665.

vicarious liability has been avoided as a criterion to impute corporate criminal liability.[51]

Contrariwise, the abovementioned principles establish that sanctions will be applied to entities controlling the respondents only where the Bank demonstrates its involvement in the prohibited practice.[52] Although on this occasion the rules appear respectful of the due process procedural safeguards, they contradict *per se* the aforesaid unified vision of corporate groups implicitly espoused by the MDBs.

Finally, the principles address the vexed question of inheritance of corporate liability. Specifically, they provide that in the case of acquisition, mergers, and other corporate events involving the debarred entity:

> a rebuttable presumption will be applied that successors and assigns are subject to any sanction imposed on their predecessors. The successor or assign may rebut this presumption by demonstrating that such application would be unreasonable. However, the business operations of the originally sanctioned entity should continue to be sanctioned.[53]

Although this criterion does not specify what happens if the corporate events occur during the investigation phase, it seems in principle adequate from a functional point of view, although it raises some concerns from a theoretical standpoint. It is fully understandable that all the decisions taken in order to restructure its affairs in the course of business cannot *per se* exempt a company from criminal liability assumed prior to such an event even if the new management has no involvement in the commission of the offense. Otherwise, firms might easily make instrumental use of such business operations in order to avoid responsibility.[54] If this is true, at the same time the fact that a company inherits criminal liability from a previous management poses serious concerns. The inheritance of corporate liability cannot represent an automatism. As a result, the adoption of a rebuttable presumption has to be surely welcomed. However, the rule does not specify in which way the successors might demonstrate that the imposition of the sanction is unreasonable. Some insights into the matter have been offered by the Bank through its Information Note, which clarifies:

> While sanctions are not automatically applied to successors or assigns, a rebuttable presumption is applied that successors and assigns are subject to any sanction imposed on their predecessors. The successor/assign may rebut this presumption by demonstrating that such application would violate the general principles adopted by the Bank [...] including that such application would impose a disproportionate penalty on the successor/assign. If the successor/assign can show to the satisfaction of the Bank that the business of the original

[51]The doctrine of "vicarious liability" represents a mechanism by which the law attributes blame on a person for the conducts of another. Therefore, such a doctrine might inherently lead to unfair and disproportionate decisions and is kept within strict limits. See David Ormerod, *Smith and Hogans's Criminal Law* (13th edn, Oxford University Press 2011), 273.

[52]The principles expressly provide that involvement may include willful blindness and a failure to supervise. See 'MDB Harmonized Principles on Treatment of Corporate Groups' (*Asian Development Bank*) (n 47) para 4.

[53]ibid.

[54]See Grasso, 'Peaks and troughs of the English deferred prosecution agreement' (n 17) 404.

> sanctioned entity is limited to a particular portion of the successor entity(ies) (e.g., particular subsidiaries within a corporate group), then the Bank may decide to limit the application of the sanction accordingly. There are likely to be cases, however, where the originally sanctioned predecessor has become so intertwined with the business of the successor or where the original business represents such a large portion of the overall business of the successor entity(ies) that such a limitation will be either impracticable or will pose an unacceptable reputational and/or fiduciary risk to the Bank Group.[55]

In its decisions, the Sanctions Board recognized that the change in management or corporate identity might warrant mitigation where the staff responsible for the perpetration of the sanctionable practice is no longer working for the investigated entity and, at the same time, no evidence suggests that the firm's current management is connected with the misconduct.[56] In order to recognize such a mitigation, the Sanctions Board used the rule provided by section 9.02(i) of the Bank's Sanctions Procedures, which provides that in determining an appropriate sanction, the SDO and Sanctions Board might consider "any other factor" they reasonably deem relevant to the sanctioned party's culpability or responsibility in relation to the misconduct.[57]

Although such a decision could be surely welcomed, it appears opportune that in the absence of a specific regulation, it should be possible for firms to avoid liability for corrupt practices perpetrated prior to the acquisition process through the development of particular procedures for anticorruption due diligence to be followed in any merger or acquisition project.[58]

4.4 World Bank's Jurisdictional Reach over Noncontractors

A critical issue that the Sanctions Board has dealt with has concerned the possibility of qualifying subjects that are external to the World Bank's contractual nexus as potential respondents in its sanctions process. Such an issue has been recently raised in *World Bank v Stephen Courtenay Chandler*,[59] where the respondent raised several

---

[55]See 'Sanctions Regime: Information Note' (*World Bank*) (n 4) 22.

[56]See *infra* note 102 and accompanying text in Chap. 6.

[57]See 'Sanctions Procedures' (*World Bank*) (n 35) Part A, 9.02(i).

[58]See Stefania Giavazzi, Francesca Cottone and Michele De Rosa, 'The ABC Model: The General Framework for an Anti-Bribery Compliance Program' in Stefano Manacorda, Francesco Centonze and Gabrio Forti (eds), *Preventing Corporate Corruption* (Springer 2014), 163.

[59]This case, which involved Mr Stephen Courtenay Chandler ("Respondent"), arose in the context of the Metropolitan Areas Urban Transport Project, which sought, to improve the quality and performance of urban transport infrastructure in the Republic of Argentina. In 2010, a consortium entered into a joint venture agreement for purposes of providing advisory services for a contract stipulated within the area of the project. In particular, the Respondent was appointed as one of the legal representatives of the consortium, which was eventually awarded a contract in 2011. Specifically, in the contract it was established that Mr Chandler had to act as the "Project Manager"

arguments to implicitly challenge the Bank's jurisdiction to pursue sanctions against him in relation to the contract. In particular, he asserted that his firm was merely a subcontractor and not a party to the contract and that neither he nor his firm did sign the contract.[60] In its decision, the Sanctions Board stated that no valid challenge to its jurisdiction was presented in the case at issue for the following three reasons: that Mr Chandler signed the consortium agreement on behalf of his firm, that the consortium agreement expressly provided that any of its legal representatives would jointly have sufficient authority to bind the consortium, and that the respondent's signature appeared on a number of advance certificates submitted by the consortium to the public authority.[61]

Nevertheless, besides the specific circumstance of the case, in the decision the Sanctions Board restated that from its perspective, "the Bank does not need the consent of or privity with a Respondent to assert jurisdiction to sanction."[62] The judging body also highlighted that, "as a general matter," it had previously rejected jurisdictional challenges by individual respondents who asserted that they were never personally in privity of contract with the Bank or the borrower.[63]

Specifically, the Sanctions Board made reference to two previous decisions that is worth to analyze. In the first one, the World Bank based its judgment on an internal information note (i.e., the World Bank Group's Sanctions Regime: Information Note of November 2011 at p. 20), which provided that "under the sanctions framework the Bank does not need the consent of or privity with a Respondent to assert jurisdiction to sanction."[64] On that occasion, additional arguments with which the respondent challenged the Bank's jurisdiction were not considered by the judging body because of their late submission.[65] The Sanctions Board dealt with the same issue again in a case related to some sanctionable practices allegedly perpetrated within the Benin Health System Performance Project.[66] In this second case, the individual respondent argued that where the Bank asserted that he had allegedly violated its Consultant Guidelines, the financial institution went beyond the scope of its jurisdiction because he was not the consultant, held no shares or financial interest in the consultant firm,

---

submitting monthly progress reports to certify the consortium's work. In October 2012, the Argentinean project implementation unit rescinded the Contract because of "the falsity of substantial information submitted by the [Consortium] . . . [in] the Progress Reports." Consequently, INT alleges that the Respondent engaged in fraudulent practices during the contract's execution by providing false information. Eventually, the World Bank imposed a sanction of debarment on Mr. Chandler for a period of three 3 years. See *World Bank v Stephen Courtenay Chandler*, [2016] Sanctions Board 86.

[60]ibid para 23.

[61]ibid para 25.

[62]ibid para 24.

[63]ibid.

[64]See *World Bank v Anonymized Respondent*, [2014] Sanctions Board 64, at para 28.

[65]ibid para 29.

[66]See *World Bank v Anonymized Respondent*, [2015] Sanctions Board 81.

and held no financial or other stake in the Bank's project.[67] In its decision, the parajudicial authority affirmed:

> The Sanctions Board may, as it has previously decided, assert jurisdiction over corporate officers, managers, and directors employed by a firm that competed for or received a contract award – even where the applicable guidelines do not refer directly to the possibility of sanctioning individuals [...] Accordingly, an interpretation of the May 2004 Consultant Guidelines to prohibit fraudulent practices by both firms and individual employees, and to permit potential sanctions against the Individual Respondent as well as the Respondent Entities to the extent that any or all of them may be found liable, would be consistent with the Sanctions Board's precedent and the sanctions framework. The Individual Respondent's objection to jurisdiction is therefore denied.[68]

The absence of pre-established criteria to determine the scope of the Bank's jurisdictional reach over noncontractors, combined with the extensive interpretation given by the Sanctions Board, not only denote that the legal framework on which the sanctions process is founded is still incomplete but also appear to be a matter of concern in relation to the position of individuals and entities that, being noncontractors, played a marginal or external role within the Bank's funded projects. Furthermore, it may represent a clear indication of the fact that the essence of the Bank's sanctions system goes beyond a merely contractual nature, characterizing what appears to be a real instrument of global governance having inherent parapublicistic features.

4.5 Sanctionable Practices

The World Bank has identified five fundamental sanctionable practices the perpetration of which may be punished through the sanctions process. They are corrupt practice, fraudulent practice, collusive practice, coercive practice, and obstructive practice. Unfortunately, no definition of such practices is offered under the Bank's Sanctions Procedures, which only provide a reference to other Bank's sources. In particular, they state:

> Such terms are defined in the Anti-Corruption Guidelines, Procurement Guidelines or Consultant Guidelines, as the case may be, under which such case is being brought (see Annex A); (ii) with respect to any case under subparagraph 1.01(c)(ii) of Section III.A, a corrupt, fraudulent, coercive, collusive or obstructive practice, as defined in the World Bank Vendor Eligibility Policy in connection with the Bank's corporate procurement; (iii) with respect to any case under sub-paragraph 1.01(c)(iii) of Section III.A, a violation of a Material Term, as defined in the VDP Terms &Conditions; and (iv) with respect to any case under sub-paragraph 1.01(c)(iv) of Section III.A, a violation of sub-section 11.05 of Section III.A.[69]

---

[67] ibid para 28.

[68] ibid para 29.

[69] See 'Sanctions Procedures' (*World Bank*) (n 35) section II, (r).

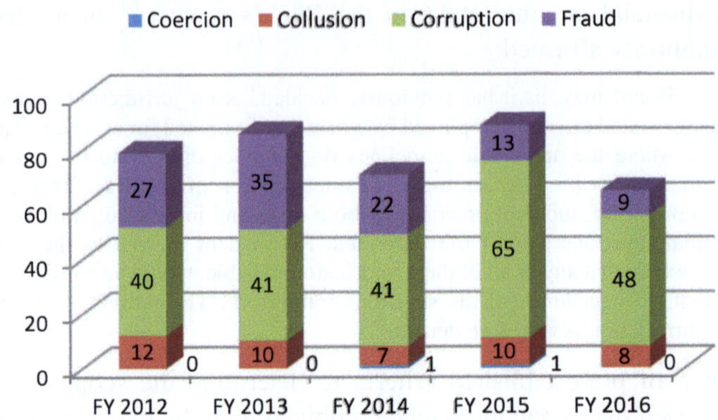

Fig. 4.1 World Bank: Type of Allegations Investigated 2012–2016 (figures expressed in number of cases). *Source*: 'The World Bank Group Integrity Vice Presidency – Annual Update – Fiscal Year 2016' (*World Bank*, Publications) 23 <http://pubdocs.worldbank.org/en/118471475857477799/INT-FY16-Annual-Update-web.pdf>

The absence of a uniform definition included in the Sanctions Procedures and the fact that the very notion of the sanctionable practices may vary depending on the type of contract under which the violation occurred, as well as on the time when the illicit behavior was perpetrated, inevitably generates a certain degree of confusion. The following parts of this chapter will offer an analysis of the various sanctionable practices based on the notions provided by the Bank's Anti-Corruption Guidelines as adopted in 2006.

As of 2012, among the five sanctionable practices, the vast majority of the Bank's cases focused on corrupt and fraudulent practices (see Fig. 4.1). It is interesting to note that no case of obstructive practice was reported and that of the 48 cases under investigation for corruption in 2016, 24 had included elements of fraud and/or collusion.

4.6 Corruption

The notion of "corrupt practice" is set forth in the October 2006 Anti-Corruption Guidelines, as revised in January 2011, at paragraph 7. Under the Guidelines, a corrupt conduct consists in "the offering, giving, receiving or soliciting, directly or indirectly, of anything of value to influence improperly the actions of another party."[70] Taking into consideration that traditionally within various domestic jurisdictions only bribery, which corresponds to "the corrupt payment, receipt or solicitation of a private favor for official action,"[71] was identified as the relevant illicit

[70]See 'Guidelines on preventing and combating fraud and corruption' (*World Bank*) (n 7) para 7(a).

[71]See Bryan A. Garner, *A Dictionary of Modern Legal Usage* (Oxford University Press 1995) 118.

conduct to be criminalized, the adoption of such a broad definition has to be welcomed. Corruption is a very broad term, which might refer to a multitude of different illicit conducts, and the abovementioned definition may include most of them. In the Anti-Corruption User Guide, the Bank offers the following example of corrupt practice:

> A company is awarded Bank-financed contracts from governments in exchange for a bribe or kickbacks. Kickbacks generally occur when a company that is awarded a contract "kicks back" money to the ministry official(s) who steered the award of the contract to that company. Typically, the kickback is a percentage of the value of the contract and, in countries with systemic corruption, the percentage is built into the cost that all bidders consider when bidding on contracts. In most cases, the money paid in bribes or kickbacks is extracted from the project financing, decreasing development impact.[72]

However, the scope of the notion of corrupt practices used by the Bank is not always so wide. Under some Bank-financed contracts, the definition of corrupt practices is different and characterized by a narrower scope. In that regard, some interesting insights were offered in *World Bank v ASDECON Corporation Company Limited*,[73] where the Sanctions Board had to verify whether or not the respondent agreed to take part in improper payments to some Implementing Agency officials. As a matter of fact, on that occasion, the judging body utilized the definition of corrupt practice as provided by the May 2002 Consultant Guidelines, paragraph 1.25(a)(i), which governed the project's procurement. This definition, although resembles the one set forth by the Anti-Corruption Guidelines, limits the scope of the sanctionable practice to bribes: "offering, giving, receiving, or soliciting of anything of value to influence the action of a public official in the selection process or in contract execution."[74]

The decision offers interesting elements on the meaning of "soliciting of anything of value." Indeed, under the circumstances of the fact, the respondent's Managing Director did not solicit any payment in his or respondent's favor, but he solicited the third party to join in a common payment to public officials in order to influence them. Therefore, the question was whether the firm's pressure on another firm to let them make improper payments to public officials might constitute "soliciting" under the applicable definition of corrupt practices.

The Sanctions Board found that such conduct might be considered as "soliciting" within the meaning of the May 2002 Consultant Guidelines. It highlighted that, from the one hand, nothing in the applicable definition of "corrupt practice" specified that one must solicit payment for oneself and, from the other, that the same definition did

---

[72]See 'The World Bank's Anti-Corruption Guidelines and Sanctions Reform – A User's Guide' (*World Bank*) 6 <http://siteresources.worldbank.org/PROJECTS/Resources/40940-1173795340221/RevisedPMNDFinaluserGuideline031607.pdf>.

[73]See *World Bank v ASDECON Corporation Company Limited*, [2012] Sanctions Board 50. For a description of the case see *supra* note 42 in Chap. 3.

[74]See 'Guidelines – Selection and Employment of Consultants by World Bank Borrowers' (*World Bank*, May 2002) para 1,25(a)(i) <https://siteresources.worldbank.org/INTPROCUREMENT/Resources/ConGuid-05-02-ev4.pdf>.

not require that the party making the solicitation must be the party that could exert the influence.[75] Thus, in the judging body's opinion, the definition might be read to include both the act of soliciting something for oneself in exchange for exerting improper influence and the act of soliciting or enticing another to give something to a third party in exchange for the third party's improper influence. In order to support this opinion, the Sanctions Board referred to the definition adopted in the Unites States in relation to the offense of "solicitation of a bribe," citing the Black's Law Dictionary, where it is defined as "the crime of asking or enticing another to commit bribery." Moreover, the judging body referred to the notion of "trading in influence," as is recognized by Article 18(b) of the United Nations Convention Against Corruption (UNCAC),[76] in order to assert that a party with influence to trade need not be a public official so long as it is someone with sufficient access to and ability to influence a public official.

Therefore, the Sanctions Board, applying the provision of paragraph 1.25(a)(i) to a case not falling within its wording, eventually construed the term "soliciting" adopting an extensive interpretation against the interests of the respondent.

The fight against the perpetration of this sanctionable practice appears to be of the utmost importance for the financial institution as it embodies the spirit of the Bank's governance and anticorruption policy.

A landmark decision by the Canadian Supreme Court in April 2016 endorsed these anticorruption efforts of international organizations. In particular, the Court affirmed:

> Corruption is a significant obstacle to international development. It undermines confidence in public institutions, diverts funds from those who are in great need of financial support, and violates business integrity. Corruption often transcends borders. In order to tackle this global problem, worldwide cooperation is needed. When international financial organizations, such as the appellant World Bank Group, share information gathered from informants across the world with the law enforcement agencies of member states, they help achieve what neither could do on their own.[77]

4.7 Fraud

Under the October 2006 Anti-Corruption Guidelines, a "fraudulent practice" consists in "any act or omission, including a misrepresentation, that knowingly or recklessly misleads, or attempts to mislead, a party to obtain a financial or other

[75] See *World Bank v ASDECON Corporation Company Limited*, [2012] Sanctions Board 50, at para 44.

[76] Article 18(b) of UNCAC requires the criminalization of the conduct consisting in: "The solicitation or acceptance by a public official or any other person, directly or indirectly, of an undue advantage for himself or herself or for another person in order that the public official or the person abuse his or her real or supposed influence with a view to obtaining from an administration or public authority of the State Party an undue advantage."

[77] See *World Bank Group v. Wallace*, 2016 SCC 15, [2016] 1 S.C.R. 207.

benefit or to avoid an obligation."[78] The Guidelines also specify that mere inaccuracy, committed through simple negligence, is not enough to constitute a sanctionable fraud. In order to act "knowingly or recklessly," the fraudulent actor must either know that the information or impression being conveyed is false or be recklessly indifferent as to whether it is true or false.[79]

In the Anti-Corruption User Guide, the World Bank offers the following example of corrupt practice:

> During the implementation of a project, the poor performance of a key consulting company raises suspicion that the capacities and qualifications of the company might have been misrepresented. An investigation reveals that the experience and credentials of the principal as well as the qualifications and certifications of the consulting firm were misrepresented in order to meet.[80]

The vast majority of the Sanctions Board's decisions deals with the illicit conduct of fraudulent practice. Therefore, the judging body has offered on many occasions insights into the definition of such a conduct. *World Bank v Income Electrix Limited*[81] appears to be one of the more illustrative judgments on this topic.

In this case, the definition of "fraudulent practice" was the one set forth in paragraph 1.14(a)(ii) of the May 2004 Procurement Guidelines governing the project's procurement. The Guidelines defined this conduct as "a misrepresentation or omission of facts in order to influence a procurement process or the execution of a contract." Subsequently, in October 2006 (i.e., after the perpetration of the illicit conducts), the definition of fraudulent practice set out in paragraph 1.14(a)(ii) of the Bank's Guidelines was revised as follows: "any act or omission, including a misrepresentation, that knowingly or recklessly misleads, or attempts to mislead, a party to obtain a financial or other benefit or to avoid an obligation."

As regards the *actus reus*, the Sanctions Board clarified that the physical component of fraudulent practices was to make "a misrepresentation of facts."[82] In the decision, the Board did not offer any definition of the term "misrepresentation," nor did it refer to the notion used in the common law legal systems.[83] Anyway, the

---

[78]See 'Guidelines on preventing and combating fraud and corruption' (*World Bank*) (n 7) para 7(b).

[79]ibid fn 13.

[80]See 'Anti-Corruption Guidelines – A User's Guide' (*World Bank*) (n 72) 6.

[81]See *World Bank v Income Electrix Limited*, [2012] Sanctions Board 46. For a description of the case see *supra* note 49 in Chap. 3.

[82]ibid para 23.

[83]Under common law, misrepresentation could be defined as "*the act of making a false or misleading assertion about something with the intent to deceive.*" See 'Misrepresentation' in Bryan A. Garner (ed), *Black's Law Dictionary* (9th edn, West 2009).

judging body considered that misrepresentation occurred on the basis of evidence from respondent[84] and the Proposed JV Partner.[85] Therefore, the Sanctions Board found it more likely than not that respondent's bid contained documents falsifying the Proposed JV Partner's signatures and misrepresenting its participation in the claimed JV arrangements.

Concerning the *mens rea*, as highlighted by the Sanctions Board, the 2004 definition of fraudulent practice did not include an explicit state of mind such as "knowing or reckless." As a matter of fact, as it has been mentioned above, this standard was adopted only lately by in October 2006. Anyway, the Sanctions Board held:

> The 'knowing or reckless' standard may be implied under the pre-October 2006 definitions, however, because the legislative history of these definitions reflects the October 2006 incorporation of this standard was intended only to make explicit the pre-existing standard for *mens rea*, not to articulate a new limitation.[86]

Furthermore, the Sanctions Board highlighted that the "fraudulent practice" required the specific intent of acting in order to influence the procurement process. In the case, the Sanctions Board deduced the existence of such an intent from the same affidavit undersigned by the Logistics Officer:

> In which he stated he signed and submitted the documents 'to ensure timely submission of the bid, as without which, I presumed that the bid would not be entertained.' The Logistics Officer's statements on record suffice to show he falsified the Proposed JV Partner's signatures with the requisite intent to influence the procurement process so that Respondent's bid would be considered eligible.[87]

To prove the mental element of the sanctionable practice, the Sanctions Board focused only on the state of mind that the agent of the conduct (i.e., the Logistics Officer) had when he was committing the fraud:

> The record of Respondent's internal findings indicates the Logistics Officer's contemporaneous awareness of wrongdoing. He stated that when the Manager contacted him after the bidding deadline, he chose not to inform the Manager [. . .] 'because he was not authorized to do so . . . and he did not want to take the blame for the failure of the bid.' The evidence thus supports a finding the Logistics Officer acted knowingly in misrepresenting the Proposed JV Partner's signatures.[88]

[84]The record contained admissions from Respondent and the Logistics Officer that the Logistics Officer signed the JV agreement and power of attorney on behalf of the Proposed JV Partner, without the latter's authorization or agreement, and submitted them with Respondent's bid for the Contract.

[85]The record included certified written submissions from the Proposed JV Partner confirming the purported signatures were false and unauthorized, and it had never accepted Respondent's proposed JV arrangements.

[86]See *World Bank v Income Electrix Limited*, [2012] Sanctions Board 46, at para 11.

[87]ibid para 25.

[88]ibid para 24.

The notion of "reckless," which was not covered in the abovementioned decision, proved to be the cause of complex interpretative issues for the Bank's officials involved in the sanctions process. In the Advisory Opinion of 2010, the Bank's General Counsel had the opportunity to offer some insights into this concept. In particular, a reference was made to two different notions used within common law jurisdictions: criminal recklessness[89] and tortious recklessness.[90] While the former is characterized by higher standards of proof because it requires the prosecutor to prove that the defendant was aware of a risk of harm, the latter can be proved merely demonstrating the occurrence of an unjustifiable risk taking consisting in the actor's deviation from the standard of due care that a reasonable person would have applied in the same circumstances. In this regard, the Counsel specified that "an approach to liability for fraudulent practice that adopted the criminal recklessness requirement [. . .] would create unreasonable evidentiary burdens for the Bank."[91] As a result, the Counsel recommended the adoption of "a permissive stance with regard to the element of knowledge."[92] Such an approach appears potentially dangerous because of its inherent inconsistency. As a matter of fact, on the one hand, the Bank has adopted a definition of fraudulent practice that closely resembles the offense of fraud, but on the other, it has considered too burdensome the adoption of the related concept of criminal recklessness. It is not a case that under common law, a stringent concept of recklessness in relation to the offense of fraud has been developed. Such a choice reflects both the fundamental rights that are at stake and the stigmatizing effects that are produced where a subject is accused of fraudulent practices. As we have already argued, these are elements that the sanctions process has in common with domestic criminal trials.[93] Consequently, the willingness to ease the work of the Bank's investigators does not appear to represent a valid justification for such a discrepancy.

In *World Bank v LTB Leitungsbau GmbH and Mr. Roland Kolitsch*,[94] the judging body offered additional insights into the notion of misrepresentation. In particular,

---

[89]See 'Advisory Opinion' (*World Bank*) (n 29) 23, para 93.

[90]ibid 24, para 97.

[91]ibid 25, para 101.

[92]ibid.

[93]See *supra* note 92 and accompanying text in Chap. 3.

[94]The case arose in the context of the Nepal-India Electricity Transmission and Trade Project, which aimed at facilitating electricity trade between the Republic of India and the Federal Democratic Republic of Nepal (the "Borrower") and increasing the supply of electricity in the territory of the Borrower. On 9 September 2011, the implementation unit for the Project issued bidding documents for a contract for the "Design, Supply, and Installation of Hetauda-Dhalkebar-Inaruwa 400 KV Transmission Line." On 29 December 2011, the Respondent Firm, as part of a joint venture, submitted a bid for the contract. INT alleged that the Respondents engaged in a fraudulent practice during the procurement process by knowingly or recklessly misrepresenting in the bid the Respondent Firm's anticipated role in the execution of the Contract. In particular, INT asserted that the Respondents represented they would perform approximately 25% of the work under the contract when, in fact, they expected the joint venture partner to perform all of the work. According to INT, the Respondent Firm's actual role was to provide its credentials in exchange for a royalty fee to help

the respondent firm was accused of committing fraudulent practices consisting in falsely declaring that it would carry out 25% of the work that the contract entailed where in reality the entire work had to be performed by the joint venture partner. In that regard, the respondent asserted that due to the fact that the representations on work allocation made in the documents submitted for the bid were merely estimations and not final, they were inherently incapable to misrepresent facts. However, the Sanctions Board did not accept this argument because, even though the joint venture agreement expressed that the partners would do the final work allocation after the award of the contract, the joint venture agreement still represented to the authorities that the respondent firm would be involved in the execution of the contract in a range of approximately 25% of the workload.[95]

4.8 Collusion

The notion of "collusive practice" is provided by paragraph 7 of the Anti-Corruption Guidelines. The provision specifies that a collusive conduct consists in "an arrangement between two or more parties designed to achieve an improper purpose, including to influence improperly the actions of another party."[96]

In the Anti-Corruption User Guide, the World Bank offers the following example of collusive practice:

> A borrowing government arrests an official of an agency that is responsible for implementing a Bank financed project on charges of financial impropriety. On the basis of that arrest and subsequent information from a contractor, an investigation of the relevant contracts is carried out, and reveals that the agency official had arranged a collusion "ring" to steer a large number of contract awards to his own company and to the companies of people known to him. To implement the collusion, the agency official influenced local officials who had a role in awarding the contracts.[97]

In *Information Computer Systems CJSC* and *BMS Consulting LLC*, the Sanctions Board had the opportunity to discuss the key elements of collusion.[98] In particular,

---

the joint venture partner qualify in the bidding process for the contract. Eventually the Sanctions Board imposed a sanction of debarment with conditional release on the Respondent entity and the individual Respondent (the general manager for export of the Respondent Firm) with a minimum period of ineligibility of 3 years and 6 months beginning from the date of this decision. See *World Bank v LTB Leitungsbau GmbH and Mr. Roland Kolitsch*, [2016] Sanctions Board 90.

[95] ibid para 26.

[96] See 'Guidelines on preventing and combating fraud and corruption' (*World Bank*) (n 7) para 7(c).

[97] See 'Anti-Corruption Guidelines – A User's Guide' (*World Bank*) (n 72) 8.

[98] The decision is related to two cases that arose in the context of the Ukrainian Social Assistance System Modernization Project, which aimed at improving the effectiveness of Ukraine's social assistance system by better targeting cash benefits and reducing the burden on beneficiaries. In practice, in 2005, the Bank and Ukraine (the "Borrower") entered into a loan agreement to provide the equivalent of US$99.4 million to support the project. As a result, in 2009, the Ukrainian competent ministry issued a first tender for the supply of the required hardware and software.

on that occasion, INT alleged that Information Computer Systems CJSC and BMS Consulting LLC engaged in collusive practices in connection with two tenders and a third bidder to ensure that the former would win the first tender and the latter would win the second one.[99] In particular, according to INT, the two companies agreed to split profits on the two tenders and the third bidder agreed to accept a small share of the profits from the first tender for its help.[100] In its decision, the Sanctions Board clarified that INT bore "the initial burden to show that it is more likely than not that the Respondents engaged in a scheme or arrangement between two or more bidders, with or without the knowledge of the Borrower, designed to establish bid prices at artificial, non-competitive levels."[101]

Then the judging body held that the investigative material supported findings that the companies perpetrated collusive practices entering into an arrangement with each other and the third bidder. Specifically, in order to assess if collusion occurred, the Sanctions Board focused on two main elements. The first one was the establishment of a scheme designed for stifling competition through arrangements deliberately introduced into the bidding to make it difficult or impossible for other market players to compete:

> Contemporaneous email evidence provided by the Former Employee demonstrates that the collusive scheme was designed to stifle competition for Tenders 1 and 2. For instance, an employee of the Second Respondent Firm emailed employees of the First Respondent Firm in May 2010 stating, 'The Parties have agreed to start working on technological and organizational shivs, considering the most dangerous competitors .... The shivs must make bidding as difficult as possible for any competitor. [The Third Bidder] will play up in the project.' According to a translator's comment in the English-language version of the email provided by INT, the term 'shiv' in the language of the original document may be understood to mean 'special requirements, arrangements, criteria that are deliberately introduced into the bidding in order to make it difficult or impossible for other market players to compete.'[102]

The second element consisted in carrying out a scheme designed to establish bid prices at artificial noncompetitive levels:

> In addition, the Arrangements Email indicates that the Respondents coordinated their bids for Tenders 1 and 2 in a way that was designed to establish bid prices at artificial

Only three companies submitted bids for this tender: Information Computer Systems CJSC, BMS Consulting LLC and a third bidder. Upon recommendation of the bid evaluation committee (the "BEC"), the Borrower and Information Computer Systems CJSC entered into a contract in October 2010 which was valued at the equivalent of approximately US$29.6 million. Then, in 2010 the ministry issued a second tender. In response, four companies submitted bids for this tender. Those firms included the abovementioned three ones plus an additional company. Upon recommendation of the BEC, in 2011, the Borrower and BMS Consulting LLC entered into a contract, which was valued at approximately US$5 million. See *World Bank v Information Computer Systems CJSC and BMS Consulting LLC*, [2016] Sanctions Board 87.

[99]ibid para 13.

[100]ibid para 19.

[101]ibid para 72.

[102]ibid para 80.

non-competitive levels. The scheme as set out in the email provides, *inter alia*, that the Second Respondent Firm "plays up to" the First Respondent Firm under Tender 1 by submitting a bid with a higher price so that the First Respondent Firm wins the bid; and the First Respondent Firm "plays up to" the Second Respondent Firm under Tender 2 by submitting a bid with a higher price so that the Second Respondent Firm wins that bid. Consistent with the Arrangements Email, the Second Respondent Firm submitted a higher bid than the First Respondent Firm for Tender 1 – and the First Respondent Firm won that tender; and the First Respondent Firm submitted a higher bid than the Second Respondent Firm for Tender 2 – and the Second Respondent Firm won that tender. While evidence that the desired influence actually materialized is not necessary to establish this element of collusive practices, it may bolster a showing of the Respondent's intent to influence, which is all that is required.[103]

4.9 Coercion

Under the October 2006 Anti-Corruption Guidelines, "coercion" consists in "impairing or harming, or threatening to impair or harm, directly or indirectly, any party or the property of the party to influence improperly the actions of a party."[104]

In the Anti-Corruption User Guide, the World Bank offers the following example of coercion:

> In a roads project, procurement for two Bank financed roads is found to be tainted by the use of intimidation of competing bidders. An investigation reveals that a company that was pre-determined to win contracts in a collusive scheme used a combination of threats to the future business interests of competitor companies or threats to the physical well being of competitors' staff, in addition to payments to "losing" bidders, to ensure that other bidders submitted inflated bids. In one instance, representatives of one company held the rival bidder's staff captive in order to force the competitor to miss the bid submission deadline. The effect of the collusion is that winning bid prices are considerably higher than they would have been through genuine competitive bidding. As a result, the project's developmental impact is eroded and confidence in the Bank's procurement system severely undermined.[105]

4.10 Obstruction

The notion of "obstructing practice" is set forth in the October 2006 Anti-Corruption Guidelines. Under the Guidelines, an obstructing conduct consists in "(i) deliberately destroying, falsifying, altering or concealing of evidence material to the investigation or making false statements to investigators in order to materially impede a Bank investigation into allegations of a corrupt, fraudulent, coercive or collusive practice; and/or threatening, harassing or intimidating any party to prevent it from disclosing

[103]See ibid at para 81.

[104]See 'Guidelines on preventing and combating fraud and corruption' (*World Bank*) (n 7) para 7 (d).

[105]See 'Anti-Corruption Guidelines – A User's Guide' (*World Bank*) (n 72) 7.

its knowledge of matters relevant to the investigation or from pursuing the investigation, or (ii) acts intended to materially impede the exercise of the Bank's contractual rights of audit or access to information."[106] The Guidelines also specify that the abovementioned rights comprise those provided for, *inter alia*, in paragraph 9(d).[107] They include the contractual provisions under which each recipient of a loan has to permit the Bank to inspect all of their accounts and records and other documents relating to the project.

In the Anti-Corruption User Guide, the World Bank offers the following example of obstructing practice:

> Based on an allegation of corruption, investigators contacted a company that was awarded a contract on a Bank financed project to audit the financial records. While the company is obligated under its contract to allow access to these records, it refused to do so. This refusal of access is itself an offense that could render the company ineligible to bid on future Bank contracts.[108]

In *Information Computer Systems CJSC and BMS Consulting LLC*, the Sanctions Board had the opportunity to address the sanctionable offense of obstructive practices.[109] From INT's perspective, the respondents' false statements to INT investigators materially impeded the investigation and, as a result, amounted to obstruction. In particular, INT asserted that, during its interviews with the respondent President and the respondent Vice President and with other employees of one of the respondent firms, the interviewees denied engaging in or knowing about the alleged corrupt and collusive practices.[110] Moreover, INT affirmed that the first respondent firm engaged in obstructive practices by "materially impeding the exercise of the Bank's inspection and audit rights by denying INT access to the First Respondent Firm's computers and refusing to permit INT to conduct an audit in May 2012."[111]

In relation to the first allegation, the Sanctions Board stated that the mere denial of a misconduct, even where it constitutes a false statement, cannot form *per se* the basis for an obstructive practice. In particular, the Sanctions Board held:

> If it were to apply INT's broad interpretation of obstructive practice as asserted here, it could lead to a separate finding of sanctionable misconduct in each instance where a Respondent is found liable for other misconduct that it had denied. In these circumstances, the Sanctions Board concludes that INT has not sufficiently alleged obstruction as a distinct count of misconduct.[112]

---

[106]See 'Guidelines on preventing and combating fraud and corruption' (*World Bank*) (n 7) para 7 (e).

[107]ibid fn 14.

[108]See 'Anti-Corruption Guidelines – A User's Guide' (*World Bank*) (n 72) 9.

[109]See *World Bank v Information Computer Systems CJSC and BMS Consulting LLC*, [2016] Sanctions Board 87. For a description of the case see *supra* note 98.

[110]ibid para 24.

[111]ibid para 25.

[112]ibid para 113.

Such a decision has to be surely welcomed as it appears to be respectful of key due process safeguards in an area characterized by considerable tensions between the need of safeguarding defense rights and the necessity of implementing an effective judicial system.

A more severe approach has been taken at the domestic level within the American jurisdiction. In particular, the decision of the U.S. Supreme Court in *Dunnigan* is emblematic of the existence of the abovementioned conflicting interests.[113] In that case, the accused person, elected to take the stand, was the sole witness in her own defense and denied all criminal acts attributed to her. However, due to the fact that her responsibility was conclusively proved during the trial, the District Court imposed a more severe sentence under the November 1989 U.S. Sentencing Guideline § 3C1.1, which stated: "If the defendant willfully impeded or obstructed, or attempted to impede or obstruct the administration of justice during the investigation or prosecution of the instant offense, increase the [defendant's] offense level by 2 levels."[114] On the contrary, in a decision that appears fully respectful of due process rights, the Court of Appeals reversed the District Court's decision to increase respondent's offense level affirming that otherwise "every defendant who takes the stand and is convicted [would] be given the obstruction of justice enhancement."[115] However, the Supreme Court eventually stated that the judge of first instance correctly enhanced the sentence because the defendant's conduct amounted to perjury. Specifically, the Court affirmed:

> The commission of perjury is of obvious relevance in this regard, because it reflects on a defendant's criminal history, on her willingness to accept the commands of the law and the authority of the court, and on her character in general [. . .] A witness testifying under oath or affirmation violates this statute if she gives false testimony concerning a material matter with the willful intent to provide false testimony, rather than as a result of confusion, mistake or faulty memory [. . .] Of course, not every accused who testifies at trial and is convicted will incur an enhanced sentence for committing perjury. As we have just observed, an accused may give inaccurate testimony due to confusion, mistake or faulty memory. In other instances, an accused may testify to matters such as lack of capacity, insanity, duress or self defense. Her testimony may be truthful, but the jury may nonetheless find the testimony insufficient to excuse criminal liability or prove lack of intent.[116]

In any case, the U.S. Supreme Court decision in *Dunnigan* does not contradict the Sanctions Board's choice in the *Information Computer Systems CJSC* and *BMS Consulting LLC*. Even if, following the U.S. Supreme Court's judgment, we were to admit that a false denial might result in a heavier sentence, it should never constitute *per se* the basis for an autonomous offense of obstruction.

As regards the second allegation, the Sanctions Board highlighted that the audit clauses for the relevant bidding documents and contracts specifically required the respondents to permit the Bank to inspect all accounts and records relating to the

[113] See *United States v. Dunnigan* (91-1300), 507 U.S. 87 (1993).

[114] ibid.

[115] ibid.

[116] ibid.

performance of the contracts.[117] Consequently, the Sanctions Board held that respondents had perpetrated obstructive practices stating that

> Considering the totality of the record, and noting that INT was never provided with access to the requested documents and that the First Respondent Firm refused to authenticate the Email File or provide INT with access to its email server, the Sanctions Board finds that it is more likely than not that the First Respondent Firm engaged in obstruction by impeding the Bank's exercise of its inspection and audit rights.[118]

---

[117]See *World Bank v Information Computer Systems CJSC and BMS Consulting LLC*, [2016] Sanctions Board 87, at para 115.

[118]ibid para 116.

Chapter 5
Defense's Rights and Rule of Evidence

5.1 INT's Duty to Provide Information of Investigation Outcomes

In order to avoid the occurrence of a Kafkian situation, any person under investigation should be aware of the specific allegations he or she is under investigation for. When accused parties are aware of the investigative body's concerns, they have the opportunity to present evidence and legal arguments directly targeted to them or, alternatively, may deliberately decide to stay silent.

In *World Bank v Development and Relief Corporation B.V.*,[1] the respondent Project Manager and the respondent Commercial Manager asserted that they were not given sufficient notice that they might be personally subject to sanctions. However, the Sanctions Board did not find that the abovementioned individual

[1]The case was commenced in relation to the activities of Development and Relief Corporation B.V., a Dutch company specialised in the supply of medical appliances, and arose in the context of the health sector projects financed by the World Bank. After the completion of the investigation the case involved six Respondents: two entities plus four individuals. In particular, at the time of the alleged misconduct Development and Relief Corporation B.V. was co-owned by its Respondent Director and Respondent Co-Owner. As the Respondent Director and the Respondent Co-Owner had agreed to wind down the Firm and divide the business between them, each established his own new firm. The Respondent Director became the sole owner of Development and Relief Corporation International B.V. (the Respondent Co-Owner's new firm is not named in the present proceedings due to the circumstance it was not involved in the case). INT alleged that Respondent Firm and Respondent Firm International, as well as the individuals involved in their management, engaged in corrupt practices by offering and/or paying five percent of the value of each awarded contract to a World Bank consultant involved in the procurement process, the Procurement Advisor. INT further alleged that Respondent Firm and Respondent Firm International engaged in fraudulent practices with respect to nine submitted bids by failing to disclose the offers and payments to the Procurement Advisor as commissions, gratuities or fees. Finally INT alleged that Respondent Firm International engaged in obstructive practices by deleting email correspondence relevant to INT's investigation. See *World Bank v Development and Relief Corporation B.V.*, [2013] Sanctions Board 60.

S. Manacorda, C. Grasso, *Fighting Fraud and Corruption at the World Bank*,
https://doi.org/10.1007/978-3-319-73824-6_5

respondents were not informed that the scope of its enquiry encompassed potential misconducts and that any misconduct would lead to public sanctions.

The judging body highlighted that basic principles of fairness require, among other protections, that interviewees be informed in due course of the possible outcome of an investigation and be provided an opportunity to mount a meaningful response to any allegations against them. In the case at issue, the Sanctions Board found that, "although sanctions proceedings are not criminal in character,"[2] INT had adopted the beneficial practice of informing interviewees of the nature of its investigations.

The circumstance that informing interviewees of the nature of the sanctions proceedings is considered as just a beneficial practice adopted by INT and is not recognized as a necessary rule of due process raises considerable concerns. Without proper information on the aims of the investigations, the interviewees are not allowed to exercise in an effective way the right to remain silent and not incriminate themselves, which are strictly connected with the presumption of innocence, which is a fundamental element of both the freedom and due process perspectives.[3] At the regional level, these rights have been recognized as an implicit element of Article 6 of the European Convention of Human Rights by the European Court of Human Rights in *Funke v France*.[4] The circumstance that the Sanctions Board tends to depict the sanctions proceedings as not criminal in character does not seem a sufficient element to justify the avoidance of such an essential guarantee of due process.

---

[2]ibid para 59.

[3]See Andrew Sanders, Richard Young, and Mandy Burton, *Criminal Justice*, (4th edn, Oxford University Press 2010) 256.

[4]In this landmark sentence the European Court of Human Rights stated: "[The applicant] claimed that the authorities had violated the right not to give evidence against oneself, a general principle enshrined both in the legal orders of the Contracting States and in the European Convention and the International Covenant on Civil and Political Rights [. . .]. In the instant case the customs had not required Mr Funke to confess to an offence or to provide evidence of one himself; they had merely asked him to give particulars of evidence found by their officers and which he had admitted, namely the bank statements and cheque-books discovered during the house search. As to the courts, they had assessed, after adversarial proceedings, whether the customs' application was justified in law and in fact [. . .]. The Court notes that the customs secured Mr Funke's conviction in order to obtain certain documents which they believed must exist, although they were not certain of the fact. Being unable or unwilling to procure them by some other means, they attempted to compel the applicant himself to provide the evidence of offences he had allegedly committed. The special features of customs law (see paragraphs 30–31 above) cannot justify such an infringement of the right of anyone "charged with a criminal offence," within the autonomous meaning of this expression in Article 6, to remain silent and not to contribute to incriminating himself. There has accordingly been a breach of Article 6 para 1 (art. 6-1)." See *Funke v. France* (1993) Series A no 256, paras 41–44.

5.2 Right to Evidence Disclosure and Quality of Evidentiary Material

Disclosure has always represented a burning issue in every justice system, and the application of proper and fair disclosure is an essential element of due process. The "golden rule" is that fairness requires that complete discovery should be made of all materials held by the prosecution that weakens its case or strengthens that of the defense.[5] Such a duty is firmly recognized at the national level within many jurisdictions. For instance, in the United States, the suppression or withholding of material evidence favorable to the accused undoubtedly constitutes a violation of constitutional guarantees of due process. Due to the fact that the decisions on disclosure rest primarily on the investigative body, which can use its discretion in determining whether or not evidence favorable to the accused should be revealed, the need for the recognition of full due process safeguards in this area is considered as paramount. At the regional level, Article 6 of the European Convention of Human Rights, which enshrines the minimum fundamental due process guarantees that should be recognized in a criminal justice system, covers also the rules on evidence disclosure. In this regard, the European Court of Human Rights clarified:

> It is a fundamental aspect of the right to a fair trial that criminal proceedings, including the elements of such proceedings which relate to procedure, should be adversarial and that there should be equality of arms between the prosecution and defence. The right to an adversarial trial means, in a criminal case, that both prosecution and defence must be given the opportunity to have knowledge of and comment on the observations filed and the evidence adduced by the other party [...] In addition Article 6 § 1 requires [...] that the prosecution authorities disclose to the defence all material evidence in their possession for or against the accused.[6]

Within the Bank's regulatory framework, disclosure is dealt with by the Sanctions Procedures. In particular, section 3.02 provides:

> In submitting a Statement of Accusations and Evidence to the SDO, INT shall present all relevant evidence in INT's possession that would reasonably tend to exculpate the Respondent or mitigate the Respondent's culpability. If any such evidence comes into INT's possession subsequently, such evidence shall be disclosed by written submission to the SDO or Sanctions Board, as the case may be.[7]

Moreover, section 5.04, which deals with the issue of "distribution of written materials," establishes that the Sanctions Board "shall" provide to the parties copies of all written submissions and evidence and any other materials related to the

[5] See 'Attorney General's Guidelines on Disclosure' (*The Crown Prosecution Service*) <www.cps.gov.uk/legal/a_to_c/attorney_generals_guidelines_on_disclosure>.

[6] See *Rowe and Davis v. The United Kingdom* (2000) ECHR 2000-II, para 60.

[7] See 'Bank Procedure: Sanctions Proceedings and Settlements in Bank Financed Projects' (*World Bank*, 28 June 2016) Part A, 3.02 <http://siteresources.worldbank.org/EXTOFFEVASUS/Resources/3601045-1377105390925/Procedure_Bank_Procedure_Sanctions_Proceedings_and_Settlements_in_Bank_Financed_Projects(6.28.2016).pdf>.

proceedings[8] and that it "may" make available to a respondent materials concerning sanctions proceedings against other respondents where they involve related accusations, facts, or matters.[9] Finally, section 7.03 provides that "except as expressly provided for in this Procedure, the Respondent shall have no right to review or obtain any information or documents in the Bank's possession."[10] The application of these rules generated relevant interpretative difficulties that the Sanctions Board tried to address.

Specifically, in *World Bank v GHD Pty Ltd,*[11] the respondent made a formal request in order to obtain additional material, including, *inter alia*, any additional exculpatory evidence possessed by INT, as well as all documents and information related to sanctions procedures against the subconsultant whose proceedings formerly ended with a settlement.[12]

INT objected to these requests asserting that they were contrary to the wording of the Sanctions Procedures and their underlying policy, including the confidentiality of settlements. Moreover, INT considered the request as unnecessary in light of respondent's no-contest position.

In order to decide the case, the Sanctions Board addressed the question whether settlements between the Bank and subconsultants would constitute "sanctions proceedings" within the meaning of section 5.04(b) of the Sanctions Procedures, which as explained above establishes that "upon approval of the Sanctions Board,"

---

[8]ibid Part A, 5.04(a).

[9]ibid Part A, 5.04(b).

[10]ibid Part A, 7.03.

[11]This case involved GHD Pty Ltd ("Respondent"), one of the biggest international network of engineers, architects and environmental scientists that employs more than 5500 people across five continents. It arose in the context of the Indonesia Infrastructure Reconstruction Enabling Project by which Indonesia sought to provide technical assistance to support the post-earthquake and tsunami emergency rehabilitation and reconstruction strategy in Aceh and North Sumatra. In July 2006 the International Development Association (IDA) and the Republic of Indonesia entered into a Multi-Donor Trust Fund for Aceh and North Sumatra Grant Agreement to provide US$ 42 million to support the project. The agreement required all consulting services to be procured in accordance with the provisions of the May 2004 Consultant Guidelines. In August 2006, the Project Implementation Unit issued a request for proposals to provide consulting services under the project. In response, GHD Pty Ltd submitted a proposal in October 2006 and was the successful bidder, so in February 2007 it entered into a contract with the Project Implementation Unit valued at approximately US$ 18 million. To help fulfill its obligations GHD Pty Ltd entered into three subconsultancy agreements with a local firm to provide professional and technical staff. GHD Pty Ltd was accused of fraudulent practices consisting in failing to make required disclosures about a "marketing fee" of about US$ 43,000 to the local firm, and of fraudulently submitting to the Project Implementation Unit housing reimbursement requests, supporting them with false documentation, for some US$ 210,000 that exceeded actual expenses. Moreover, Respondent used false supporting documentation to request fraudulently a reimbursement for US$ 150,000 as vehicle and transportation expenses. See *World Bank v GHD Pty Ltd,* [2013] Sanctions Board 56.

[12]For an analysis of the Bank's settlement process see *infra* notes 125–154 and accompanying text in Chap. 6.

documents relating to other sanctions proceedings may be made available to the respondent.

From the Board's perspective, because the Sanctions Procedures expressly refer solely to materials relating to sanctions proceedings and provide that, besides those documents, the respondent shall have no right to obtain any other information in the Bank's possession, only where settlements were considered as falling within the category of sanctions proceedings could the related documents be made available to respondents.

In this respect, the judging body held that the settlement agreements could not be considered as part of sanctions proceedings for the following reason. Notwithstanding the circumstance that the Sanctions Procedures do not offer any definition of the terms "settlement" and "sanctions proceedings," the Sanctions Board deduced from a literal reading of sections 11.01(a),[13] 11.02(a),[14] and 11.03(d)[15] that the two notions should be markedly distinct because "they repeatedly refer to settlements as distinct from sanctions proceedings."[16] Accordingly, the judging body rejected the respondent's request considering that the settlement at issue did not fall within the meaning of section 5.04(b) of the Sanctions Procedures.

The solution adopted by the Sanctions Board raises relevant concerns because it appears to be based on a restrictive interpretation of the term "sanctions proceedings." Firstly, the recognition of a formal distinction made merely on the basis of the way in which respondents have decided to face the INT accusations appears inconsistent with the "informal rule of evidence" by which the entire sanctions process should be inspired.[17] Moreover, such an interpretation could not be considered satisfying as far as it is related to a provision whose rationale is to grant respondents procedural safeguards allowing them to access materials that could potentially constitute an indispensable exculpatory evidence. Therefore, in order to fairly answer the needs for due process, an extensive interpretation of the term "sanctions proceedings" should have been more appropriate. Besides, despite the circumstance that section 5.04 refers to "sanction proceedings," it does not expressly deny that materials related to settlement agreements could be made available to respondents.

---

[13]Section 11.01(a) provided that "At any time during sanctions proceedings, INT and one or more Respondents, acting jointly, may request the Evaluation Officer for a stay of proceedings for the purpose of conducting settlement negotiations." This provision is now included in Part B of the Sanctions Procedures. See 'Sanctions Procedures' (*World Bank*) (n 7) Part B, 1(a).

[14]Section 11.02(a) provides that "At any time prior to or during sanctions proceedings [. . .] INT and one or more Respondents party thereto may submit a signed copy of any settlement agreement." This provision is now included in Part B of the Sanctions Procedures. See ibid Part B, 2(a).

[15]Section 11.03(d) provides that "If a settlement agreement is to become effective prior to the commencement of sanctions proceedings, the terms of the agreement shall have the same effect as if sanctions proceedings had been commenced and concluded with the outcome [. . .] as may be specified in the agreement." This provision is now included in Part B of the Sanctions Procedures. See ibid Part B, 3(d).

[16]See *World Bank v GHD Pty Ltd*, [2013] Sanctions Board 56, para 30. For a description of the case see *supra* note 11.

[17]See 'Sanctions Procedures' (*World Bank*) (n 7) Part A, 7.01.

As regards the respondent's request to obtain additional exculpatory evidence possessed by INT, it is appreciable that the Sanctions Board determined that any additional evidence in INT's possession that could reasonably be considered as exculpatory or mitigating should be admitted. In fact, as the judging body argued, the rule under section 3.02 (which obliges INT to present all relevant evidence in its possession that would reasonably tend to exculpate the respondent or mitigate its culpability) is provided "as a matter of fundamental fairness and is essential to the Sanctions Board's ability to identify and weigh all relevant factors in reaching its sanctions decisions."[18] As a result, the Sanctions Board asked INT to produce such evidence and granted the respondent the opportunity to review and comment upon such additional evidence.[19]

Notwithstanding such a satisfactory determination, the respondent argued that INT submitted irrelevant and duplicative materials, continuing to withhold potentially exculpatory or mitigating evidence. As a consequence, respondent submitted a motion to dismiss the case with prejudice or, alternatively, to estop INT from asserting aggravation or contesting mitigation due to "INT's purported withholding of potential mitigating evidence in violation of fundamental fairness, due process, and INT's obligations under the Sanctions Procedures."[20] In particular, the respondent asserted that the additional evidence they obtained from INT was belated, incomplete, and mostly duplicative or nonprobative.[21]

However, the Sanctions Board found that respondent failed to establish grounds that would warrant an exceptional remedy as summary dismissal and that, although it found "the piecemeal presentation of evidence on both sides[22] regrettable, it ultimately considered the issue not so prejudicial as to warrant the requested dismissal or estoppel."[23]

The issue arising from the regulations on evidence discovery, as provided by section 3.02, is related to the lack of control that both respondent and the same Sanctions Board can exercise in order to verify if INT effectively discloses all exculpatory evidence in its possession. Indeed, there is no legal or practical instrument that respondent can utilize to oversee the document selection activity made by INT. Such a question is even more relevant considering that INT demonstrated so far, on the one hand, the constant intention of limiting respondent's access to the Bank's materials and, on the other, a substantial partiality similar to the one that characterizes prosecutors within domestic criminal justice systems.

[18]See *World Bank v GHD Pty Ltd*, [2013] Sanctions Board 56, para 32.

[19]ibid.

[20]ibid para 19.

[21]ibid.

[22]The Sanctions Board noted that the Respondents "did not pursue the issue of purportedly missing evidence in the timeliest or most consistent fashion," and that they adopted "inconsistent positions through the proceedings, alternatively seeking to obtain certain additional evidence, then seeking exclusion of the same evidence from record." See ibid para 35.

[23]ibid para 37.

Another issue that has emerged in relation to evidence is related to its intrinsic quality. For instance, in *World Bank v Karl Storz GmbH & Co. KG*,[24] the respondent argued that a set of exhibits, which contained transcripts of some of the interviews conducted by INT, were patchy and of limited quality because sections of the interviews that were not transcribed were inaudible.[25] Although the Sanctions Board acknowledged that it could not determine the content of the inaudible sections of the transcripts, it affirmed that there was nothing to suggest that those sections were material and that it would consider the quality of the transcripts of interview in the context of the record as a whole when assessing their evidentiary weight.[26] As a result, the judging body not only confirmed its informal approach to the rule of evidence but also showed for the umpteenth time that such an approach is used to the detriment of the accused. Such an attitude, which denotes that in the vast majority of cases the Sanctions Board prefers to take a stance that is definitely in line with the position expressed by INT, makes the need to adopt full due process safeguards even more compelling.

5.3 Right to a Hearing

In *World Bank v GHD Pty Ltd*,[27] the respondent formally requested in its Response a hearing under section 6.01 of the Sanctions Procedures. In its Reply, INT asserted that no hearing was necessary because respondent contested only the sanction, without disputing on its liability. From INT's point of view, a hearing might be requested only if it related to the accusations against a respondent.

The issue is regulated by section 6.01 of the Sanctions Proceedings, which at the time of the decision established:

> The Respondent or INT may request that the Sanctions Board hold a hearing on the accusations against the Respondent. Such requests shall be made exclusively in the

[24] The case arose in the context of the Health Sector Reform Project, which aimed at providing more accessible medical services in the Republic of Romania ("the Borrower"). In May 2009, the Romanian Ministry of Health issued bidding documents for the procurement of maternity and neonatal care equipment. The Respondent successfully entered into a contract with the Borrower having a value of €1,999,988. INT alleged that the Respondent engaged in corrupt practices by offering and paying commissions to a World Bank consultant involved in the procurement process. The Sanctions Board imposed a sanction of fixed-term debarment for a period of 2 years. See *World Bank v Karl Storz GmbH & Co. KG*, [2017] Sanctions Board 95.

[25] ibid para 19.

[26] ibid para 20.

[27] See *World Bank v GHD Pty Ltd*, [2013] Sanctions Board 56, para 37. For a description of the case see *supra* note 11.

> Respondent's Response or in INT's Reply [. . .] If no such request is made, the Sanctions Board shall review the case and render its decision on the basis of the existing record, in accordance with Section 8.02(a), without a hearing.[28]

Therefore, although there were no doubts that under such provision hearings represented a mere possibility depending on the request of the parties,[29] it did not appear clear if, upon request, the respondent or INT had a full right to obtain that a hearing was effectively held. Taking into consideration that the right to a hearing is widely recognized as a procedural entitlement essential to safeguard the fundamental right to a fair process, this was an issue of critical importance.[30]

In order to solve the abovementioned threshold matter, the Sanctions Board had the opportunity to construe the rule established by the abovementioned version of section 6.01. In particular, the judging body held that this provision "does not state that, where a party has requested a hearing, the Sanctions Board may deny such hearing at its discretion or upon other's party objections."[31]

Therefore, by means of such reasoning, it seemed that the Sanctions Board had intended to recognize a general right of the parties to obtain a hearing, if requested.

Moreover, answering directly to the issue raised by INT, the Sanctions Board held that section 6.01 did not "require that Respondents must specifically deny liability [. . .] in order to justify a hearing." In this regard, the Sanctions Board called attention to the circumstance that the oral presentations and exchanges at a hearing might clarify points of fact or law relevant to the determination of sanctions, as well as liability. Furthermore, the Sanctions Board held that the hearing could be considered as an instrument to encourage cooperation. Considering all those factors, the Sanctions Board proceeded with a hearing.[32]

However, notwithstanding the strength of such a pronouncement, the question if the Sanctions Board might reserve for itself the possibility of denying a request for a hearing where it considered it inappropriate or merely dilatory remained unanswered.

---

[28] At the time of the decision the version of this section was the following: "The Respondent or INT may request that the Sanctions Board hold a hearing on the accusations against the Respondent. Such requests shall be made exclusively in the Respondent's Response or in INT's Reply [. . .] If no such request is made, the Sanctions Board shall review the case and render its decision on the basis of the existing record, in accordance with Section 8.02(a), without a hearing."

[29] As a mere example, in decision *World Bank v Contech Devices Pvt. Ltd.* neither Respondent nor INT requested a hearing, therefore the Sanctions Board's decision was entirely based on the case written record. See *World Bank v Contech Devices Pvt. Ltd.*, [2012] Sanctions Board 54. For a description of the case see *infra* note 3 in Chap. 6.

[30] For instance, this tenet is enshrined in Article 6 of the European Convention on Human Rights that provides: "In the determination of his civil rights and obligations or of any criminal charge against him, everyone is entitled to a fair and public hearing within a reasonable time by an independent and impartial tribunal established by law." See Convention for the Protection of Human Rights and Fundamental Freedoms [1950], Article 6.

[31] See *World Bank v GHD Pty Ltd*, [2013] Sanctions Board 56, para 27.

[32] ibid.

The issue seems now resolved under the new version of section 6.01 adopted as of 2016, which in clearer terms states:

> Upon request by the Respondent in its Response or by INT in its Reply, or upon decision by the Sanctions Board Chair, the Sanctions Board will hold a hearing on the accusations against the Respondent.[33]

As a result, under this new provision, no discretionary power seems to be left to the judging body as to whether to allow a hearing to be held if requested by the parties.

It is interesting to note that the right to request a hearing is regulated in diverse ways within the different MDBs' sanctioning procedures.[34] For instance, under the Enforcement Policy and Procedures of the European Bank for Reconstruction and Development, while a hearing could be held only on request of the respondent, the Chief Compliance Officer (i.e., the investigative body of the Bank) may not request a hearing.[35] Moreover, the Sanctions Procedures of the Inter-American Development Bank expressly provide that the parties do not have any right to a hearing and that only the Sanctions Committee has a discretionary power to hold, when considered appropriate, hearings.[36]

Another concern relating to the right to a hearing appears to be raised from the circumstance that the Bank's Sanctions Procedures provide that "the hearing shall remain confidential and shall not be open or available to the public."[37] Such a

---

[33]See 'Sanctions Procedures' (*World Bank*) (n 7) Part A, 6.01.

[34]For a comparison between the various MDBs' sanctioning systems see Norbert Seiler and Jelena Madir, 'Fight Against Corruption: Sanctions Regimes of Multilateral Development Banks' (2012) 15(1) *Journal of International Economic Law* 5.

[35]Section 8.6 of EBRD's Enforcement Policy and Procedures provides that: "Should the Respondent wish to make oral representations to the Enforcement Committee [. . .] The Enforcement Committee may also request oral representations of both parties on its own volition. In the case where oral representations are to be made, the Enforcement Committee shall provide the Respondent and the Chief Compliance Officer (CCO) no less than thirty (30) days' notice of the date, time and location of the hearing. At the hearing: (1) The Respondent may be self-represented or represented by counsel or any other person authorised by the Respondent, at the expense of Respondent. (2) The CCO shall be present and/or represented by counsel or by any other person appointed by the CCO. There shall be no live witness testimony at the hearing. Oral representations shall be informal and shall be limited to the arguments and evidence contained in the Appeal Record." See 'Enforcement Policy and Procedures: The mechanism to combat fraud and corruption in EBRD projects' (*European Bank for Reconstruction and Development*, November 2015) s 8.6 <www.ebrd.com/news/publications/policies/enforcement-policy-and-procedures.html>.

[36]Section 11.3 of IADB's Sanctions Procedures provides that "neither the Office of Institutional Integrity nor a Respondent shall have a right to a hearing. The Sanctions Officer shall make his/her Determination on the basis of the Record and without a hearing. The Committee may, in its discretion, hold such hearings as it deems appropriate. In such case, the Committee shall determine the nature, length and form of any such hearing." See 'Sanctions Procedures' (*Inter-American Development Bank*) s 11.3 <http://idbdocs.iadb.org/wsdocs/getdocument.aspx?docnum=39676437>.

[37]See 'Sanctions Procedures' (*World Bank*) (n 7) Part A, 6.03(a).

provision could not be considered compatible with jurisdictional requirements by domestic courts and with the right to a fair trial.[38]

5.4 Time Limits for Submitting the Written Response to the Sanctions Board

The decision *World Bank v ASDECON Corporation Company Limited*[39] offers interesting elements on the interpretation of time limits provided in order to allow respondents to appeal against the first-tier decision issued by the Suspension and Debarment Officer (SDO). Section 5.01(a) of the Sanctions Procedures provides that the respondent may contest the case by submitting to the Sanctions Board a written Response within 90 days after delivery of the Notice of Sanctions Proceedings issued by the Bank's SDO. Furthermore, section 4.04 establishes that if the respondent does not contest the accusations or the sanction recommended by the SDO in the Notice within 90 days after its delivery, this sanction shall enter immediately into force. As provided by the same provision, the SDO shall promptly issue a specific Notice of Uncontested Sanctions Proceedings.[40]

In the abovementioned case, the Evaluation Officer (now SDO) issued a Notice of Sanctions Proceedings on June 15, 2011, whereas the respondent submitted the written Response on September 16, 2011, i.e. 3 days after the time limit of 90 days established by section 5.01(a) expired.[41]

Notwithstanding such delay in submitting the Response, the Sanctions Board *de facto* deemed the appeal as valid.

On the point the respondent raised, as a threshold matter, an issue of general fairness in relation to section 5.01(a) arguing that the limit of just 90 days was not fair in comparison to the huge amount of time granted to the Bank's officials, precisely 3 years to INT for the investigations and 2 more years to the Evaluation Officer (now SDO) for the Notice. However, the Sanctions Board rejected such

[38] See Laurence Boisson de Chazournes and Edouard Fromageau, 'Balancing the Scales: The World Bank Sanctions Process and Access to Remedies' (2012) 23(4) *European Journal of International Law* 963, 987.

[39] See *World Bank v ASDECON Corporation Company Limited*, [2012] Sanctions Board 50. For a description of the case see *supra* note 42 in Chap. 3.

[40] See *supra* notes 143–145 in Chap. 3 and accompanying text.

[41] The other two companies condemned by the SDO did not submit any Response. Therefore, the Evaluation Officer issued the Notice of Uncontested Sanctions Proceedings on September 20, 2011 stating that "no response having been submitted to the Sanctions Board [...] within the specific period [...] the sanctions recommended by the EO in the Notice are deemed uncontested for purposes of Section 4.04 of the Sanctions Procedures." The sanctions recommended by the SDO against them entered into force as of September 20, 2011. See paragraph 7 of the Notice of Uncontested Sanctions Proceedings issued by the SDO on 20 September 2011, Sanctions Case: no. 117.

argument on the ground that the respondent has the possibility to ask for an extension of time for submitting its written Response, as provided under section 5.02(b) of the Sanctions Procedures,[42] whereas in this case respondent did not avail itself of this option.

Although the Sanctions Board held that respondent's arguments of prejudice in its submission deadlines lacked foundation, it did not declare the Response to be void and turned to the merits, omitting to indicate the reasoning behind this procedural decision.

Analyzing this part of the decision, it seems that the time limit of 90 days provided under section 5.01(a) of the Sanctions Procedures is not considered by the Sanctions Board as a mandatory period because its expiration does not prevent the Sanctions Board from judging the grounds of a Response. This appears to be true at least where the Response has been lodged before the issuance of the Notice of Uncontested Sanctions Proceedings by the SDO. It follows that the exact moment in which the first-tier decision enters into force does not correspond with the expiration of the term of 90 days provided under section 5.01(a) but is strictly related to the issuance of the Notice of Uncontested Sanctions Proceedings by the SDO.

In addition, the provision under section 5.02(b) of the Sanctions Procedures establishing "Extensions of Time Periods for Filing Submissions" offers some evidence supporting this argument.

This argumentation implies that any possible delay of the SDO in issuing the Notice of Uncontested Sanctions Proceedings has direct effects on the respondent's right to submit a Response after the expiration of the abovementioned time limit. The absence of certainty in relation to such a fundamental procedural rule raises serious concerns because it may lead to a differentiated and as such unfair treatment of respondents, which can be merely based on the timeliness of SDO's action.

5.5 Standard of Proof and Shift of the Burden of Proof

Before analyzing the issues related to the standard of proof, it has to be highlighted that the entire sanctions system is inspired by an informal approach to the rule of evidence.[43] As clarified by the Bank's General Counsel in the Advisory Opinion of 2010:

> INT may present any kind of evidence. Therefore, "best evidence" is clearly not a requirement [...] Where best evidence is not available, Section 7.01 permits INT to present whatever circumstantial evidence it can marshal to support an allegation or factual assertion. At the same time, it is entirely up to the EO [now SDO] and the Sanctions Board, in their

[42] Such section establishes that: "Upon request by INT or the Respondent, a reasonable extension of any time period for the filing of submissions may be granted as a matter of discretion by the Sanctions Board Chair, by notice to both parties." See 'Sanctions Procedures' (*World Bank*) (n 7) Part A, 5.02(b).

[43] ibid Part A, 7.01.

discretion, to evaluate and weigh the evidence, so they may freely decide that circumstantial evidence proffered by INT is insufficient to support the relevant allegation or assertion.[44]

The standard of proof adopted by the Bank consists in the balance of probabilities. In other words, the *quantum* of evidence that must be presented by INT before the SDO or the Sanctions Board has to be enough to satisfy the judging bodies it was more likely than not that the alleged sanctionable practice occurred.[45] As a result, the Bank adopted a standard of proof essentially similar to the one that is traditionally used within the common law jurisdictions in civil proceedings to determine disputed questions of fact in adjudication.[46] This has been confirmed also by the Bank's General Counsel, who affirmed that "this standard of proof is understood as being equivalent the 'preponderance of the evidence,' essentially the standard to be found in civil cases in most jurisdictions."[47] Within the same countries, by contrast, prosecutors in criminal proceedings must prove their case beyond reasonable doubt, which means that the accused must be acquitted unless the judge is sure of his/her guilt.[48] In this regard, the Bank's General Counsel clarified:

> Certainly, the standard is not meant to be in any way equivalent to "beyond a reasonable doubt" that prevails in criminal law. Therefore, the decision maker may still be left with 'reasonable doubts' about the culpability of the Respondent and nevertheless impose a sanction.[49]

Taking into consideration the punitive nature of the sanctions that the Bank may impose through the sanctions process, such a decision of applying a standard of proof that offers weaker guarantees to respondents represents *per se* a matter of considerable concern.[50]

There is also a difference between the *quantum* of evidence that must be presented by INT before the SDO in order to obtain a temporary suspension or the recommendation of a sanction and the *quantum* of evidence required before the Sanctions Board to obtain the imposition of a final sanction. In the former case, the accusations have to be supported only by "sufficient evidence,"[51] whereas in the

[44]See 'Advisory Opinion on Certain Issues Arising in Connection with Recent Sanctions Cases' (*World Bank*, 15 November 2010) 10, para 44 <http://siteresources.worldbank.org/INTLAWJUSTICE/214574-1300377840517/23440937/AdvisoryOpinion.pdf>.

[45]Such a choice has been reiterated during the harmonization process of the MDBs' Sanctions procedures see *supra* note 163 and accompanying text in Chap. 1.

[46]See Mike Redmayne, 'Standards of Proof in Civil Litigation' (1999) 62(2) *The Modern Law Review* 167.

[47]Interestingly, the Counsel also added that "when this nomenclature adopted in 2004, it was felt that the phrase 'more likely than not' would be more understandable to non-lawyers." See 'Advisory Opinion' (*World Bank*) (n 44) 11, para 45.

[48]See *Woolmington v DPP* [1935] A.C. 462 HL.

[49]See 'Advisory Opinion' (*World Bank*) (n 44) 11, para 46.

[50]See *supra* notes 92–94 and accompanying text in Chap. 3.

[51]See 'Sanctions Procedures' (*World Bank*) (n 7) Part A, 4.01.

latter the requirement is the "preponderance" of the evidence.[52] As explained by the Bank's General:

> Sufficiency of evidence differs from the preponderance of evidence required for the imposition of sanctions by the Sanctions Board, since, at the time that the EO [now SDO] reviews a proposed Notice of Temporary Suspension or Notice of Sanctions Proceedings, the EO [now SDO] will not have seen any counter-evidence from the Respondent. The EO [now SDO] therefore generally looks simply at the evidence presented in either type of Notice . . . to determine whether a reasonable person would conclude, considering all relevant circumstances, that it was more likely than not that the Respondent had engaged in a Sanctionable Practice.[53]

Moreover, the Counsel specified that, although it is not the SDO's duty to make the respondent's case, it is appropriate for the Bank's official to consider other inferences that might be drawn from the evidence presented by INT beyond the inferences made by the investigators.[54] Serious doubts arise from such a way of interpreting the standard of proof within the first tier of the sanctions process. In truth, the absence of an adversarial process does not seem to assure at the present time a fair outcome of the SDO's decisions.

In *World Bank v Income Electrix Limited*,[55] the Sanctions Board confirmed that, as provided by section 8.02(b)(i) of the Sanctions Procedures, the standard of proof consists in determining if it is "more likely than not" that respondent engaged in a sanctionable practice. Moreover, the judging body specified that "more likely than not" means that, upon consideration of all the relevant evidence, a preponderance of the evidence supports findings that the respondent engaged in a sanctionable practice. In this way, the Sanctions Board acknowledged that the requested standard of proof is equivalent to the one demanded in civil cases under common law. Furthermore, the Sanctions Board restated the rule provided by section 7.01 of the Sanctions Procedures by which no formal rule of evidence has to be applied, affirming: "the Sanctions Board has discretion to determine the relevance, materiality, weight and sufficiency of all evidence offered; formal rules of evidence do not apply."[56]

The Sanctions Board also confirmed the rule on the shifting of the burden of proof provided by section 8.02(b)(ii) of the Sanctions Procedures, stating:

> INT shall have the burden of proof to present evidence sufficient to establish that it is more likely than not that the Respondent engaged in a Sanctionable Practice. Upon such a showing by INT, the burden of proof shall shift to the Respondent to demonstrate that it is more likely than not that the Respondent's conduct did not amount to a Sanctionable Practice.[57]

---

[52] ibid Part A, 8.02(b)(i).

[53] See 'Advisory Opinion' (*World Bank*) (n 44) 11, para 48.

[54] ibid 11, para 49.

[55] See *World Bank v Income Electrix Limited*, [2012] Sanctions Board 46. For a description of the case see *supra* note 49 in Chap. 3.

[56] ibid para 9.

[57] ibid para 10.

A later decision[58] appears extremely relevant as to the abovementioned flexible approach that, under section 7.01 of the Sanctions Procedures, can be adopted by the Sanctions Board when considering all probative evidence. In this case, the judging body found that INT did not meet its burden of proof. On that occasion, INT alleged that a certificate submitted by the respondent in order to participate in the Bank-financed project was a forgery and contained false statements and a false signature. Consequently, INT accused the respondent of fraudulent practices. However, the Sanctions Board found that INT had not met its burden of proof to show that it was more likely than not that the certificate was forged. Actually, the judging body found significant weaknesses in the evidence presented by INT. From the Sanctions Board's perspective, the record contained only limited indicia of falsity, consisting in INT's transcripts of an interview with the purported signatory. Such transcripts apparently revealed that the interviewee denied that he had signed the certificate, considered it as a fraud, and stated he even did not remember the respondent. However, the judging body showed some concerns with respect to the reliability of those transcripts. For instance, it was not clear why the interviewee, when asked from INT, refused to provide a signature sample without giving any explanation other than the following comment: "If I say it's not mine, believe me."[59] Moreover, the Board showed concerns about the credibility of the interviewee. Taking into consideration all these factors, the Sanctions Board discounted the weight of INT's records also because their content was not reaffirmed in any other statements signed by the interviewee and was not corroborated by the legal entity for which the interviewee worked.

The importance of such a decision is that the Sanctions Board clarified the degree of discretion that it and the SDO have in determining the relevance, materiality, weight, and sufficiency of all evidence offered. In particular, it was stated in the decision that

> Consistent with Section 7.01 of the Sanctions Procedures, the Sanctions Board recalls that it adopts a flexible approach when considering all probative evidence, and does not require that INT support every forgery allegation with predetermined types of testimonial or documentary evidence – which, depending on the circumstances, may not always be available. At the same time, the Sanctions Board bases its findings on the record as presented, which in this case does not support a finding of forgery by of a preponderance of evidence [...]

[58]The case arose in the context of the Cartagena Water Supply, Sewerage and Environmental management Project in Colombia. It aimed at improving sanitary conditions, water and sewerage services and their sustainability, as well as at facilitating the environmental clean-up of water bodies within the affected territory. On 20 September 2006, the Respondent submitted its bid providing a performance certificate purportedly signed by an individual on behalf of an entity. INT alleged that the certificate was a forgery containing false statements and a false signature. Consequently, it accused the Respondent of fraudulent practices. Eventually, the Sanctions Board held that it was not more likely than not the Respondent engaged in the alleged sanctionable practice and, as a result, declared the proceedings terminated. See *World Bank v Undisclosed Respondent*, [2013] Sanctions Board 59.

[59]ibid para 21.

> Accordingly, the burden does not shift to Respondent to demonstrate that it is more likely than not that Respondent did not use a forged Certificate.[60]

Therefore, in the case at issue, the Sanctions Board decided that, due to the absence of the purported issuer's written confirmation of forgery, of a signature sample from the purported signatory and of any other corroborating evidence, the record presented did not support findings of forgery by a preponderance of the evidence and, accordingly, decided to terminate the sanction proceeding against the respondent, including the temporary suspension imposed by the Evaluation Officer.

5.6 Restrictions on Respondents' Physical Access to Evidentiary Documents

In *World Bank v Development and Relief Corporation B.V.*,[61] the Sanctions Board considered INT's various arguments regarding potential restrictions on the respondents' physical access to some of INT's additional evidence.

In particular, the Sanctions Board originally granted INT's request to restrict respondents' access to evidence to in-camera review in accordance with section 5.04 (e) of the Sanctions Procedures. As a matter of fact, although the normal rule established by section 5.04(a) provides that respondents have to be provided, in a timely manner, with copies of all written submissions and evidence, section 5.04 (e) of the Sanctions Procedures introduces the following exception:

> Upon request by INT, the Sanctions Board may provide that certain pieces of evidence be made available to the Respondent solely for review at a designated Bank country office or such other place as the Sanctions Board Chair may designate for such purpose. The Respondent may request the Sanctions Board Chair, in consultation with INT, to designate another place upon a showing that review at such location would present an undue burden. Such materials shall be available for review during normal business hours, for as long as the Respondent may reasonably request, but the Respondent shall not be authorized to make copies of such materials.[62]

The Sanctions Board reached this decision taking into account the confidentiality of certain types of personnel information included in the staff record submitted by INT.[63] However, on second thought, the judging body noted that the staff rule on confidentiality of personnel information permitted the release of basic employment data such as name, employment status, employment dates, job title, and department

---

[60] ibid para 25.

[61] See *World Bank v Development and Relief Corporation B.V.*, [2013] Sanctions Board 60. For a description of the case see *supra* note 1.

[62] See 'Sanctions Procedures' (*World Bank*) (n 7) Part A, 5.04(e).

[63] See *World Bank v Development and Relief Corporation B.V.*, [2013] Sanctions Board 60, para 55.

to persons outside the Bank Group. On that basis, the Sanctions Board eventually found no grounds to limit the respondents to in-camera review.[64]

In reality, INT had even requested that those staff records originally attached to the reply be completely withheld from the respondents due to confidentiality concerns under section 5.04(c) of the Sanctions Procedures, which provides:

> The Sanctions Board may, in its discretion and upon request by INT, agree to the withholding of particular evidence submitted to the SDO or the Sanctions Board, upon a determination that there is a reasonable basis to conclude that revealing the particular evidence might endanger the life, health, safety, or well-being of a person or constitute a violation of any undertaking by the Bank in favor of a VDP participant. In the event that the Sanctions Board denies INT's request, INT shall have the option to withdraw such evidence from the record or to request withdrawal of the Notice.[65]

In that regard, the Sanctions Board did not accept INT's arguments that the evidence came within any of the exceptional circumstances included in this section and consequently denied the investigative body's request to withhold evidence from the respondents.[66]

5.7 Live Witness Testimony

Under the Sanctions Procedures, section 6.03(b)(iv), no live witness testimony shall be taken, except that one or more witnesses may be called and questioned by members of the Sanctions Board only. The aforesaid provision is very clear on the point specifying that

> No live witness testimony shall be taken, except that one or more witnesses may be called and questioned by members of the Sanctions Board only. The Respondent or its authorized representative may make a statement during the hearing. There shall be no crossexamination, although rebuttal evidence may be presented during the hearing.[67]

In *World Bank v Income Electrix Limited*,[68] the Sanctions Board dealt with this aspect of the sanctions proceedings and affirmed:

> It may call any witness to testify at its discretion [. . .]. Regardless of who may have initially proposed a particular witness to testify, it is for the Sanctions Board to determine whether such testimony may be useful and permitted.[69]

---

[64] ibid para 56.

[65] See 'Sanctions Procedures' (*World Bank*) (n 7) Part A, 5.04(c).

[66] See *World Bank v Development and Relief Corporation B.V.*, [2013] Sanctions Board 60, para 56.

[67] See 'Sanctions Procedures' (*World Bank*) (n 7) Part A, 6.03(b)(iv).

[68] See *World Bank v Income Electrix Limited*, [2012] Sanctions Board 46. For a description of the case see *supra* note 49 in Chap. 3.

[69] ibid para 20.

Indeed, in the present case, notwithstanding that respondent had offered to make the Logistics Officer available for questioning at the hearing, the Sanctions Board ultimately determined not to exercise its discretion to call the witness. It is important to note that a key element for taking the present decision was a written affidavit submitted by the Logistics Officer in which he stated that he signed and submitted the documents "to ensure timely submission of the bid, as without which, I presumed that the bid would not be entertained"[70] and that "neither [the Manager] nor any other staff of [Respondent] had ever instructed and/or encouraged me to sign on behalf of [the Proposed JV Partner] under any circumstances whatsoever."[71] Therefore, the Sanctions Board took its decision without having the possibility to delve into this key evidence or allowing a fundamental witness to clarify its statements.

Significant matters of concerns arise from such a provision. Granting one who is accused of an illicit conduct that amounts to a crime the right to confront a witness is widely recognized as a fundamental due process safeguard. At the domestic level, the rule prohibiting hearsay from being admitted as evidence because of the inability of the other party to cross-examine the maker of the statement is recognized by many jurisdictions and even enshrined at the constitutional level. For instance, the Sixth Amendment of the US Constitution expressly establishes that "in all criminal prosecutions, the accused shall enjoy the right [...] to be confronted with the witnesses against him."[72] The confrontation clause established by this Amendment, which includes a cluster of fair trial rights and is considered to be the heartland of American constitutional criminal procedure, is designed to promote the truth.[73] As argued by Amar, this clause might naturally lead to such ultimate objective because

> First, [it] may discourage deliberate perjury by prosecution. witnesses, who might be ashamed to tell their lies with the defendant in the room, and afraid that their lies will not stand up to open scrutiny. Second, by simply allowing a defendant to hear a witness's story, the clause may help an innocent defendant to figure out where the witness might be mistaken (perhaps in all good faith). Third, the clause enables the defendant not merely to hear the witness's story, but to directly question and cross-examine it – to show the jury and the public where the holes are – and to invite the witness herself to supplement, or clarify, or revise the story, so that the jury and the public may hear the *whole* truth.[74]

As a matter of fact, the purpose of the adversarial system where, under the direction of the judging authority, the opposing sides present evidence, examine witnesses, and conduct cross-examinations is to afford an opportunity to elicit

---

[70]ibid para 25.

[71]ibid para 28.

[72]See 'Constitution of the United States – Amendment VI (1791)' (*United States Senate*) <www.senate.gov/civics/constitution_item/constitution.htm#amdt_5_1791>.

[73]See Akhil Reed Amar, 'Sixth Amendment First Principles' (1996) 84(4) *Georgetown Law Journal* 641, 688.

[74]ibid.

answers that will impeach the veracity, capacity to observe, impartiality, and consistency of the witness.[75]

At the regional level, the defendant's right to examine witnesses is enshrined in Article 6(3) of the European Convention of Human Rights, which states that everyone charged with a criminal offense has the minimum right "to examine or have examined witnesses against him and to obtain the attendance and examination of witnesses on his behalf under the same conditions as witnesses against him."[76] As it has been clarified by the European Court of Human Rights, such a right can be restricted only in exceptional cases.[77]

The rule that witnesses have to appear for their interrogation in person (principle of live testimony), as well as the right to confront a witness, is also recognized by the procedural rules of the International Criminal Court (ICC). As a matter of fact, although before the ICC the taking of evidence may be directed by the presiding judge, witness interrogation generally follows the adversarial model.[78] Again at the international level, a research conducted on the cases brought before the International Criminal Tribunal for Rwanda demonstrated the importance of the principle of live testimony showing that more than 50% of the prosecution witness appearing in these trials testified in a way that was seriously inconsistent with their pretrial statements.[79]

As a result, the decision taken by the Bank to rely mainly on written evidence and not allow the parties to cross-examine the witnesses in the rare cases where they are summoned by the Sanctions Board appears not only to infringe the fundamental due process rights of the respondents but also to undermine the determination of the truth.

---

[75]See Charles T. McCormick, 'The Scope and Art of Cross-Examination' (1952) 47(2) *Northwestern University Law Review* 177, 179.

[76]See the See Convention for the Protection of Human Rights and Fundamental Freedoms [1950], Article 6(3).

[77]In *Doorson v The Netherlands* the Court held that: "It is true that Article 6 (art. 6) does not explicitly require the interests of witnesses in general, and those of victims called upon to testify in particular, to be taken into consideration. However, their life, liberty or security of person may be at stake, as may interests coming generally within the ambit of Article 8 (art. 8) of the Convention. Such interests of witnesses and victims are in principle protected by other, substantive provisions of the Convention, which imply that Contracting States should organise their criminal proceedings in such a way that those interests are not unjustifiably imperilled. Against this background, principles of fair trial also require that in appropriate cases the interests of the defence are balanced against those of witnesses or victims called upon to testify." See *Doorson v The Netherlands* (1996) ECHR 26, para 70.

[78]See Kai Ambos, *Treatise on International Criminal Law*, vol 3 (Oxford University Press 2016) 464.

[79]ibid 470.

5.8 Evidential Value of Party's Silence

In *World Bank v ASDECON Corporation Company Limited*,[80] the Sanctions Board offered a careful reasoning on the evidence value of silence in the sanctioning proceedings. Indeed, in this case, INT relied primarily on the statement given by the third party's representative asserting that the Executive Director of the consortium told him that there was a commitment to pay 17% of the contract to Implementing Agent officials as a management fee.[81] Moreover, INT considered the silence of the Director on this point as showing that respondent agreed to participate in the bribe. On the contrary, respondent asserted that this silence did not show *per se* assent to any bribe.

As a preliminary remark, it has to be highlighted that the rule of evidence that is provided by the Sanctions Procedures on the matter is very broad, denoting a lack of certainty. Section 7.01 of the Procedures provides that the Sanctions Board has discretion to determine the relevance, materiality, weight, and sufficiency of all evidence.[82] Therefore, the Sanctions Board had the possibility to determine the relevance of a party's silence without referring to any particular rule.

The judging body held that silence could indicate two different things: on the one hand, it could indicate a party's assent or acquiescence; on the other, it may just reflect a lack of agreement, engagement, trust, or comprehension. Then it stated that the way of determining what is the real value of silence in a given case is to verify whether the silent party heard and understood what was being said and whether the silence in response to what was being said was, under the circumstances, so unnatural as to amount to implied acquiescence.[83]

Therefore, it seems that the Sanctions Board has adopted an interpretation of silence that rejects the traditional "safe-harbour" conception of defendant's silence on the wake of the reforms that inspired many common law jurisdictions during the last decades. Under such an approach, in some circumstances, it is possible to draw inferences against the defendant from his or her silence.[84]

In the case under analysis, after a thorough evaluation, the Sanctions Board eventually found that the "persistent silence [of the Executive Director] – in the face of repeated attempts to make unexplained reallocations that happen to

---

[80]See *World Bank v ASDECON Corporation Company Limited*, [2012] Sanctions Board 50. For a description of the case see *supra* note 42 in Chap. 3.

[81]ibid para 29.

[82]See *supra* note 60 and accompanying text.

[83]See *World Bank v ASDECON Corporation Company Limited*, [2012] Sanctions Board 50, at para 30.

[84]Under the UK Criminal Evidence Order Act 1988, for instance, it is possible for the finder of fact to infer proof of the accused's guilt from his silence at trial. See Thomas P. Quinn Jr, 'Judicial Interpretation of Silence: The Criminal Evidence Order of 1988' (1994) 26 *Case Western Reserve Journal of International Law* 365.

correspond to the amount of the alleged improper payment at issue – is more likely than not a sign Respondent had agreed to the payment scheme."[85]

Taking into consideration that the sanctions process does not provide respondents with full due process safeguards, in order to avoid any further imbalance in favor of the Bank's investigative body, the system should have allowed respondents to refuse to testify and prevent any adverse inference to be drawn from their silence.

5.9 Request for a Stay of Proceedings

In *World Bank v Dutchmed B.V.*,[86] the Sanctions Board had the opportunity to address the vexed question of the relationship between the sanctions process and other criminal proceedings in which respondents are involved at the domestic level. In particular, the respondent submitted to the Sanctions Board a request for a stay of proceedings and for the production of evidence on the ground that it had the status of suspect in a national criminal proceedings. Specifically, the respondent argued that, having such a status, the necessity of safeguarding its right against self-incrimination and the inability to interview witnesses for its defense "make it premature for the Sanctions Board to examine the case substantively."[87] In this regard, the respondent expressly invoked the due process safeguards enshrined in Article 6 of the European Convention on Human Rights.[88]

It is interesting to note that from INT's perspective, the request had "no basis in the sanctions framework or in the facts of the case" and that, *inter alia*, the respondent's request "should be denied insofar as it attempts to connect sanctions proceedings with national criminal procedures."[89]

---

[85]See *World Bank v ASDECON Corporation Company Limited*, [2012] Sanctions Board 50, at para 37.

[86]The case arose in the context of the Health Sector Reform Project, which aimed at providing more accessible medical services in the Republic of Romania ("the Borrower"). In May 2008, the Romanian Ministry of Health issued bidding documents for the procurement of medical equipment for the emergency services of municipal and local hospitals. The Respondent submitted bids for all the lots included in the procurement process and successfully entered into contracts with the Borrower for several lots. INT alleged that the Respondent engaged in corrupt practices by offering and paying commissions to a World Bank consultant involved in the procurement processes for those tenders and by offering and paying for personal trips for five staff members of the Romanian project management unit in order to influence the award of the contracts. Finally, INT alleged that the Respondent engaged in an obstructive practice by refusing to permit the Bank's investigators to conduct an audit as requested. The Sanctions Board imposed a sanction of debarment with conditional release after a minimum period of ineligibility of 14 years. See *World Bank v Dutchmed B.V.*, [2017] Sanctions Board 93.

[87]ibid para 23.

[88]ibid para 31.

[89]ibid para 35.

Eventually, the Sanctions Board denied the respondent's request for a stay of proceedings for the following reasons:

> In reaching this determination, the Sanctions Board took into account that sanctions proceedings are solely administrative in nature and intended to ensure that the Bank's fiduciary duty is fulfilled and that the proceeds of its financings are used for their intended purposes. The Sanctions Board noted that its proceedings are carried out in accordance with the World Bank Group's sanctions framework, as approved by its member country shareholders. The Sanctions Board further noted that the sanctions framework does not provide for a stay of proceedings due to any concurrent criminal, civil, or administrative proceedings before a national court or other tribunal. In addition, the Sanctions Board observed that the conduct of these proceedings does not prejudice the Respondent's right to raise its asserted privilege against self-incrimination in the context of the pending national criminal proceedings; and that whether the Respondent may successfully raise the privilege is a matter for the national tribunal's consideration, not the Sanctions Board. Finally, the Sanctions Board determined that the Respondent's asserted inability to interview the specified witnesses does not constitute a basis for granting a stay of proceedings, as the Respondent has been given a full opportunity to respond to the case made out by INT.[90]

Such a decision raises serious concerns and cannot be positively welcomed for a variety of reasons. Firstly, the Board unduly reiterates the minimalist approach to the application of due process safeguards adopted by the Bank justifying it on the basis that the sanctions process is labeled as having administrative nature. In reality, the severity of the sanction imposed (i.e., debarment with conditional release after a minimum period of ineligibility of 14 years) and the circumstance that for the same conducts the respondent was subject to criminal proceedings at the national level are emblematic of the punitive nature of the sanctions process and of the need for the recognition of full due process safeguards. Secondly, the fact that the sanctions framework does not provide for a stay of proceedings due to any concurrent criminal, civil, or administrative proceedings does not appear as a valid argument to deny a stay of proceedings where it is reasonable to grant it. As we have already argued, although the Bank's sanctions framework is extremely fragmented and inevitably lacunose,[91] section 11 of the Sanctions Board Statute provides for a safety valve[92] expressly allowing the Board to take decisions on all matters not addressed in the sanctions framework.[93] Moreover, the possibility of granting a stay of proceedings is not unknown to the sanctions process. As a matter of fact, the rules that discipline the settlement agreements provide for such a request that may be

[90]ibid para 26.

[91]See *supra* notes 22–27 and accompanying text in Chap. 3.

[92]See 'WBG Policy: Statute of the Sanctions Board' (*World Bank*, 18 October 2016) <http://siteresources.worldbank.org/EXTOFFEVASUS/Resources/3601045-1377105390925/WBG_Policy_Statute_of_the_Sanctions_Board_(10.18.2016).pdf>.

[93]For instance, the Sanctions Board used such a provision in order to deal with requests for reconsideration, which are not addressed by the Bank's sanctions framework. See *infra* notes 95–109 and accompanying text.

submitted at any time during sanctions proceedings and shall be granted as a matter of course.[94] Finally, the Sanctions Board did not take in adequate consideration the serious prejudice that a respondent might suffer due to its decisions in the context of the pending national proceedings. It has not to be underestimated the fact that the decisions taken by an international organization that enjoys credibility and authoritativeness as the World Bank does may inherently exert a substantial degree of influence on the wider public and the domestic judicial authorities. Consequently, where fundamental rights are at stake like when a respondent is subject to domestic criminal proceedings, a stay of proceedings should be granted or, at least, the publication of the Bank's sanctioning decision should be postponed until the end of such national proceedings.

5.10 Principle of Finality

In *World Bank v De Lorenzo of America Corp. S.A. de C.V.*,[95] the statutory and procedural framework included the Sanctions Board Statute as revised on September 15, 2010, and the Sanctions Procedures as adopted on January 1, 2011 (subsequently revised in 2016).

Both Article XIV of the Statute and section 8.03(a) of the Sanctions Procedures establish the principle of finality of Sanctions Board decisions. As a matter of fact, Article XIV of the Statute provides that Sanctions Board's decisions "shall be final and without appeal"; section 8.03(a) of the Sanctions Procedures stated that each Sanctions Board decision "shall be final and shall take effect immediately."[96]

[94] See *infra* notes 134–136 and accompanying text in Chap. 6.

[95] The case concerned a Request for Reconsideration filed by Respondent with regard to Sanctions Board Decision no. 49 (2012) – Sanctions Case no. 130, by which the Sanctions Board debarred Respondent with conditional release after a minimum period of two years for fraudulent practices. Respondent asked the Sanctions Board "to clarify" to original decision no. 49 (2012) in order that the two-year minimum period of debarment be calculated to have begun with the temporary suspension in April 2011, instead of the date of the issuance of the decision no. 49, in May 2012. The Request for Reconsideration principally asserted that calculating the debarment period to begin on the date of the decision would penalize Respondent for exercising its right of appeal to the Sanctions Board. Moreover Respondent highlighted that the decision contained no indications that the Sanctions Board wished to increase the two-year debarment recommended by the SDO. INT, in its Comments on the Request for Reconsideration, asserted that the decision appeared to have taken into account as a mitigating factor the period of temporary suspension served by Respondent. In any case, INT highlighted that there was no basis to grant the Respondent for reconsideration as Respondent did not raise any facts falling within the category of exceptional circumstances under the standards set out in Sanctions Board Decision no. 43. See *World Bank v De Lorenzo of America Corp. S.A. de C.V.*, [2013] Sanctions Board 57.

[96] The new version of section 8.03 of the Sanctions Procedures, as amended in 2016, currently provides: "The decision of the Sanctions Board shall be final and without appeal, and shall be binding on the parties to the proceedings. The decision shall take effect immediately, without prejudice to any action taken by any government under its applicable law."

As already set forth by the Sanctions Board in the earlier Decision No. 43 (2011), the principle of finality is:

> [. . .] a fundamental aspect of any judicial or quasi-judicial process, including international administrative tribunal proceedings [. . .] Finality is essential to provide certainty to the parties and others with an interest in the proceedings, prevent re-litigation of claims already adjudicated, conserve judicial resources, and encourage respect for adjudicated outcomes (*res judicata*).[97]

In truth, neither the Statute nor the Sanctions Procedures address whether the Sanctions Board may reopen or reconsider its own decisions. However, the Statute states:

> In all matters not addressed in the WBG Sanctions Framework, the Sanctions Board shall follow the instructions of the Sanctions Board Chair for the operation of the Sanctions Board.[98]

In the case at issue, the judging body took into account the considerations expressed by the Sanctions Board Chair in the abovementioned Decision No. 43 (2011). On that occasion, the Sanctions Board Chair convened a plenary session[99] to determine the Sanctions Board's competence to review requests for reconsideration. Under the standards set out in Sanctions Board Decision No. 43 (2011), the specific preclusion of appeal provided by Article XIV of the Statute and section 8.03(a) of the Sanctions Procedures did not necessarily prevent the Sanctions Board's own reconsideration of its decisions. As a matter of fact, even if finality is an essential aspect of any judicial or quasi-judicial process, it must on occasion yield in narrowly defined and exceptional circumstances in order to satisfy fundamental principles of fairness.[100] In particular, in Decision No. 43 (2011), the Sanctions Board specified:

> In the absence of guidance on how to define such exceptional circumstances under the Statute and Procedures, the Bank's legislative history, or the Sanctions Board previous jurisprudence, the Sanctions Board looked to general principles of law, as demonstrated by leading international and national practice.[101]

Considering such general principles and practice, in the abovementioned decision, the Sanctions Board concluded:

---

[97]See Sanction Board Decision no. 43 (2011), paragraph 14.

[98]See 'Statute of the Sanctions Board' (*World Bank*) (n 92) s III(A)(11).

[99]As provided by section 8 of Sanctions Board Statute: "For plenary sessions, the Sanctions Board will require the – virtual or in person – presence of the full five (5) member Sanctions Board. A plenary session may be convened by the Sanctions Board Chair when, in his/her opinion: (a) the complexity of a case requires such a session; (b) it is necessary to address a question affecting the operation of the Sanctions Board, including the application of the Code of Conduct and the rules on confidentiality; (c) it is necessary to address a question of its competence under paragraph 2 above; or, (d) any other matter warranting consideration by the full Sanctions Board." See 'Statute of the Sanctions Board' (*World Bank*) (n 92) s III(A)(8).

[100]See *World Bank v Undisclosed Respondent*, [2011] Sanctions Board 43, at para 15.

[101]ibid paras 15–24.

> A final decision may be reconsidered only in exceptional circumstances such as the discovery of newly available and potentially decisive facts, fraud or other misconduct in the original proceedings, or a clerical mistake in the issuance of the original decision"[102] whereas "Mere attempts to re-argue or re-litigate a case, or Respondent's failure to timely or effectively present previously available facts or related evidence to the Sanctions Board [. . .] do not warrant reconsideration.[103]

Taking those principles into consideration, in *World Bank v De Lorenzo of America Corp. S.A. de C.V.*, the Sanctions Board did not find that exceptional circumstances warranting reconsideration of the original decision occurred and, consequently, denied to reopen the question.

In general terms, it can be positively welcomed the circumstance that the Sanctions Board, in the absence of a specific rule, decided for the possibility of yielding the finality of its own decisions. Such a safety valve represents a fundamental legal tool in order to safeguard respondents' rights. Although at the moment the criteria conceived by the Sanctions Board are quite vague, and would clearly necessitate further development in order to guarantee the predictability of the future Board's judgments on reconsideration, the utilization of a mere illustrative list of hypotheses has to be positively hailed because it will still allow enough room for improvement.

Some additional comments may be made in the light of this decision. In particular, the judging body expressly recognized that, when necessary, it has recourse to general principles of law, as demonstrated by leading international and national practice. The recourse to "external sources" for filling the unavoidable lacunae that the Bank's sanctioning system intrinsically has and assigning a higher level of authoritativeness to Sanctions Board's judgments present some problematic aspects in relation to the absence of any criterion that the judging body should follow in order to select the relevant international and domestic principles.[104]

The Sanctions Board had the opportunity to consider again the issues related to the principle of finality in *World Bank v E.C. De Luna Construction Corp. and Mr. Eduardo C. De Luna*.[105] On this occasion, the respondents based their request for reconsideration, among other things, on the two following arguments. Firstly, they affirmed that developments following their debarment in 2009 justified a review of their sanctions of indefinite debarment.[106] Secondly, they argued that the retroactive application of "beneficial rules"—i.e., rules favorable to respondents—to "finalized judgement[s]" is a "generally accepted principle in disciplinary proceedings in international and national jurisdictions." Consequently, from the

[102]ibid para 25.

[103]ibid paras 26–27.

[104]See *supra* notes 38–46 and accompanying text in Chap. 3.

[105]The decision relates to a request for reconsideration of Sanctions Board Decision no. 4 (2009) and/or Sanctions Board Decision no. 84 (2015), according to which the Respondents were debarred for an indefinite period of time for collusive practices. The Sanctions Board denied the Respondents' request for reconsideration. See *World Bank v E.C. De Luna Construction Corp. and Mr. Eduardo C. De Luna,* [2016] Sanctions Board 89.

[106]ibid para 5(i).

respondents' perspective, because the 2010 Bank's Sanctions Guidelines could not justify indefinite debarment, they should be applied retroactively in their case within the category of "beneficial rules."[107]

However, the Sanctions Board did not find any circumstances that would justify a reconsideration. In relation to the first issue, the judging body stated that the respondents submitted evidence that they already referenced, but failed to include, in previous phases of the proceedings. Consequently, the Sanctions Board did not consider the submitted record as constituting newly available facts. In particular, the evidence was from 2009 (i.e., the year of the original decision), and the respondents did not offer any explanation or evidence as to why they were not able to include this evidence in their previous requests.[108] As regards the second argument, the Sanctions Board declined to consider the Bank's adoption of the 2010 Sanctioning Guidelines as an exceptional circumstance and noted, *inter alia*, that the respondents could not point to any international law rule or precedent that would support the retroactive application of beneficial rules in finalized cases. Moreover, the judging body affirmed that the materials cited by the respondents concerned criminal and disciplinary proceedings, where instead sanctions proceedings are administrative in nature.[109]

5.11 Statute of Limitations

In *World Bank v Concept Pharmaceuticals Limited*,[110] the judging body addressed, as a threshold matter, a respondent's jurisdictional challenge related to the statute of limitations.

Respondent argued that the allegations against it would have been time-barred by the 10-year statute of limitations under section 4.01(d)(i) of the Sanctions Procedures.

This question did not give rise to any particularly complex issue of judicial interpretation because the judging body simply adhered to the wording of the provision. Under section 4.01(d)(i) of the Sanctions Procedures, a case shall be closed if "a Sanctionable Practice in connection with a contract the execution of which was completed more than ten (10) years prior to the date on which the Statement of Accusations and Evidence was submitted to the Evaluation Officer." Therefore, the Sanctions Board, adopting a black-letter approach, rejected the threshold matter raised by the respondent, reasoning as follows:

---

[107]ibid para 5(ii).

[108]ibid para 11.

[109]ibid para 12.

[110]See *World Bank v Concept Pharmaceuticals Limited*, [2012] Sanctions Board 47. For a description of the case see *supra* note 60 in Chap. 3.

> the Statement of Accusations and Evidence was submitted to the Evaluation Officer on March 1, 2010. Therefore, the allegations against Respondent would be time-barred if Respondent had completed execution of its [...] contract before March 1, 2000. The record shows Respondent signed the contract for TB I in December 2000 – so could not have begun, let alone completed, execution of the TB I contract until after March 1, 2000.[111]

Notwithstanding such a straightforward reasoning, various concerns arise from the way in which section 4.01(d)(i) has been formulated.

Firstly, there are no doubts that, for the purpose of applying the statute of limitations, the provision considers relevant the mere passage of the time elapsed during INT's investigations. As stated in the abovementioned section, the submission of the INT's Statement of Accusations and Evidence to the SDO definitely interrupts the accruement of limitation periods.[112] The consequence of such provision is that the passage of time that elapses from the conclusion of the investigations to the final decision issued by the Sanctions Board is irrelevant for the purpose of the statute of limitations. This rule is applicable notwithstanding the circumstance that the sanctioning proceedings could last several years. In the present case, for instance, the judging body did not take into consideration the circumstance that the first and second tiers of the proceedings lasted more than 2 years (INT submitted the Statement of Accusations and Evidence to the Evaluation Officer on March 1, 2010, and the definitive decision was issued by the Sanctions Board on May 30, 2012).

A second concern is related to the statute of limitations' date of accrual. As specified by section 4.01(d)(i), limitation periods run from the completion of the execution of contracts. Therefore, such provision does not take into account the considerable period of time that could potentially elapse between the moment in which the sanctionable practice has been perpetrated and the one in which the execution of the related contract is completed. Such argument is even more relevant in consideration of the circumstance that many contracts related to Bank-financed projects have a long duration due to their considerable complexity and high value.

Therefore, in the light of the above argumentations, a question of general fairness could be raised in relation to how the rule on limitations periods has been conceived by the Bank's Sanctions Procedures. In particular, it seems that the 10-year statute of limitations, being substantially granted to allow INT conducting its investigations, is definitively excessive.

Anyway, to be comprehensive, it must be noted that the Sanctions Board tends to consider in determining appropriate sentences the passage of significant time as a mitigating factor.

---

[111] ibid para 20.

[112] As provided by the Sanctions Procedures: "In order to initiate sanctions proceedings, INT shall submit to the Evaluation Officer a Statement of Accusations and Evidence [...]" See 'Sanctions Procedures' (*World Bank*) (n 7) Part A, 3.01(b).

Chapter 6
Sanctions and Sentencing Practices

6.1 Indefinite or Fixed-Term Debarment

Sanctions vary according to the severity of offenses and the evidence presented against respondents. They impose different costs on the concerned firms and individuals. The Bank issued Sanctioning Guidelines in order to offer guiding criteria to the SDO and the Sanctions Board.[1] The document specifies that the guiding principles "are not meant to be prescriptive in nature, but to provide guidance to those who have the discretion to impose sanctions on behalf of the" Bank.[2] In *World Bank v Contech Devices Pvt. Ltd.*,[3] the Sanctions Board clarified:

> While the Sanctioning Guidelines themselves state they are not intended to be prescriptive in nature, they provide a point of reference to help illustrate the types of considerations potentially relevant to a sanctions determination. They further suggest potentially applicable ranges of increases or decreases from a proposed base sanction of debarment with the possibility of conditional release after three years.[4]

It follows a brief illustration of all the available sanctions appearing in order of decreasing severity.

---

[1]See 'World Bank Group Sanctioning Guidelines' (*World Bank*, 1 January 2011) <http://siteresources.worldbank.org/EXTOFFEVASUS/Resources/WorldBankSanctioningGuidelines.pdf>.

[2]ibid 1.

[3]The case arose in the context of the Bangladesh Health, Nutrition and Population Sector Program in which the People's Republic of Bangladesh (the Borrower) entered in 2005. In May 2009, the Respondent submitted a bid and was awarded a contract for the supply of 720,000 sets of intrauterine contraceptive devices for US$135,936. The Respondent was accused of fraudulent practices consisting in submitting forged documents. For the perpetration of such a sanctionable practice the Sanctions Board imposed on the Respondent a fixed-term debarment of one year. See *World Bank v Contech Devices Pvt. Ltd.*, [2012] Sanctions Board 54.

[4]ibid para 32.

S. Manacorda, C. Grasso, *Fighting Fraud and Corruption at the World Bank*,
https://doi.org/10.1007/978-3-319-73824-6_6

Debarment, or exclusion from the current or future bidding process, is the interdictory sanction governed by paragraph 1.16(d) of the Procurement Guidelines, which provides:

> [The World Bank] will sanction a firm or individual, at any time, in accordance with the prevailing Bank's sanctions procedures, including by publicly declaring such firm or individual ineligible, either indefinitely or for a stated period of time: (i) to be awarded a Bank-financed contract; and (ii) to be a nominated sub-contractor, consultant, supplier, or service provider of an otherwise eligible firm being awarded a Bank-financed contract.[5]

The indefinite (or permanent) debarment is the most punitive action that the Sanctions Board may impose. When a firm or individual has engaged in a flagrant form of fraud or corruption, indefinite debarment excludes that entity from multilateral funded projects[6], whereas under the fixed-term debarment, the respondent is declared ineligible to do further business with the Bank for a fixed amount of time.

The Bank's Sanctioning Guidelines specify that permanent debarment "is generally only appropriate in cases where it is believed that there are no reasonable grounds for thinking that the Respondent can be rehabilitated through compliance or other conditionalities."[7] Moreover, the Guidelines recommend that in ordinary circumstances, permanent debarment is only applied to natural persons, closely held companies by such persons, and shell companies.[8]

As regards fixed-term debarment, the Guidelines clarify that such a sanction may be applied where no reasonable purpose would be served by imposing conditions and the proposed debarment is for a relative short period of time. As a result, under the new Guidelines, fixed-term debarment plays only a residual role and cannot be considered a the "baseline" sanction. The same document gives the example of a firm that has already in place a robust corporate compliance program or of a sanctionable practice merely involving isolated acts of employees who have already been terminated.[9]

In the case of a firm, the ineligibility extends to any firm or individual who the debarred firm directly or indirectly controls, so allowing a very extended application of the sanctions. Specularly, where it is an individual that is to be debarred, the ineligibility extends to any firm that the debarred person directly or indirectly

[5]See 'Guidelines: Procurement of Goods, Works, and Non-Consulting Services under IBRD Loans and IDA Credits & Grants' (*World Bank*, January 2011, Revised July 2014) 1.16(d) <http://pubdocs.worldbank.org/en/492221459454433323/Procurement-GuidelinesEnglishJuly12014.pdf>.

[6]See 'Bank Procedure: Sanctions Proceedings and Settlements in Bank Financed Projects' (*World Bank*, 28 June 2016) Part A, 9.01(c) <http://siteresources.worldbank.org/EXTOFFEVASUS/Resources/3601045-1377105390925/Procedure_Bank_Procedure_Sanctions_Proceedings_and_Settlements_in_Bank_Financed_Projects(6.28.2016).pdf>.

[7]See 'Sanctioning Guidelines' (*World Bank*) (n 1) E.

[8]ibid.

[9]ibid B.

No.	RESPONDENT	COUNTRY	SANCTIONABLE PRACTICES	LENGTH OF DEBARMENT
1	Information Computer Systems CJSC	Ukraine	Collusive, Corrupt and Obstructive Practices	22 years and 6 months
2	Mr. Alexander Fedchenko	Ukraine	Collusive and Corrupt Practices	11 years and 6 months
3	Mr. Ngyyen Phuong Quy	Vietnam	Fraudulent and Collusive Practices	11 years
4	SFC Vietnam Investment Development for Environment Corp.	Vietnam	Fraudulent and Collusive Practices	10 years
5	Mr. Nikolay Dovzhenko	Ukraine	Collusive and Corrupt Practices	8 years and 6 months

Fig. 6.1 World Bank: The Five Longest Debarment Imposed in 2016. *Source*: 'The World Bank Group Integrity Vice Presidency – Annual Update – Fiscal Year 2016' (*World Bank*, Publications*)* 35 <http://pubdocs.worldbank.org/en/118471475857477799/INT-FY16-Annual-Update-web.pdf>

controls. Under such a rule, the identification of all the links between the blacklisted firms and individuals might pose enormous problems,[10] especially at the transitional level. Suffice here to mention the common business practice consisting in the use of shell companies or the anonymity protection that many jurisdictions still offer to beneficial owners.

In 2016, the Bank debarred a total amount of 58 entities, with the longest debarment set to 22.5 years (see Fig. 6.1).

This interdictory sanction can be imposed prior to or after the award of a contract. In the latter case, the borrower may continue the execution of the contract, providing that additional due diligence is applied.[11] As a result of the debarment, after the effective date of the suspension, the blacklisted individual or entity shall never sign any new contract or amendment to an existing contract.[12] In the case of violation, a declaration of misprocurement will be issued by the Bank during the award process or after it if a fraud is discovered later on. As regards the declaration of misprocurement, paragraph 1.16(c) of the Procurement Guidelines provides:

> [The World Bank] will declare misprocurement and cancel the portion of the loan allocated to a contract if it determines at any time that representatives of the Borrower or of a recipient of any part of the proceeds of the loan engaged in corrupt, fraudulent, collusive, coercive, or obstructive practices during the procurement or the implementation of the contract in question, without the Borrower having taken timely and appropriate action satisfactory to

[10]See Laurence Folliot-Lalliot, 'Introduction to the World Bank's policies in the fight against corruption and conflict of interests in public contracts' in Jean-Bernard Auby, Emmanuel Breen and Thomas Perroud (eds), *Corruption and Conflicts of Interest* (Edward Elgar 2014) 243.

[11]ibid 244.

[12]ibid.

the Bank to address such practices when they occur, including by failing to inform the Bank in a timely manner at the time they knew of the practices.[13]

Taking into consideration that the Bank does not have any direct power over the country representatives and civil servants, who are often enmeshed in the corrupt activities perpetrated by the debarred firms or individuals, the possibility of ordering the reimbursement of the loan represents an effective economic leverage to encourage the national authorities in taking appropriate actions against the persons involved in the illicit activities.[14]

It has to be also highlighted that under the new transparency policy of the Bank, in the case of debarment (with or without conditions), the names of the debarred entities and the sanction they have received are published on the Bank's website.[15] Due to the serious harm to respondents' reputation that such a publication might cause, this can be considered as an additional indirect sanction imposed by the financial institution.

6.2 Debarment with Conditional Release

Over the course of time, the Bank has gradually moved to the system of conditional debarment, under which the sanctioned party is subject to ineligibility and is released from debarment only if it demonstrates compliance with certain remedial, preventative, or other conditions for release, after a minimum period of debarment.[16]

As specified in the Sanctioning Guidelines, debarment with conditional release currently represents the "baseline" sanction that should normally be applied absent the considerations that would justify another sanction.[17] The rationale behind such a choice is to encourage the respondent's rehabilitation and to mitigate further risk to Bank-financed activities.[18]

Although the sanctioned party may not be released prior to the defined debarment period, even if they meet the conditions prior to the period's lapse, it can be specified in the decision that compliance with certain conditions like cooperation or remedial measures may reduce the minimum period of debarment originally established.[19]

---

[13]See 'Procurement Guidelines' (*World Bank*) (n 5) 1.16(c).

[14]See Folliot-Lalliot, 'Introduction to the World Bank's policies' in *Corruption and Conflicts of Interest* (n 10) 247.

[15]See 'World Bank Listing of Ineligible Firms & Individuals' (*World Bank*) <http://web.worldbank.org/external/default/main?contentMDK=64069844&menuPK=116730&pagePK=64148989&piPK=64148984&querycontentMDK=64069700&theSitePK=84266>.

[16]See 'Sanctions Procedures' (*World Bank*) (n 6) Part A, 9.01(d).

[17]See 'Sanctioning Guidelines' (*World Bank*) (n 1) II(A).

[18]ibid.

[19]ibid.

Examples of conditions that respondents might be normally required to meet are the implementation of an integrity compliance program and the adoption of other actions to improve business governance, of remedial measures to address the misconduct for which the respondent was sanctioned,[20] of disciplinary actions against employees.[21]

The function of monitoring and supervising integrity compliance by sanctioned companies and of deciding whether the compliance conditions established by the SDO or the Sanctions Board have been satisfied is undertaken by the Integrity Compliance Office (ICO), whose office has been established in September 2010 by INT.[22]

As the Independent Advisory Board (IAB) highlighted in its report of February 2014, "as of December 31 2013, 177 entities had been sanctioned with compliance conditions, including 25 entities subject to debarment with conditional early release under the pre-2010 sanctions procedures and 152 parties subject to conditional sanctions following the 2010 sanctions reforms."[23] The panel also underlined that some companies do not engage with an integrity compliance program accepting continuing debarment from the Bank and some others cease to trade after the imposition of the sanction.[24]

The panel clarified that ICO works with debarred entities in two different ways. On some occasions, the Office enters into an agreement on the selection of a suitable monitor for a compliance program. In other cases, ICO works with companies in order to develop a suitable compliance program, which will be reviewed and possibly approved by the Office.[25] In particular, the IAB observed:

> If the Bank imposes a penalty of conditional non-debarment, or debarment with conditional release, it is to induce a party to comply with remedial, preventive or other conditions to improve governance and integrity. Whether a company does improve governance and integrity will depend very much on the quality of the compliance program and the effectiveness of implementing it. In large organisations, a compliance program will require the commitment of senior Board and management personnel and could extend to a very high number of employees.[26]

---

[20]ibid.

[21]See 'Sanctions Procedures' (*World Bank*) (n 6) Part A, 9.01(d).

[22]See 'Sanctions & Compliance' (*World Bank*) <http://www.worldbank.org/en/about/unit/integrity-vice-presidency/sanctions-compliance>.

[23]See 'Independent Advisory Board (IAB) 2013 Annual Report' (*World Bank*, February 2014) 9 <http://siteresources.worldbank.org/PROJECTS/Resources/40940-1244163232994/IAB-2013-ANNUAL_REPORT-FINAL-28FEB14.pdf>.

[24]ibid 10.

[25]ibid.

[26]ibid.

6.3 Conditional Nondebarment

In the case of conditional nondebarment, the respondent is not debarred but is subject to specific conditions that have to be satisfied within a set time frame. In other words, the sanctioned party is required to comply with certain remedial, preventative, or other conditions to avoid debarment.[27] If the conditions, which are similar to the ones that can be imposed in case of debarment with conditional release,[28] are not observed, the respondent is then debarred. This sanction is commonly applied where there are clear circumstances that indicate that a direct debarment should not be applied. In this regard, the Sanctioning Guidelines illustrate two cases in which such a sanction may be "generally" imposed. Conditional nondebarment can be considered appropriate when respondents have demonstrated that they have taken comprehensive voluntary corrective measures. This sanction can also be imposed on parents and other affiliates of respondents in cases where, notwithstanding the fact they were not directly involved in the sanctionable practice, the misconduct was the result of their systemic failure to supervise.[29] As in the case of debarment with conditional release, the Bank's official who undertakes the function of monitoring integrity compliance by sanctioned parties and deciding whether the compliance conditions have been satisfied is the Integrity Compliance Office (ICO).[30]

6.4 Letter of Reprimand

This sanction is imposed in less serious cases, where even conditional nondebarment might be disproportionate to the illicit conduct.[31] The letter of reprimand can be published on the Bank's website. Although in this case the sanctioned entity or individual will continue to be eligible to participate in the Bank-financed projects, this public identification is hardly without cost; indeed, as it has been highlighted in relation to the publication of the debarred entities' names, the publication of the letter of reprimand may potentially cause serious harm to respondents' reputation and, consequently, place them at a disadvantage in competition for international contracts. The letter of reprimand will be removed after a determined amount of time as specified in the same document.

The content of the letter commonly includes the following elements: the respondent's details, a reference to the case, a brief description of the perpetrated

---

[27] See 'Sanctions Procedures' (*World Bank*) (n 6) Part A, 9.01(b).

[28] See *supra* notes 16–21 and accompanying text.

[29] See 'World Bank Group Sanctions Regime: An Overview' (*World Bank*, 8 October 2010) 4 <http://siteresources.worldbank.org/EXTOFFEVASUS/Resources/Overview-SecM2010-0543.pdf>.

[30] See *supra* note 22 and accompanying text.

[31] See 'Sanctions Procedures' (*World Bank*) (n 6) Part A, 9.01(a).

sanctionable practice, the public admonishment, and the period of time during which the letter will be available on the Bank's website. As a mere example, see the following content of the letter of reprimand issued against Sinohydro Corporation Limited in June 2016:

> Dear Respondent,
>
> In its Decision No. 88 (the "Decision"), the Sanctions Board found that the record supported a conclusion that the Respondent had engaged in a fraudulent practice. In particular, the Sanctions Board found that it was more likely than not that the Respondent had recklessly misrepresented commissions paid or to be paid to an agent in order to influence the procurement process for a World Bank-financed contract.
>
> The present letter shall serve as a reprimand for the Respondent's engagement in a fraudulent practice. In its determination of this sanction, the Sanctions Board took into account all applicable sanctioning factors, as stated in the Decision at Section V.C.
>
> Pursuant to the Decision, this letter shall be posted on the World Bank's website as of today for a period of one (1) year.[32]

In this case,[33] the SDO recommended the imposition of a debarment with conditional release for the respondent with a minimum period of ineligibility of three (3) years.[34] The Sanctions Board found more likely than not that the respondent engaged in fraudulent practices paying a commission to a local consulting firm without disclosing the payment in the bidding documents.[35] However, the judging body also found that mitigation was to be warranted because the respondent demonstrated to have implemented an effective compliance program that "would appear to address the type of misconduct in this case."[36] As a result, the Sanctions Board decided to impose a letter of reprimand instead of the debarment with conditional release.[37]

---

[32]See 'Sanctions Case no. 372 – Letter of Reprimand' (*World Bank*, 29 June 2016) <http://siteresources.worldbank.org/INTOFFEVASUS/Resources/3601037-1346795612671/SanctionsCaseNo.372-LetterofReprimand.pdf>.

[33]The case arose in the context of the OMVS Felou Hydroelectric Project, which aimed at augmenting the supply of low-cost hydroelectricity to national power utilities and developing a nucleus of a cooperative power-pooling mechanism in West Africa. The project implementation units determined that Sinohydro Corporation Limited was the lowest qualified bidder and awarded the contract to the firm. The World Bank's Integrity Office alleged that the Respondent engaged in fraudulent practices in its Bid and the Bidding Letter by knowingly misrepresenting commissions paid or to be paid to agents in relation to the Contract. Specifically, the investigators asserted that in response to a requirement in the Bidding Documents and the Bidding Letter to disclose such commissions, the Respondent stated "[n]one," although it intended to pay, and later paid, commissions to a local consulting firm. According to Integrity Office, the representative of the Respondent who prepared the Bid and the Bidding Letter (the "Respondent's Employee") acted knowingly and with the intent to influence the procurement process. See *World Bank v Sinohydro Corporation Limited*, [2016] Sanctions Board 88.

[34]ibid para 4.

[35]ibid para 25.

[36]ibid para 53.

[37]ibid para 62.

The Sanctions Procedures do not provide the publication of the letter as mandatory. As a result, on some occasions, the Bank may impose a formal letter of private reprimand to the respondent, whose anonymity is then protected.[38]

6.5 Restitution and Financial Remedies

The sanctioned party may be required to make restitution to the borrower or to any other party or take actions to remedy the harm caused by its illicit conduct.[39] As specified in the sanctions process overview issued in 2010, restitution proved to be difficultly applicable largely due to lack of clear criteria as to how to calculate the *quantum* to be returned and determine the relevant recipient. Consequently, the overview specified that appropriate cases where such a sanction should be imposed may include those where the damage caused by the misconduct is clear and quantifiable.[40] Similarly, in the Sanctioning Guidelines, it is clarified that restitution, as well as financial and other remedies, "may be used in exceptional circumstances," including those involving fraud in contract execution where there is a quantifiable amount to be restored to the client country or project.[41]

In any case, rather than as an autonomous sanction, restitution orders can be used as conditions that respondents have to respect in order to avoid debarment in case of conditional nondebarment or to be released from a debarment with conditional release. For instance, in *World Bank v MVV decon GmbH*, the Sanctions Board established that the ineligibility period should be applied to the respondent only if,

[38]For instance, this occurred in the Sanction Board case no 91. This case arose in the context of the 2004 Emergency Baghdad Water Supply and Sanitation Project, which sought to restore basic water supply and sanitation services for the Iraqi capital of Baghdad. The Respondent was the only firm invited to bid in 2005 for the supply and installation of vertical pumps for the AbuNawas Raw Water Pumping Station. On 21 August 2005 the Respondent entered into a contract, which was valued at US$2,127,400. INT alleged that the Respondent engaged in a fraudulent practice by misrepresenting in the commission paid or to be paid to its agent in relation to the contract, which was secretly increased from approximately 2% to 5%. Specifically, INT argued that the Respondent concealed the actual commission to avoid additional scrutiny in light of the fact that the Respondent was subject to an investigation for paying bribes through the Agent in connection with the United Nation's Oil for Food Program. The Sanctions Board found that it was more likely than not that the Respondent's employees misrepresented in the bidding documents the commission to be paid to the agent and that the evidence supported a finding of fraudulent practice. Considering the full record and all the factors of the case, the Sanctions Board issued a formal letter of private reprimand to the Respondent on the date of this decision, without prejudice to the Respondent's eligibility to participate in Bank-Financed Projects. See *World Bank v Anonymized Respondent*, [2016] Sanctions Board 91.

[39]See 'Sanctions Procedures' (*World Bank*) (n 6) Part A, 9.01(e).

[40]See 'Sanctions Regime: An Overview' (*World Bank*) (n 29) 4, fn 6.

[41]See 'Sanctioning Guidelines' (*World Bank*) (n 1) II(F).

among other conditions, it "has restituted an amount of US$ 144,546 to the Borrower."[42]

6.6 Sentencing Practice

As provided in the preamble of the Sanctioning Guidelines, the Bank's sentencing aims are the exclusion of corrupt actors from access to Bank financing (i.e., debarment) and deterrence. Moreover, rehabilitation, through the imposition of conditions designed to improve the ethical culture of sanctioned parties and reduce recidivism, is considered a key means to reduce integrity risks.[43]

Criminal law scholars assume that there are three alternative courses to the problem of setting sentencing rationales: to declare a single rationale, to allow sentencers a fairly free choice among several rationales, to declare a primary rationale providing, however, that in certain cases another rationale might be given priority.[44] Nevertheless, the approach embodied by the Bank is related to a mixed and multifaceted sentencing system. As a matter of fact, more than a rationale of sentencing operate simultaneously within that system in order to let the judging body identify the more appropriate sanction. It is an approach that seems to invite inconsistency, by requiring the Sanctions Board to consider a variety of different purposes that are often divergent. In particular, the aims expressly taken into

[42]This case involved MVV decon GmbH, a German advisory and engineering services company, and arose in the context of the Russian Enterprise Housing Divestiture Project that sought to accelerate the sustainable divestiture of enterprise housing throughout Russia by demonstrating within the participating cities a combination of housing reforms and investments designed to transfer housing to the private sector and lower its operating cost. In July 1996 the International Bank for Reconstruction and Development (IBRD) and the Russian Federation entered into a loan agreement to provide approximately US$ 300 million in support of the project. In November 1999 six Russian cities and the Project Implementation Unit entered into a contract with a Consortium of consulting companies to provide technology advisory services to monitor the effectiveness of energy efficiency improvements in residential buildings. The Consortium was a joint venture between Respondent's legal predecessor and two other consultants. The contract began in November 1999 and expired in November 2001. Respondent's legal predecessor was accused of engaging in fraudulent practices submitting, during the period above-mentioned, falsified invoices, timesheets and monthly status reports used to overbill the Project Implementation Unit for 159 work days totalling US$ 144,546. See *World Bank v MVV decon GmbH*, [2012] Sanctions Board 53.

[43]See 'Sanctioning Guidelines' (*World Bank*) (n 1) 1.

[44]For instance, the third approach has been operating in England and Wales since 2003, with desert or proportionality as the primary rationale and others aims having priority in certain cases. Section 142 of the Criminal Justice Act 2003 provides that: "Any court dealing with an offender in respect of his offence must have regard to the following purposes of sentencing—(a) the punishment of offenders, (b) the reduction of crime (including its reduction by deterrence), (c) the reform and rehabilitation of offenders, (d) the protection of the public, and (e) the making of reparation by offenders to persons affected by their offences." See Andrew Ashworth, *Sentencing and Criminal Justice* (5th edn, Cambridge University Press 2010) 76.

consideration by the Sanctioning Guidelines are incapacitation, deterrence, and rehabilitation.

Concerning incapacitation, the Guidelines state that the first Bank's sentencing aim is represented by the exclusion of corrupt actors from access to Bank financing by means of debarment. The wording of the Guidelines directly evokes the incapacitative rationale, designed to deal with corrupt actors in such a way as to make them incapable of offending for substantial periods of time.

Moreover, the Guidelines utilize the concept of deterrence, where they highlight that the sanctions process is designed to discourage both the respondent (specific deterrence) and others (general deterrence) from engaging in future sanctionable practices. Finally, it is expressly identified a rehabilitative purpose, grounded on the imposition of conditions designed to improve the integrity culture of sanctioned parties and reduce recidivism, in the belief that those conditions might enable corrupt actors to modify their attitude and behaviors.

The Sanctioning Guidelines do not cite explicitly desert as one of the sentencing rationales and proportionality as a consequence in terms of measures. Nevertheless, it could be considered another valid purpose capable to guide the Sanctions Board in determining the appropriate sanction. As a matter of fact, the severity of the misconduct and the magnitude of harm represent, as provided by section 9.02 of the Sanctions Procedures, the first two factors that the Sanctions Board has to take into consideration to determine the appropriate sanction.[45] Indeed, these two concepts evoke the main factors that, under the proportionality principle, are utilized in order to assess the seriousness of offenses and on which the severity of sanctions should be based. Considering that the proportionality principle is strictly connected with the just desert theory, it is then possible to affirm that desert represents one of the rationales, if not the main rationale, of the Bank's sanctioning practice.

6.7 Consistency and Predictability in World Bank Sentencing

In *World Bank v Zhonghao Overseas Construction Eng. Co. Ltd.*,[46] the Sanctions Board offered several and significant elements about its interpretation of sentencing practice. The Board clarified that to identify the appropriate sanction to be imposed

[45]However under the Sanctioning Guidelines those two factors are labelled as aggravating factors (Sanctioning Guideline s IV), circumstance that could considered a source of confusion.

[46]The case involved Zhonghao Overseas Construction Eng. Co., Ltd. ("Respondent"), a Chinese private joint-stock enterprise incorporated in October 2001 with a registered capital of 150 million yuan, and arose the context of the Sudan Emergency Transport and Infrastructure Development Project, which sought to rehabilitate and develop critical roads and transport infrastructure in Southern Sudan; improve critical urban infrastructure in the major towns of Southern Sudan; and build capacity for planning, construction, and the sustainable operation, maintenance and management of the infrastructure in Southern Sudan. In December 2005, the International Development

on respondents, it was necessary to take into account "the factor of proportionality across Respondents subject to sanction based on the same misconduct."[47] In particular, the judging body had to assess the adequacy of the Deputy General Manager's uncontested sanction recommended by the EO (now SDO), which consisted in a debarment for a minimum period of 3 years subject to conditional release. Therefore, the Sanctions Board on the one hand offered interesting hints on what the rationales of sentencing adopted in the sanctions process were; on the other, it showed its clear willingness to avoid disparities in sentencing.

The issue about disparities in sentencing evokes the problems related to consistency and fairness of decisions, as well as accountability and transparency of sentencing decision making. In this regard, the Sanctions Board follows a sensible approach to sentencing, establishing that respondents subject to sanction based on the same misconduct should be treated similarly. In other words, it attempts to avoid unwarranted inconsistencies in sentencing practices and to meet the demands of fairness, which requires that similar cases be dealt with in a similar manner. However, it appears that the Sanctions Board does not consider inconsistency in its sentencing decisions as an exceptional case on which a request for reconsideration can be granted.[48]

Anyway, in order to ensure that the Sanctions Board's decisions are consistent in their approach and the outcomes reasonably predictable, the Bank issued on January 1, 2011, the abovementioned Sanctioning Guidelines. They are meant to "provide a guidance to those who have the discretion to impose sanctions on behalf of the WBG."[49]

Association ("IDA") and the Government of Southern Sudan entered into a Memorandum of Agreement to provide US$ 50 million for the Project through the Multi-Donor Trust Fund for Southern Sudan. The tender at issue was for a contract to reconstruct a section of road in Southern Sudan required bidders to demonstrate "experience in works of a similar nature and size for each of the last five years." In March 2008, Respondent submitted a bid signed by the Deputy General Manager as Respondent's authorized signatory. Pursuant to the tender requirements, Respondent's bid included as proof of prior work experience a purported contract agreement with a Nigerian state government for a road project in that state. INT alleged that the Deputy General Manager forged the contract agreement by substituting the name of the actual contractor with that of Respondent's Nigerian subsidiary. Anyway, with the belief that the contract agreement was genuine, the Bid Evaluation Committee requested a no-objection letter from the World Bank to award the tender to Respondent. The Bank requested further documentation and in response, Respondent provided three letters purportedly issued by the Nigerian state government to confirm Respondent's substantial completion of the Nigerian road project, and a fourth letter in Respondent's name itemizing its work details for the project. After additional due diligence, however, the Bid Evaluation Committee concluded several of the letters contained false and/or misleading information. It consequently revised its recommendation, and the tender was awarded to another bidder. See *World Bank v Zhonghao Overseas Construction Eng. Co. Ltd.*, [2012] Sanctions Board 48.

[47] ibid para 49.

[48] See *World Bank v E.C. De Luna Construction Corp. and Mr. Eduardo C. De Luna*, [2016] Sanctions Board 89.

[49] See 'Sanctioning Guidelines' (*World Bank*) (n 1) 1.

The Guidelines indicate that "the base sanction for all misconduct is 3 year debarment with conditional release,"[50] specifying "that debarment with conditional release should normally be applied absent the considerations that would justify another sanction."[51] The other sanctions are then outlined (from paragraphs B to F of Sanctioning Guideline section II) as follows: debarment, conditional nondebarment, letter of reprimand, permanent debarment, restitution, and other remedies. The Guidelines indicate for all sanctions the conditions for their application, as well as the aggravating and mitigating factors capable to entail, respectively, an increase or a reduction of the sentence.[52]

Therefore, the Bank adopted, in order to structure the Sanctions Board's discretion, a solution very similar to the one followed in the US and in the UK for criminal offenses, which is the arrangement of guidelines designed to provide different ranges of sentence for different levels of seriousness of each type of conduct and to indicate a common starting point. It is a technique whose aim is to provide a framework within which the court can locate the particular conduct it is dealing with and then reflect the facts of that case (notably, the aggravating and mitigating factors) by placing it appropriately within or outside the relevant range. Nevertheless, the degree of bindingness of guidelines as recognized within the common law legal systems and in the Bank's Guidelines is different. While the former generally leaves a limited scope for judicial discretion for deciding on a sentence of a different kind or outside the range,[53] the latter is not intended to be compulsory being conceived as a mere guidance. Indeed, the same Bank's Sanctioning Guidelines state that they "are not meant to be prescriptive in nature."

Having said that, although the Guidelines provide numerical references (in years) to be applied in case of aggravating factors and percentage of sentence reduction in case of mitigating factors, it is not possible to interpret them in a mathematical fashion, whereby each individual ingredient should increase or reduce the notional sentence by a prescribed amount. This is a conception consistent with the great degree of flexibility, which characterizes the Sanctions Board proceedings in every aspect.[54]

---

[50]ibid I.

[51]ibid II(A).

[52]The sanctioning guidelines identify the aggravating factors as follows: Severity of the Misconduct (1–5 years for this category); Harm Caused by the Misconduct (1–5 years for this category); Interference with Investigation (1–3 years for this category); Past History of Adjudicated Misconduct (10 years). Under Sanctioning Guideline s V the mitigating factors are: Minor Role in Misconduct (up to 25%); Voluntary Corrective Action Taken (up to 50%; a greater reduction may be warranted in exceptional circumstances); Cooperation with Investigation (up to 33%, however, in extraordinary circumstances, a greater reduction may be warranted). See ibid IV.

[53]Just to make few examples, in Minnesota "the sentencing judge must find, and record, substantial and compelling reasons why the presumptive guidelines sentence would be too high or too low in a given case," and in England and Wales, the Coroners and Justice Act 2009 expressly provides that courts "must follow" any relevant guidelines unless the court is satisfied that it would be contrary to the interests of justice to do so.

[54]In the Sanctions Board Decision no. 56 (Sanctions Case: no. 177) the judging body states that formal rules "do not apply in the Bank's sanctions proceedings."

6.8 Criteria for Determining the Sanction: Severity of the Misconduct and Magnitude of Harm

In *World Bank v MVV decon GmbH*,[55] the judging body dealt with the first two criteria that under section 9.02(a) and (b) of the Sanctions Procedures have to be taken into consideration to determine an appropriate sanction. They are the severity of the misconduct and the magnitude of harm.

Indeed, these two concepts evoke the main factors that, under the proportionality principle, are utilized in order to assess the seriousness of an offense and on which the severity of sanctions should be based.[56]

If this is true, however, under the Sanctioning Guidelines, those two factors are labeled as aggravating factors.[57] The circumstance that those elements are treated under the Procedures as determining the seriousness of an offense and under the Guidelines as aggravating factors could cause some confusion from a theoretical point of view.[58] In truth, in the absence of any specific procedural rule disciplining aggravating and mitigating factors, all those elements contribute toward the determination of the general seriousness of the sanctionable practice.

It emerges that under those criteria, the same elements of the fact can be used by the Sanctions Board to both determine what should be the basic sanction and evaluate the applicability of additional aggravating factors. Such an overlap might lead to heavier sentencing decisions that would be, as such, unfair. This situation is aggravated by the fact that, in the absence of any formal rule, the approach adopted by the Sanctions Board consists in considering the totality of the circumstances and all potential aggravating and mitigating factors to determine an appropriate sanction avoiding any mechanistic determination.[59] The problem here lies in the fact that, in its reasoning, the Board does not clarify the way in which it conducts its comparative judgment and how it arrives at the resulting synthesis of all the elements of the fact. Consequently, the respondents are not enabled to appreciate the weight that the judging body gives to such elements and to evaluate the fairness and consistency of its decisions.

The confusion caused by the absence of predetermined criteria of sentencing evaluation has emerged, for instance, in *World Bank v MVV decon GmbH*. In this case, to determine the appropriate sentence, the Sanctions Board considered three

[55]See *World Bank v MVV decon GmbH*, [2012] Sanctions Board 53. For a description of the case see *supra* note 42.

[56]See Ashworth, *Sentencing and Criminal* (n 44) 104.

[57]See 'Sanctioning Guidelines' (*World Bank*) (n 1) IV(A), IV(B).

[58]This theoretical uncertainty is even made worse because mitigating circumstances are expressly indicated as an autonomous factor by section 9.02(e) of the Sanctions Procedure. To the contrary, section 9.02 never refers explicitly to aggravating circumstances.

[59]The Sanctions Board defines its sentencing practice as "a case-by-case analysis tailored to the specific facts and circumstances presented in each case." See *World Bank v Anonymized Respondent*, [2016] Sanctions Board 91, para 36.

elements listed in section IV.A.1 of the Sanctioning Guidelines as aggravating circumstances.[60] Firstly, the judging body considered the repeated pattern of conduct[61] consisting in the respondent's multiple submission of several types of falsified documents, including invoices, time sheets, status reports over an extended period. From the Sanctions Board's point of view, such a circumstance warranted an aggravating treatment. Moreover, the judging body considered the participation of respondent's management at the time of the misconduct as justifying aggravation. Indeed, section IV(A)(4) of the Sanctioning Guidelines suggests that aggravation should apply if an individual within high-level personnel of the organization participated in, condoned, or was willfully ignorant of the misconduct. In the present case, the Sanctions Board reached its decision on the ground that the respondent admitted that members of its former management participated in the misrepresentations notwithstanding that at the time of the proceedings those individuals were no longer employed by the respondents. Finally, as requested by INT's Reply, the Sanctions Board had to assess the use of sophisticated means that is a potential aggravating factor set out by section IV(A)(2) of the Guidelines.[62] The judging body held that, in its opinion, the submission of falsified documents in order to perpetrate the fraudulent practice was not so sophisticated or complex as to warrant aggravation.

To assess the seriousness of the conduct, then the Sanctions Board had to evaluate, as requested by section 9.02(b) of the Sanctions Procedures, the magnitude of the harm caused by the misconduct. It is interesting to note that while the Sanctions Procedures do not contain any definition of this concept and do not offer any criterion to evaluate it, section IV(B) of the Sanctioning Guidelines indicate just two elements (the harm to public safety/welfare and the degree of harm to projects) that, due to their intrinsic inadvertency, could be considered as typical aggravating factors rather than general criteria to determine the seriousness of a conduct. In any case, the Sanctions Board stated that none of the abovementioned factors were present in the case. However, it decided to take into account the financial harm inherent in overbilling the "Borrower under the Contract."[63] It has to be highlighted that the Sanctions Board did not clarify the criteria used in order to evaluate this financial harm, nor did it declare the amount of relevance given to such an element.

---

[60]The other elements that were not considered in this decision but that are nevertheless listed in the Guidelines in order to determine the severity of the misconduct are the central role in misconduct and the involvement of public official or World bank staff.

[61]See 'Sanctioning Guidelines' (*World Bank*) (n 1) IV(A)(1).

[62]As it has been specified by the Guidelines, this concept "includes the complexity of the misconduct (e.g., degree of planning, diversity of techniques applied, level of concealment); the number and type of people or organizations involved; whether the scheme was developed or lasted over a long period of time; if more than one jurisdiction was involved."

[63]See *World Bank v MVV decon GmbH*, [2012] Sanctions Board 53, at para 56.

6.9 Aggravating Factors

The Sanctioning Guidelines include detailed treatment of aggravating factors, with indicative ranges for sentence increases.

Specifically, the Guidelines identify four general categories of aggravating factors, which can be applied by the SDO and the Sanctions Board. The less serious category is represented by any conduct of interference with the Bank's investigations carried out by the respondent. Such a category includes two groups of conducts. The first is represented by physical activities aimed at interfering with INT's investigative process like deliberately destroying, falsifying, altering, or concealing evidence material or making false statements to investigators.[64] The second includes activities of intimidating or bribing a witness. For both types of conduct, the Guidelines recommend a sentence increase ranging from 1 to 3 years.[65]

Some concerns arise from the close similarity shared by this category of aggravating circumstances and the conduct that is the constituent element of the sanctionable practice of obstruction. As a matter of fact, the notion of obstructing practice, as set forth in the October 2006 Anti-Corruption Guidelines, consists in "deliberately destroying, falsifying, altering or concealing of evidence material to the investigation or making false statements to investigators in order to materially impede a Bank investigation into allegations of a corrupt, fraudulent, coercive or collusive practice; and/or threatening, harassing or intimidating any party to prevent it from disclosing its knowledge of matters relevant to the investigation or from pursuing the investigation." The legal framework developed by the Bank does not allow to differentiate between the sanctionable practice and the aggravating factor. As a result, the same type of conduct might be theoretically used, on the one hand, to determine the respondent's liability and the basic sentence to be imposed and, on the other, to justify the application of the abovementioned circumstances and the resulting increase of the sentence.

Other two general categories of aggravating factors include the severity of the misconduct and the harm caused through it.[66] Examples of the types of conduct falling within these categories are the presence of a repeated pattern of conduct,[67]

---

[64]See 'Sanctioning Guidelines' (*World Bank*) (n 1) IV(C)(1).

[65]ibid.

[66]It is interesting to note that, to the contrary, the lack of harm is not included by the Sanctioning Guidelines among the mitigating factors. As a consequence, from the Sanctions Board's perspective the absence of harm, even where supported by evidence, has to be considered as a merely neutral fact that does not justify any mitigation. See *World Bank v Karl Storz GmbH & Co. KG*, [2017] Sanctions Board 95, para 42. For a description of the case see *supra* note 24 in Chap. 5.

[67]In *World Bank v Zhonghao Overseas Construction Eng. Co. Ltd.*, the Sanctions Board considered the use of five forged documents in one course of conduct, within the same Bank-financed project and a short period of time, as a misconduct that, being characterized by a repetitive nature, merited aggravating treatment. See *World Bank v Zhonghao Overseas Construction Eng. Co. Ltd.*, [2012] Sanctions Board 48, para 39. For a description of the case see *supra* note 46.

the use of sophisticated means[68] such as the number and type of participants in the misconduct and their level of organization, the role played by the individuals involved in the illicit acts, the involvement of public servants or Bank's officials, and the degree of harm caused to the Bank-financed project.[69] For all the types of conduct included in these two categories, the Guidelines recommend a sentence increase ranging from 1 to 5 years.[70] As it has been already highlighted, serious concerns arise from the circumstance that the same elements of the fact falling within these two general categories can be used by the Sanctions Board to both determine what should be the basic sanction and evaluate the applicability of additional aggravating factors.[71]

Finally, the Bank considers recidivism as the most serious aggravating factor. The Guidelines recommend a sentence increase of 10 years in case of "past history of adjudicated misconduct." Interestingly, the Guidelines specify that "prior history must involve misconduct other than the misconduct for which the Respondent is being debarred and that it can include debarments by another MDB."[72]

6.10 Mitigating Factors

Differently from the aggravating circumstances, section 9.02(e) of the Sanctions Procedures expressly provides that the Sanctions Board shall consider mitigating circumstances in order to determine an appropriate sanction. The same provision includes as possible mitigating factors the fact that "the sanctioned party played a minor role in the misconduct, took voluntary corrective action or cooperated in the investigation or resolution of the case, including through settlement."[73] Moreover, Part V of the Sanctioning Guidelines is entirely dedicated to mitigating factors and includes indicative ranges for sentence reductions. The document indicates as potential factors of mitigation circumstances such as the minor role in misconduct, the voluntary corrective action taken, and the cooperation with investigation. For each mitigating circumstance, the Sanctioning Guidelines recommend a sanction reduction of certain percentage points. Specifically, the performance of voluntary corrective actions is the circumstance that may warrant the greater sanction

[68]In *World Bank v Karl Storz GmbH & Co. KG*, the Sanctions Board considered the following circumstances as sufficient elements to warrant aggravation: the use of a variety of tactics including receipt of confidential bid information from a public official; the use of an alias by the public official for purposes of the Agreement with the Respondent; and the use of an intermediary to make a payment to a public official's Swiss bank account." See *World Bank v Karl Storz GmbH & Co. KG*, [2017] Sanctions Board 95, para 40.

[69]See 'Sanctioning Guidelines' (*World Bank*) (n 1) IV(A)(1–5), IV(B)(1–2).

[70]ibid.

[71]See *supra* notes 55–63 and accompanying text.

[72]See 'Sanctioning Guidelines' (*World Bank*) (n 1) IV(D).

[73]See 'Sanctions Procedures' (*World Bank*) (n 6) Part A, 9.02(e).

reduction, i.e. of up to 50%.[74] The Guidelines identify four types of voluntary corrective actions. The first is represented by the "cessation of misconduct."[75] Then the Guidelines mention the taking of disciplinary actions, or other remedial steps, against the responsible individuals.[76] The third type of voluntary corrective action is the establishment or enhancement of an effective corporate compliance program.[77] From the Sanctions Board's perspective, such programs have to be characterized also by a certain specificity so that they can potentially address the type of misconduct at issue in the relevant case.[78] Finally, the same mitigating factor can be recognized where the respondent voluntarily addresses any inadequacies in contract implementation or returns funds obtained through the misconduct.[79] As specified by the Guidelines, the timing of these voluntary corrective actions may be indicative of the extent to which they reflect the respondent's genuine remorse and intention to reform.

Another category of mitigating factors, which may result in a sanction reduction of up to 33%, is the cooperation with INT over the course of the investigation.[80] Different kinds of conducts fall within such a category. Specifically, this mitigating factor might be recognized where the respondent has provided substantial assistance in the investigation,[81] through voluntary disclosure and/or presenting[82] truthful, complete, and reliable information.[83] As specified by the Guidelines, in this case, the nature and extent of the assistance, as well as its timeliness, have to be considered in order to assess the relevance of the mitigating factor. The conduction of effective

---

[74]The Guidelines specify that in exceptional circumstances, such actions may result in an even greater reduction. See 'Sanctioning Guidelines' (*World Bank*) (n 1) V(B).

[75]ibid V(B)(1).

[76]ibid V(B)(2).

[77]ibid V(B)(3).

[78]In *World Bank v Karl Storz GmbH & Co. KG*, the Sanctions Board warranted the mitigation taking into consideration that, *inter alia*, the Respondent hired compliance officers, issued a comprehensive global Code of Conduct, increased compliance training of its senior staff members worldwide, and implemented due diligence proceedings for consultancy agreements. See *World Bank v Karl Storz GmbH & Co. KG*, [2017] Sanctions Board 95, para 46. For a description of the case see *supra* note 24 in Chap. 5.

[79]See 'Sanctioning Guidelines' (*World Bank*) (n 1) V(B)(4).

[80]The Guidelines specify that in exceptional circumstances, such actions may result in an even greater reduction. See ibid V(C).

[81]ibid V(C)(1).

[82]For instance, in *World Bank v MVV decon GmbH*, the Sanctions Board granted mitigation because the Respondent's managers met with INT on several occasions and provided relevant information. See *World Bank v MVV decon GmbH*, [2012] Sanctions Board 53, at para 58. For a description of the case see *supra* note 42.

[83]In *World Bank v GHD Pty Ltd*, the Sanctions Board granted mitigation because the Respondent corresponded with INT and made relevant personnel available for interviews, including the manager and other employees involved in the preparing the fraudulent documentation. See *World Bank v GHD Pty Ltd*, [2013] Sanctions Board 56, para 73. For a description of the case see *supra* note 11 in Chap. 5.

internal investigations of the misconduct, whose outcomes have to be shared with INT,[84] is mentioned as another circumstance that may warrant mitigation.[85] A third type of conduct that falls within this category is admissions or full and affirmative acceptance of guilt or responsibility for misconduct over the course of the investigation.[86] The last type of conduct included in this category is the voluntary restraint from bidding on Bank-financed tenders pending the outcome of an investigation.[87] Finally, the Guidelines recommend a sanction reduction of up to 25% where the respondent plays a minor role in the misconduct.[88] Such a marginal role is recognized, for instance, if no individual with decision-making authority participated in, condoned, or was willfully ignorant of the misconduct.

In *World Bank v MVV decon GmbH*,[89] the Sanctions Board offered some insights into the role that mitigating factors play in determining the sentence to be imposed. In particular, in verifying if mitigating circumstances were present, the Sanctions Board considered that the respondent's cooperation deserved mitigating treatment. In particular, the Sanctions Board reached this decision on the ground that the respondent's managers met with INT on several occasions and provided information and documentation relevant for the investigation. Moreover, the judging body held that the respondent's voluntary corrective action deserved as well mitigating credit. It has to be highlighted that the Sanctions Board held that the respondent bore the burden of presenting evidence to show any voluntary corrective action taken.[90] Specifically, the respondent offered the proof of both the implementation of an enhanced corporate compliance program and the compensation for damages. Precisely, respondent provided detailed description and documentation of the compliance system[91] and implemented it prior to INT's initiation of the sanctions proceedings.[92] Regarding the restitution, respondent offered compensation for

[84]In *World Bank v GHD Pty Ltd*, the Sanctions Board did not apply mitigation for the internal investigations conducted by the Respondent because, although such activities were carried out and the related outcomes were shared with the Asian Development Bank, it refused to share its findings with INT without unreasonable conditions. See ibid para 73.

[85]See 'Sanctioning Guidelines' (*World Bank*) (n 1) V(C)(2).

[86]ibid V(C)(3).

[87]ibid V(C)(4).

[88]ibid V(A).

[89]See *World Bank v MVV decon GmbH*, [2012] Sanctions Board 53.

[90]ibid para 59. The Sanctions Board held the same also in the No.45 (2011) at para 72.

[91]The compliance system included: a requirement all employees pass corporate compliance training, including a general orientation on Respondent's corporate compliance policies as well as a course tailored to the employee's specific unit; additional compliance training required for employees upon reaching certain managerial levels; provision of quarterly remainders to all employees regarding the corporate compliance program; any periodic checks to ensure new employees receive training.

[92]The Sanctioning Guidelines provide that: "The timing of the action may indicate the degree to which it reflects genuine remorse and intention to reform, or a calculated step to reduce the severity of the sentence." See 'Sanctioning Guidelines' (*World Bank*) (n 1) V(B)(1).

damages up to US$ 144,545 to demonstrate its willingness to take responsibility for the misconduct.

Finally, it has to be mentioned that, apart from the case of indefinite debarment, respondents debarred for a minimum period in excess of 10 years may petition for a reduction of the minimum period of debarment after 10 years have elapsed.[93]

6.11 Other Relevant Factors in Determining the Sentence

Under section 9.02(i) of the Sanctions Procedures, the judging body may consider "any other factor" it "reasonably deems relevant to the sanctioned party's culpability or responsibility in relation to the Sanctionable Practice." In *World Bank v Income Electrix Limited*,[94] the Sanctions Board had the opportunity to offer some insights into such a provision. In particular, it used such an extremely broad provision to recognize as a mitigating factor the passage of significant time from when the Bank became aware of potential sanctionable misconducts to the commencement of sanctions proceedings. In particular:

> [the Sanctions Board took] into consideration that over three years, and possibly closer to four years, elapsed from when the Bank learned of the false signatures between April and July 2007, to the issuance of the Notice at the end of March 2011.[95]

From such a statement, it emerges that in the opinion of the Sanctions Board, the passage of time during the second tier is not taken into consideration as a mitigating factor.

In *World Bank v ASDECON Corporation Company Limited*,[96] the Sanctions Board offered additional arguments on the relevance of the passage of time during sanction proceedings. Indeed, the Sanctions Board addressed respondent's contention about the unjustified and prejudicial delay of almost 5 years from the start of INT's investigation to the issuance of the Notice of Sanctions Proceedings.

In the opinion of the Sanctions Board, such passage of time could affect the proceedings in three different ways.

Firstly, it could be relevant for limitation periods given that, under section 4.01 (d) of the Sanctions Procedures, it set out a statute of limitations of 10 years.

Secondly, the Sanctions Board held that any delay may affect the relevance, materiality, weight, and sufficiency of evidence. In particular, the Board highlighted that a considerable procedural delay could be relevant if it compromises the respondent's ability to gather evidence for its defense, for instance, limiting a particular

---

[93]See 'Sanctions Regime: An Overview' (*World Bank*) (n 29) 4, para 15.

[94]See *Bank v Income Electrix Limited*, [2012] Sanctions Board 46. For a description of the case see *supra* note 49 in Chap. 3.

[95]ibid para 43.

[96]See *World Bank v ASDECON Corporation Company Limited*, [2012] Sanctions Board 50. For a description of the case see *supra* note 42 in Chap. 3.

witness's ability to recollect events or respondent's ability to obtain specific relevant documents.

The judging body also stated that the passage of time is relevant in relation to the determination of an appropriate sanction.[97] In particular, the Sanctions Board tends to consider the passage of significant time from when the Bank became aware of potential sanctionable misconduct to the point of sanctions proceedings as a mitigating factor under section 9.02(i) of the Sanctions Procedures.

In *World Bank v MVV decon GmbH*,[98] the judging body offered other insights into the role that any other factor might play in determining the sentence to be imposed.[99] In particular, the Sanctions Board considered relevant to that end two circumstances: the passage of time and the change in management/corporate identity. Concerning the former, the Sanctions Board confirmed that the passage of significant time from when the Bank became aware of potential sanctionable misconduct to the point of sanctions proceedings can be considered as a mitigating factor.[100] A long delay clearly may impact respondent's ability to investigate the matter, gather evidence, and defend itself. In the abovementioned case, the Sanctions Board evaluated that the extended delay warranted substantial mitigation. It took into consideration that the Bank became aware of the misconduct in 2004, while the Notice was issued in 2011, i.e. 7 years later.[101] In the same decision, the Sanctions Board identified a new element that can fall within the broad category of "any other" mitigating factors. Specifically, it considered that respondent's corporate structure had substantially evolved over the past decade since the misconduct had been perpetrated.[102] The judging body established that the successive changes in respondent's management since the time of the misconduct justified a mitigating treatment,

---

[97]This seems to be a firm determination of the Sanctions Board. See, e.g., Sanctions Board Decision no. 38 (2010) at para 54 (noting the passage of time may impact on the weight the Sanctions Board attaches to the evidence presented, and also may impact on the fairness of the process for the Respondents); Sanctions Board Decision no. 44 (2011) at para 77 (considering as a mitigating factor the substantial passage of time – six years – between the Bank's receipt of notice of potential sanctionable practices and the initiation of sanctions proceedings).

[98]See *World Bank v MVV decon GmbH*, [2012] Sanctions Board 53. For a description of the case see *supra* note 42.

[99]The Sanctions Board didn't find completion of contractual obligations a mitigating factor (see Sanction Board Decisions no. 52/2012; 44/2011; 29/2010. In this case, Respondent argued that its misconduct was not severe because the project was completed, but the Sanctions Board observed while incomplete performance in a project as a result of a Respondent's misconduct may be considered an aggravating factor, the completion of contractual obligations is not a mitigating factor in itself. Nor the judging body considered the absence of past misconduct as a mitigating factor because "even a single instance of submitting falsified documents would constitute sanctionable misconduct." (See also Sanction Board Decisions no. 52/2012 and no. 41/2010). Finally, the Sanctions Board didn't evaluate the adverse consequences of debarment as a mitigating factor.

[100]See also Sanction Board Decisions no. 6/2009; no. 46/2012; no. 47/2012; no. 48/2012; no. 50/2012.

[101]See *World Bank v MVV decon GmbH*, [2012] Sanctions Board 53, para 65.

[102]For an analysis of such a legal issue see *supra* notes 53–58 and accompanying text in Chap. 4.

considering that the staff members responsible for the misconduct were no longer working for respondent.[103]

6.12 Relevance of Presentence Provisional Measures

In *World Bank v Contech Devices Pvt. Ltd.*[104] and in the subsequent request for reconsideration,[105] the Sanctions Board offered interesting insights into the question related to presentence provisional measures served by respondents.

Over the course of the investigations, respondent had served one-year debarment sentence through its earlier period of temporary suspension and, in its request for reconsideration, asked for the deduction of the period of temporary suspension already served from the period of ineligibility to participate in Bank-financed projects imposed by the final decision. The Sanctions Board stated that "Respondent cannot substitute its prior temporary suspension, which is a provisional measure, for its final published debarment."[106] It seems that the judging body does not assign to the prior temporary suspension the same value of the final debarment sentence. In reality, they differ only in relation to the circumstance that the final decision is published on the Bank's website and, as such, can be considered more stigmatizing. However, both those measures share a most relevant feature, which is the ineligibility from Bank-financed projects. Consequently, a fairer sentencing practice should give a similar weight to the earlier period of temporary suspension and the period of debarment imposed by its final decision.

A thorny question arises from this decision. It consists in the difficult task of assessing the value of presentence provisional measures imposed on respondents. The deduction, from the debarment imposed by the final decision of the period of ineligibility suffered after the issuance of a temporary suspension measure, should be recognized on the ground of two general principles. On the one hand, such a deduction should avoid to substantially punish a respondent twice for the same fact; on the other, it should prevent discrimination in punitive treatment between respondents based on the length of the proceedings. At the domestic level, presentence provisional measures are generally recognized as relevant. They can be identified with the period the defendant has already suffered in custody during

---

[103]See *World Bank v MVV decon GmbH*, [2012] Sanctions Board 53, para 66.

[104]See *World Bank v Contech Devices Pvt. Ltd.*, [2012] Sanctions Board 54. For a description of the case see *supra* note 3.

[105]The case concerned a Request for Reconsideration filed by Respondent with regard to Sanctions Board Decision no. 54 (2012), by which the Sanctions Board debarred Respondent for one year for fraudulent practices. See *World Bank v Contech Devices Pvt. Ltd.*, [2013] Sanctions Board 58.

[106]ibid para 14.

criminal proceedings before the final sentence is determined. For instance, in *R v SAE*,[107] it is stated:

> [A]llowance is made for pre-sentence custody but only in circumstances where such pre-sentence custody is exclusively referable to the crime for which the offender has been sentenced.[108]

In the Bank's sanctioning system, the question at issue is covered by section 9.02 (h) of the Sanctions Procedures, which provides:

> The SDO or Sanctions Board, as the case may be, shall consider the following factors in determining an appropriate sanction: [...] The period of temporary suspension already served by the sanctioned party.[109]

Such a provision must be regarded as incomplete because it does not answer the fundamental question of how the measure already served by respondents should be taken into account or counted. In this case, the EO (now SDO) recommended in the Notice of Sanctions Proceedings a debarment with conditional release proposing that respondent be declared ineligible for any Bank-financed projects provided, however, after a minimum period of ineligibility of 2 years, respondent might be released from ineligibility. Such a decision was issued on June 30, 2011, and the respondent was also temporarily suspended to participate in any Bank-financed projects since then. The final decision was passed by the Sanctions Board on October 16, 2012, i.e. more than one year later. In its judgment, the Board sentenced for a debarment without conditional release, stating that respondent be declared ineligible for any Bank-financed projects for a period of one year beginning on October 16, 2012. As a consequence of such a decision, the respondent was substantially declared ineligible for any Bank-financed projects for an overall period of 28 months. Therefore, even if at first sight the Sanctions Board imposed a more lenient measure than the one applied by the EO (now SDO), it should be asserted that the sentence imposed by the Board was in reality more severe.[110] However, it is not possible to find in the reasoning of the Board any element that should justify such an increase. In fact, the Sanctions Board recognized that two mitigating factors were applicable in the case: the circumstance that the respondent cooperated in the investigations or

---

[107]See *R v SAE* (unrep, 3/4/97, NSWCCA) at 7.

[108]In some jurisdictions it is considered more desirable to backdate a sentence to take into account presentence custody, rather than to discount. For instance, section 47(2) of the Crimes (Sentencing Procedure) Act 1999 (New South Wales Consolidated Acts) states that "a court may direct that a sentence of imprisonment: is taken to have commenced on a day occurring before the day on which the sentence is imposed" and section 47(3) specifies that "in deciding the day on which the sentence is taken to have commenced, the court must take into account any time for which the offender has been held in custody in relation to the offence or, in the case of an aggregate sentence of imprisonment, any of the offences to which the sentence relates."

[109]See 'Sanctions Procedures' (*World Bank*) (n 6) Part A, 9.02(h).

[110]In truth, it is necessary to specify that in the case at issue, besides the period of debarment imposed, the Sanctions Board judgment appears in a way more lenient than the SDO's decision because, differently from the first tier decision, it did not subject the end of the debarment period to any form of condition.

resolution of the case[111] and that it had been also subject to a national debarment measure.[112] As regards the period of temporary suspension already served by the respondent, the Board failed to clarify how and to what extent such a period should influence its sentencing decisions. As a matter of fact, the judging body included in its decision a statement devoid of any real content merely affirming that the period of temporary suspension already served by the respondent had to be taken into account for the purpose of determining the sanction.[113] It has to be mentioned that, in deciding a subsequent request for reconsideration of Judgment 54 of 2012, the Board seems to consider the earlier period of temporary suspension as one of the circumstances deserving "due consideration and mitigating credit."[114] However, such a clarification cannot be deemed as exhaustive because it does not allow respondents to appreciate the weight that the Sanctions Board gives to the period of temporary suspension already served and consequently to assess the fairness of its sentencing decision. It also appears that the judging body has never decided that no further period of ineligibility was to be imposed in consideration of the period of temporary suspension already served by respondent.

In the light of the above argumentations, it could be considered very appropriate for the Bank to further specify the provision of section 9.02(h) of the Sanctions Procedures, which, as it is currently set out, could be considered as a potential source of unfairness and discrimination based on elements, such as the length of sanctioning proceedings, that are not connected with respondents' culpability.

6.13 Relevance of Potential Adverse Consequences of Debarment

The detriment that debarment of leading companies operating in key economic sectors could cause to domestic markets (both in terms of development and competition) emerges as an issue that the Sanctions Board has to consider when determining an adequate sanction. In particular, in *World Bank v Ultra Computers Company*,[115] the Sanctions Board had to evaluate if those adverse consequences of debarment could be treated as a mitigating factor. In that case, Ultra Computers Company (the respondent) argued that, due to the circumstance that it was the Azerbaijan leading IT firm, its debarment would have had anticompetitive effects

[111]See *World Bank v Contech Devices Pvt. Ltd.*, [2012] Sanctions Board 54, para 39.

[112]ibid para 43.

[113]ibid para 41.

[114]See *World Bank v Contech Devices Pvt. Ltd.*, [2013] Sanctions Board 58, at para 13.

[115]See *World Bank v Ultra Computers Company*, [2013] Sanctions Board 61. For a description of the case see *supra* note 52 in Chap. 3.

on the Azerbaijani market and that its exclusion from tendering would have significantly limited the World Bank's choice of partners.[116] As mentioned above, although no provision expressly deals with this aspect, the Sanctions Procedures provide the Sanctions Board with great freedom of maneuver in identifying atypical factors that can have an impact on the sentencing decision.[117] As a matter of fact, section 9.02, which establishes the factors affecting the sanction decision, provides:

> The SDO or Sanctions Board, as the case may be, shall consider the following factors in determining an appropriate sanction: [. . .]: (i) any other factor that the SDO or Sanctions Board, as the case may be, reasonably deems relevant to the sanctioned party's culpability or responsibility in relation to the Sanctionable Practice.[118]

In the case at issue, the judging body did not exclude the possibility of considering such an element. As a matter of fact, notwithstanding that the Sanctions Board denied the respondent's request, it implicitly admitted such a possibility in its reasoning:

> As the Respondents fail to establish the relevance of their arguments under this framework, and in any event have not provided evidence to support their assertion of anticompetitive effects, the Sanctions Board does not accept this argument.[119]

6.14 Role of Excusing or Exempting Circumstances

Another issue that deserves some attention is whether and in which way the Bank's sanctions process recognizes justifying, excusing, or exempting circumstances or conditions that can affect respondents' liability.

The Sanctions Board dealt with such legal question in *World Bank v General Consulting Training and TEAM Engineering & Management Cons.*[120] In this case,

---

[116]In previous judgments the Sanctions Board (decision no. 53 of 2012 at para 69; no. 60 of 2013 at para 140; no. 58 of 2013 at para 12) denied to treat as a mitigating factor the asserted adverse consequences of debarment. In those decisions, however, the alleged adverse consequences were directly related to Respondents' future revenues and business opportunities. It does not surprise than that in such circumstances the Sanctions Board reached a negative decision. In particular, in its decision no. 58 of 2013 at para 10(i), the judging body clarified that: "Any financial loss Respondent may assert from its ineligibility is not a cognizable mitigating factor but rather the natural consequence of suspension and debarment as envisioned under the Bank's sanction system."

[117]See *supra* notes 94–103 and accompanying text.

[118]See 'Sanctions Procedures' (*World Bank*) (n 6) Part A, 9.02(i).

[119]See *World Bank v Ultra Computers Company*, [2013] Sanctions Board 61, at para 50.

[120]The case involved General Consulting Training ("Respondent"), a company founded in 1999 in Palestine for the purpose of providing consulting and training services for private and government employers and other entities within Palestine, and arose in the context of the West Bank and Gaza Local Government Capacity Building Project, which intended to improve local governance and accountability, and thereby foster the efficient and sustainable economic, social and physical development of the urban and rural areas in the parts of West Bank and Gaza under the jurisdiction of the Palestinian Authority. In March 2005 the International Development Association ("IDA") as

which arose in the context of a development project to be undertaken in Palestine, it emerged that among the bidding documents, the respondents submitted the curriculum vitae of a professional consultant, who in reality never agreed to participate in the project. Such a submission was consequently considered by INT as a fraudulent practice. In its response, the respondent asserted that it had no intent to commit fraud and signed and submitted the consultant's curriculum vitae in consideration of the circumstance that the conditions in West Bank and Gaza made it difficult to communicate and, in any case, it thought it had the consultant's approval to do so. In particular, the respondent highlighted that the local conditions in which he had to operate were represented by the "very critical and difficult political and security situation" in Gaza in 2007. It asserted that while it believed that he had secured the consultant's oral authorization to participate, the situation made it impossible to reach local experts directly to obtain their consent and signatures. Nevertheless, the Sanctions Board did not consider difficult local conditions an excuse for fraudulent behaviors. The judging body supported its decision stating:

> had local conditions prevented the Consortium from timely obtaining proper approvals and signatures from any consultants, the Respondent Partner should have communicated this fact to MDF [the Palestinian Authority's Municipal Development Fund]. In any event, the Respondent Partner presents no evidence the Respondent Partner or Consortium ever tried to contact the Consultant directly or verify the oral authorization purportedly given to the recruiter before submitting the Proposal.[121]

---

administrator of the Denmark Grant Agreement, and the Palestine Liberation Organization for the benefit of the Palestinian Authority entered into a Trust Fund Grant Agreement to finance the Project. The Trust Fund Grant Agreement required consultant services to be procured in accordance with, *inter alia*, the provisions of section I of the May 2004 Consultant Guidelines regarding fraud and corruption. In December 2006, the Palestinian Authority issued bidding documents for a contract that would, *inter alia*, prepare for and supervise system implementation, develop appropriate financial policies and procedures, and advise on software selection. The bidding documents required each bidder to include the names of the professional staff who would work under the contract, the role each person would play, and each person's curriculum vitae signed by the staff themselves or by the authorized representative of the Professional Staff. In relation to the bid, the Respondent Firm and the Respondent Partner acted as a consortium. The Respondent Partner tasked a third party to recruit professional consultants from Gaza. Shortly thereafter, the recruiter provided the Respondent Partner with the CV of a freelance consultant from Gaza. The fraud allegations in the Cases arise from questions regarding this consultant's participation in the Contract. Actually, the recruiter authorized using the consultant's CV although he didn't inform the consultant of the usage of his CV before submitting the proposal. The Consortium presented the consultant as a confirmed participant in the bidding process, naming the consultant as one of the professional staff proposed to work on the contract. Moreover, the Respondent General Manager signed and submitted a commitment letter on the consultant's behalf. Then, the Respondent General Manager contacted the consultant to discuss his participation in the contract but he stated he intended to emigrate from the region, and he did not want to be included in the Proposal. Consequently, the Consultant told INT he had not agreed to be part of the Proposal, and contends he never discussed the Contract with anyone except the Respondent General Manager. As the cases against Respondent Firm and Respondent Partner arise from a common set of facts and related allegations of misconduct, the Sanctions Board addressed both cases in this decision. See *World Bank v General Consulting Training and TEAM Engineering & Management Cons.*, [2012] Sanctions Board 51,

[121]ibid para 94.

Considerable concerns arise from the abovementioned reasoning of the Sanctions Board. When the judging body assessed the liability of the respondent and, in particular, the presence of the *mens rea* element, it just compared the conduct perpetrated with the formal requirement provided by the contract. The words of the judging body appear emblematic of such an approach:

> the Respondent Partner's lack of diligence in this respect stands in contrast to its written representation in the Proposal, which read: 'We hereby declare that all the information and statements made in this Proposal are true and accept that any misinterpretation contained in it may lead to our disqualification'.[122]

Such a simplistic approach might potentially sow the seed of a judicial trend based on strict liability.[123]

The circumstance of submitting a bid not compliant with the wording of the agreement cannot suffice *per se* to prove the presence of the mental element required by the fraudulent practice. This is especially true when there are other circumstances that could affect the subjective element such as the presumed consent of the entitled person or the presence of a defense. Both the common law and the civil law legal systems recognize some justifying, excusing, or exempting circumstances or conditions. It could be argued that the critical political and security situation in which Gaza was in 2007 could have been taken into account in order to assess whether it corresponded to a state of impossibility sufficient to deem the respondent as not liable or less liable. Under common law, where a duty or a specific action is imposed, it can be considered a defense a situation in which it is impossible for the defendant to fulfill that duty or carry out the action.[124] Therefore, irrespective of the elements that emerged in the case at issue, to assess the liability of respondents in a fairer way, the Sanctions Board should not address these issues in such simplistic and formal way.

---

[122]ibid para 72.

[123]Indeed, the utilization of strict liability as a form of *mens rea* is widely criticised by scholars even if in some jurisdiction some strict liability offenses still exist. These is due to the real sense of unfairness in convicting someone for a conduct that was neither intentional nor negligent. In the US, for instance, it has been argued that the imposition of strict liability might be held to be unconstitutional as contrasting with Art 3 (Freedom from Inhuman or Degrading Treatments), Art 8 (Respect for Privacy), Art 10 (Freedom from Expression), and possibly Art. 7 (Guarantees against Retrospectivity). In Europe the greatest controversy has been over whether strict liability offenses infringe the presumption of innocence guaranteed under Art 6(2) of the European Convention of Human Rights. In this regard, notwithstanding the European Court has held that in principle the contracting States may, under certain conditions, penalize a simple or objective fact as such irrespective of whether it results from criminal intent o from negligence, the overriding concern is that a trial should be fair and the presumption of innocence is a fundamental right directed to that end. See David Ormerod, *Smith and Hogans's Criminal Law* (13th edn, Oxford University Press 2011), 159.

[124]ibid 401.

6.15 Alternatives to Sanctions: Negotiated Resolution Agreements

The Bank has established a settlement procedure that can lead to the conclusion of cases without carrying out a full investigation. The related agreements, which are called "Negotiated Resolution Agreements (NRAs)," can represent an effective instrument to save precious resources and foster good governance:

> Negotiated resolution agreements (NRAs), or settlements, are intended to be an efficient mechanism to resolve investigations without relying on full sanctions proceedings. Settlements can save the WBG considerable resources, while providing certainty of result for the party under investigation. Settlements will generally lead to quicker and more efficient resolution of investigations, as well as provide the WBG with an opportunity to acquire invaluable information through the cooperation of the party under investigation. Finally, settlements promote a forward leaning approach by generally requiring sanctioned firms to implement adequate compliance programs.[125]

The settlement agreements, which seem inspired by the model of the deferred prosecution agreements adopted at the domestic level in the United States[126] and more recently in England and Wales,[127] can be defined as a tool by which it is possible to divert from the ordinary sanctions procedure in order to deal with sanctionable practices allegedly committed within Bank-financed projects.

It appears that under the Bank's rules, investigated parties have the right to be invited to negotiate an NRA. As a matter of fact, the Bank's documents specify that the settlement process begins with the premise that "every subject of an INT investigation has a right to consider the option of settlement" and that, prior to launching the formal proceedings, "the subject of an INT investigation is generally advised of the WBG's settlement process."[128] It is also provided that, although a settlement may be pursued at any stage of an investigation or sanctions proceedings, a case is more likely to end in settlement before sanctions proceedings begin.[129] In reality, the final decision as to whether or not to use the settlement procedure rests on INT. Indeed, the Bank's documents specify that "before commencing settlement

---

[125]See 'World Bank Group Settlements: How Negotiated Resolution Agreements Fit Within the World Bank Group's Sanctions System' (*World Bank*, Sanctions & Compliance) 3 <http://pubdocs.worldbank.org/en/415101449169634523/Settlement-Process-Note.pdf>.

[126]See Julie R. O'Sullivan, 'How Prosecutors Apply the "Federal Prosecutions of Corporations" Charging Policy in the Era of Deferred Prosecutions, and What That Means for the Purposes of the Federal Criminal Sanction' (2014) 51 *American Criminal Law Review*, 29.

[127]See Costantino Grasso, 'Peaks and troughs of the English deferred prosecution agreement: the lesson learned from the DPA between the SFO and ICBC SB Plc' (2016) 5 *Journal of Business Law*, 388.

[128]See 'How Negotiated Resolution Agreements Fit Within the Sanctions System' (*World Bank*) (n 125) 3.

[129]ibid.

negotiations, INT must be satisfied that the particular case warrants a negotiated resolution in lieu of pursuing a traditional sanctions proceeding."[130] To this end, INT has to take into consideration several criteria such as whether an accused party has admitted culpability, whether settlement will result in resource savings to the Bank, whether an accused party has agreed to cooperate or is cooperating with INT's investigation, and whether an accused party has taken corrective measures or has shown that it will no longer be a significant fiduciary risk to the Bank.[131] Consequently, only the Bank's investigative body might take the decision if, according to the specific circumstances of each case, it is appropriate to enter into an NRA instead of pursuing the full investigation of the alleged sanctionable practices. In any case, INT is responsible for the drafting, negotiation, and execution of NRAs.

In order to ensure that all subjects entering into a settlement agreement do so voluntarily and of their own free will, the Bank requires also an affidavit to be attached to each NRA. This document aims at guaranteeing that the involved party has gained an understanding of the sanctions process and of the consequences deriving from the agreement.[132]

Whenever a subject expresses an interest in pursuing a negotiated resolution, that subject is provided with a standardized Term Sheet, which outlines the key terms that every NRA should contain.[133]

Part B of the Sanctions Procedures is entirely devoted to the settlement process. The procedural rules establish that "at any time during sanctions proceedings, INT and one or more Respondents, acting jointly, may request the SDO for a stay of proceedings for the purpose of conducting settlement negotiations."[134] Such a request for a stay of proceedings shall be granted as a matter of course.[135] Moreover, the document specifies:

> At any time prior to or during sanctions proceedings and prior to the issuance of a decision by the Sanctions Board [. . .] INT and one or more Respondents may submit a signed copy of any settlement agreement to which they are parties to the SDO for review [. . .] Such submission shall automatically stay sanctions proceeding then pending with respect to any case or cases so specified in the settlement agreement, including any proceedings before the Sanctions Board.[136]

The agreement is subject to review by the World Bank's General Counsel, and the SDO is charged with reviewing it to assess, on the one hand, if the respondent

[130]ibid.

[131]ibid.

[132]ibid.

[133]ibid.

[134]See 'Sanctions Procedures' (*World Bank*) (n 6) Part B, 1(a).

[135]ibid Part B, 1(c).

[136]ibid Part B, 2(a).

entered into the agreement freely and fully informed of its terms and free of duress and, on the other, if the terms of the agreement are broadly consistent with the Sanctioning Guidelines.[137] In particular, the Sanctions Procedures specify that "the SDO shall review the settlement agreement to ensure that the terms of the agreement do not manifestly violate sub-paragraphs 9.01 or 9.02 of Part A,"[138] which are the provisions covering respectively the range of possible sanctions and the factors affecting the sanction decision. Although such a degree of control is surely appreciable, the SDO's room for maneuver appears too limited.[139] Moreover, the involvement of the Sanctions Board as the key supervisory body would have been preferable, it being the sole parajudicial body that shows a certain degree of independence of the Bank within the sanctions process.[140] As a result, currently the system does not seem to ensure in a reasonable way that settlement agreements are reached in a completely fair manner.

The Bank has introduced two principal types of settlements: definitive settlement agreements and deferral agreements. The former, which effectively end the sanctions proceedings, may (or may not)[141] include compliance by the respondent with certain conditions.[142] As clarified in the Sanctions Procedures:

> If the settlement agreement provides for the definitive disposition, in whole or in part, of the case subject to sanctions proceedings, the case [. . .] shall be closed as of the effective date of the agreement or any other such date specified in said agreement, on such terms, including the imposition of such sanctions on the Respondent, as may be stipulated in the agreement.[143]

---

[137]See 'The World Bank Group Integrity Vice Presidency – Annual Update – Fiscal Year 2014' (*World Bank*, Publications) 35 <http://siteresources.worldbank.org/EXTDOII/Resources/588920-1412626296780/INT_Annual_Update_FY14_WEB.pdf>.

[138]See 'Sanctions Procedures' (*World Bank*) (n 6) Part B, 2(b).

[139]The SDO's review is limited to either accepting or rejecting the settlement agreement and he or she may not impose any sanction other than the sanction stipulated in the agreement or otherwise modify the agreement in any other respect. As a matter of fact the Sanctions Procedures specifies that "upon confirmation by the SDO that the terms of the settlement agreement do not manifestly violate [the Bank's sentencing practice] or any guidance issued by the Bank in respect thereof, the SDO shall impose the sanction therein stipulated." See ibid Part B, 2(c).

[140]See *supra* note 147 and accompanying text in Chap. 3.

[141]The Sanctions Procedures provide that "unless the settlement agreement otherwise expressly provides, compliance by the Respondents with the terms and conditions thereof shall be deemed conditions for release from debarment or conditions for non-debarment, as the case may be." See 'Sanctions Procedures' (World Bank) (n 6) Part B, 3(c).

[142]See 'World Bank Group's Sanctions Regime: Information Note' (*World Bank*) 25 <http://siteresources.worldbank.org/EXTOFFEVASUS/Resources/The_World_Bank_Group_Sanctions_Regime.pdf>.

[143]See 'Sanctions Procedures' (World Bank) (n 6) Part B, 3(a).

The deferral agreements "freeze"[144] sanctions proceedings for a period of time pending compliance by the respondent with certain conditions, upon the fulfillment of which the case is then settled.[145] In this regard, the Sanctions Procedures provide:

> If the settlement agreement provides for the deferral of proceedings for a period of time pending compliance by the Respondent with specified conditions, proceedings shall be deemed stayed for the period specified in the agreement, so long as the Respondent remains in compliance with such conditions. Unless the agreement otherwise expressly provides, upon expiration of the deferral period and compliance by the Respondent with all conditions specified therefore in the agreement, the case shall be closed. All statute of limitations and other time periods specified in these Procedures shall be tolled during the pendency of such deferral.[146]

Disappointingly, the Bank has not adopted the same regime of transparency used in relation to the Sanctions Board's decisions, and the settlement process appears still cloaked in a shroud of secrecy.[147] As a matter of fact, it is not currently possible to access the text of any NRA or even the abovementioned standardized Term Sheet. As a result, a comprehensive analysis of this legal instrument is difficult to be carried out. What emerges clearly from some press releases of the Bank, however, is that the imposition of the standard punitive measures is included in the terms of the agreements and that through an NRA the investigated party does not necessarily avoid the cross-debarment regime.[148] For instance, on October 31, 2016, the Bank made it known that it entered into a settlement with Honeyomar Ventures Ltd and that, under the terms of the NRA, the firm accepted to be debarred for 18 months. The Bank's press release also clearly stated that the debarment of Honeyomar qualified for cross-debarment by other MDBs.[149] Again, on February 8, 2017, the Bank announced that it entered into an NRA with Lao-Asie Consultants Group, which was debarred for 18 months following the acknowledgement of the perpetration of corrupt practices, and also with Sequeira Ingenieros, S.A., which was debarred for multiple collusive and fraudulent practices. Again, in the press release, the Bank specified that "the

[144]The Bank's Information Note clarifies that: "Deferral agreements result in an immediate deferral of proceedings. Any materials submitted to the EO [now SDO] are not considered withdrawn, but rather their consideration by the EO is suspended. The deferral agreement may specify whether or not any temporary suspension will be lifted or maintained. Any pending period for submission of a pleading runs anew if proceedings resume. (For example, if the deferral occurs after an Explanation but before submission of a Response, the Respondent has a full ninety (90) days to submit its Response if proceedings resume)." See 'Sanctions Regime: Information Note' (*World Bank*) (n 142) 25.

[145]ibid.

[146]See 'Sanctions Procedures' (World Bank) (n 6) Part B, 3(b).

[147]See *supra* notes 34–38 and accompanying text in Chap. 2.

[148]See *supra* notes 166–174 and accompanying text in Chap. 1.

[149]See 'World Bank Group Announces Settlement with Honeyomar Ventures Ltd' (*World Bank*, Press Release, 31 October 2016) <www.worldbank.org/en/news/press-release/2016/10/31/world-bank-group-announces-settlement-with-honeyomar-ventures-ltd>.

aforementioned sanctions are part of Negotiated Resolution Agreements and qualify for cross-debarment by other MDBs."[150]

Some additional clarifications on the way in which the settlement process works are offered by the Bank's Sanctions Process Information Note, which explains:

> In appropriate circumstances, sanctions also may be imposed on a Respondent through a negotiated resolution of the case. Under this mechanism, sanctions cases may be resolved by negotiations between INT and a Respondent at any stage of the sanctions process up to the issuance of a decision by the Sanctions Board, or during the investigation stage prior to the commencement of sanctions proceedings.[151]

The rewarding nature of the settlement process is quite obscure. In other words, what is not clear is whether the investigated parties that enter into an NRA are entitled to obtain a discount on the sanction and, if so, to what extent. A provision that seems to allow respondents to qualify for such a discount is section 9.02(e) of the Sanctions Procedures, which includes settlements among the factors that the Sanctions Board has to take into account to determine the appropriate sanction, expressly considering them as a mitigating circumstance. However, the Sanctioning Guidelines do not expressly include settlements among the mitigating factors. Part V (C) of the Guidelines lists a series of activities denoting a certain degree of cooperation with investigation and identifies them as mitigating factors, for which a reduction of the sanction up to 33% may be warranted.[152] Consequently, it seems that typically the decision of entering into an NRA with the Bank could fall within such a category of mitigating factors. Nonetheless, the fact that the Guidelines do not expressly mention settlements as an element that justifies *per se* a discount on sanctions still raises doubts about the abovementioned entitlement and its precise extent. As a result, there is the risk that a respondent would be granted exactly the same amount of sentence reduction if, having carried out one or more of the activities included in Part V of the Sentencing Guidelines, it decided to face all the phases of the sanctions process. Moreover, even if it could be uncommon, a respondent might theoretically conclude a settlement agreement with the Bank without carrying out any of the abovementioned activities. In particular, the degree of cooperation offered by the respondent may significantly vary. At the same time, the conduction of internal investigations, the admission of responsibility, as well as the exercise of a voluntary restraint from bidding, are not laid down as mandatory requirements to be satisfied in the negotiation of an NRA.

As it is specified in the Information Note, where the SDO has to confirm that the agreement complies with the Bank's sanctioning practice, he or she has to evaluate if the agreed sanction, if any, is "broadly consistent with the Bank's Sanctioning

[150] See 'World Bank Announces Three Negotiated Resolution Agreements' (*World Bank*, Press Release, 8 February 2017) <www.worldbank.org/en/news/press-release/2017/02/08/world-bank-announces-three-negotiated-resolution-agreements>.

[151] See 'Sanctions Regime: Information Note' (*World Bank*) (n 142) 8.

[152] In extraordinary circumstances a greater reduction may be warranted. See 'Sanctioning Guidelines' (*World Bank*) (n 1) V(C).

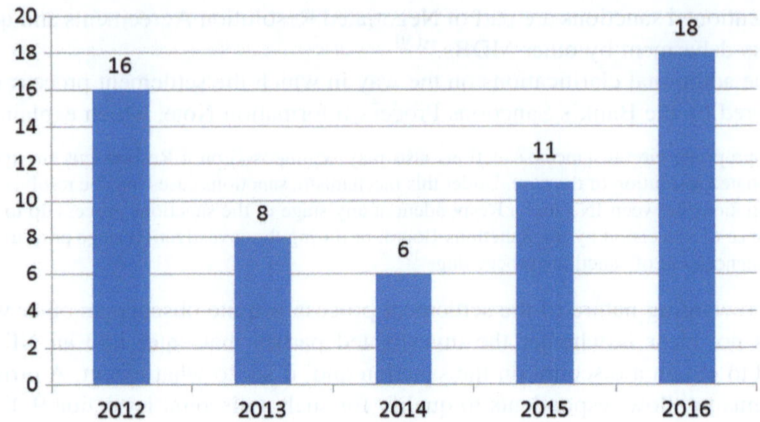

Fig. 6.2 Amount of Negotiated Resolution Agreements. *Source*: 'The World Bank Group Integrity Vice Presidency – Annual Update – Fiscal Year 2016' (*World Bank*, Publications) 25 <http://pubdocs.worldbank.org/en/118471475857477799/INT-FY16-Annual-Update-web.pdf>

Guidelines" and that "the settlement is then reflected in a sanction imposed" by the relevant SDO.[153] In the absence of other expressed criteria, it may be argued that the use of the word "broadly" leaves some room for negotiation as to the amount and nature of the sanction to be imposed through the NRA.

Anyway, taking into consideration the current figures (see Fig. 6.2), it appears that the settlement process plays still a quite marginal role within the sanctions system, with the number of investigated parties that have decided to use it over the course of the last 5 years being rather limited.[154]

6.16 Sanctions Board's Involvement in the Settlement Procedure

As mentioned above, matters of concern arise from the absence of any role played by the Sanctions Board in relation to the settlement procedure. As it has been illustrated, where the parties decide to enter into an NRA, it rests solely on the SDO the duty to review the proposed agreement. Such a choice does not seem adequate, especially where the parties choose to enter into an NRA during the second tier of the sanctions process.

[153]ibid 9.

[154]See 'The World Bank Group: Mutual Enforcement Of Debarment Decisions Among Multilateral Development Banks' (*World Bank*, 3 March 2010) 6 <http://siteresources.worldbank.org/INTDOII/Resources/Bank_paper_cross_debar.pdf>.

In *World Bank v General Consulting Training and TEAM Engineering & Management Cons.*,[155] the EO (now SDO) recommended the imposition of a debarment with conditional release after a minimum period of 3 years for the respondent firm and the respondent General Manager.[156] Over the course of the second tier of the proceedings, the respondents, which agreed to enter a guilty plea and accepted full responsibility for their actions, submitted a request to the Sanctions Board for the imposition of a less severe sanction, i.e. a one-year public debarment.[157] INT did not oppose their request for the following reasons: they unconditionally admitted to engaging in a fraudulent practice and accepted responsibility for their actions, they did not show a repeated pattern of misconduct, they cooperated fully with INT, the respondent General Manager was already working with counsel on an effective compliance program for the respondent firm.[158] What happened in practice was that the parties submitted an informal settlement agreement to the Sanctions Board. The reasons why they did not avail of the possibility of asking for a stay of proceedings and presenting a formal agreement to the EO (now SDO) do not emerge from the text of the decision. However, the main reason seems to be that the Bank's official had already recommended a much heavier sanction to be imposed. In its decision, the judging body sustained that, where the parties to a case have agreed upon liability and appropriate sanctions, the parties "should most expeditiously resolve such matter through settlement in accordance with Article XI[159] of the Sanctions Procedures."[160]

Although the parties may request for a stay of proceedings for the purpose of conducting settlement negotiations at any time during sanctions proceedings,[161] from the perspective of the judging body, where for any reason a case is presented on appeal rather than resolved through settlement, the Sanctions Board conducts a full *de novo* review. In other words, the Board deems itself not constrained by the parties' views or informal agreements or bound by the parties' consensus in the absence of a formal settlement agreement. Consequently, the Board feels free to set aside any informal proposal submitted by the parties and to impose any sanction it considers appropriate. Indeed, in the abovementioned case, the judging body applied a different sanction from the one requested by the parties. Offering such a restrictive interpretation, the Sanctions Board lost the opportunity to come up with a solution in

[155]See *World Bank v General Consulting Training and TEAM Engineering & Management Cons.*, [2012] Sanctions Board 51. For a description of the case see *supra* note 120.

[156]ibid para 5.

[157]ibid para 22.

[158]ibid para 25.

[159]Under the new Sanctions Procedures the matter is addressed by Part B. See 'Sanctions Procedures' (World Bank) (n 6) Part B.

[160]See *World Bank v General Consulting Training and TEAM Engineering & Management Cons.*, [2012] Sanctions Board 51, at para 26.

[161]See 'Sanctions Procedures' (World Bank) (n 6) Part B, 1(a).

relation to the deficiencies from which the structure of the settlement procedure presently suffers.

The formal mechanism for the settlement of sanctions currently implemented by the Bank raises serious concerns. As mentioned above, under this mechanism, the negotiated resolution of cases can take place at any stage of the sanctions process up to the issuance of a decision by the Sanctions Board. However, independently of the process phase in which it is presented, the settlement agreement is always subject to review by the SDO to confirm, *inter alia*, that the agreed sanction does not entail a manifest violation of the Bank's Sanctioning Guidelines. The circumstance that the SDO represents the sole official designed to evaluate any proposed agreement could correspond to a source of unfairness, especially where the officer has already manifested an implicit dissent against a possible agreement, for instance, having recommended a more severe sanction than the one on which INT and respondents have mutually agreed. Consequently, such a rule might *de facto* nullify the opportunity given to the parties for entering into an NRA also within the second tier of the sanctions process. The impossibility for the parties to submit their agreement to the Sanctions Board not only appears inconsistent with the abovementioned opportunity granted to them but also may have significant and negative repercussions on the rights of respondents depriving them of the possibility of obtaining an alternative assessment of the compatibility of a proposed NRA with the Bank's Sanctioning Guidelines. As a result, it would be more appropriate if the duty to review the proposed agreements rested on the judging authority actually involved in the phase of the sanctions proceedings in which the agreement is submitted, this without taking into consideration that, as it has been already argued, a general and direct involvement of the Sanctions Board at any stage of the settlement process would be in any case desirable.

6.17 Voluntary Disclosure Program

In the seventies, voluntary disclosure programs had been already introduced within national jurisdictions, and with the passage of time, they have been used by government agencies with increasing frequency. Under these programs, corporations voluntarily disclose illegal practices to the authorities. This reporting activity has been defined by Arlen and Kraakman as an *ex post* policing measure, which aims at raising the probability that corporate criminal activities will be detected and sanctioned.[162] As the authors observed, it is particularly relevant in relation to intentional misconducts that are often difficult to detect because they are deliberately hidden.[163] From the corporate perspective, reporting an illicit behavior can substitute or

[162]See Jennifer Arlen and Reinier Kraakman, 'Controlling corporate misconduct: An analysis of corporate liability regimes' (1997) 72(4) *New York University Law Review* 687, 706.

[163]ibid.

complement sanctioning it internally, whereas from the governments' perspective, it not only ensures that detected misconduct is sanctioned but also increases the probability of detection and reduces the costs of investigations.[164]

Such a voluntary disclosure is encouraged by national agencies through the promise of a *quid pro quo*, which usually consists in the imposition of a more lenient sanction.[165] In exchange, the voluntary disclosure programs can provide government agencies with the information needed to carry out their enforcement functions without the monetary and manpower constraints on agency resources that stem from investigations.[166]

Over the course of the last decade, these programs have acquired a significant relevance both at the domestic and international levels. The United States initiatives, which aimed at fighting tax evasion by means of several rounds of offshore voluntary disclosure programs (OVDP),[167] and the issuance of the OECD guidance on voluntary disclosure programs, which reflects the wealth of practical experience gained by 47 countries in relation to the implementation of those programs to foster tax compliance,[168] are emblematic of the fact that their adoption has become extremely widespread.

The Bank launched its Voluntary Disclosure Program (VDP) in 2006 as a "response to a shared desire by the Bank and companies that want to help level the playing field and assure others adhere to internationally accepted standards of business conduct."[169] In the VDP Guidelines, it is specified that the purpose of the program is to enhance the Bank's ability to fight against corruption by partnering with the private sector by means of an initiative that provides participants with incentives to disclose their knowledge of fraud or corruption and comply with the Bank's rules and guidelines.[170]

In order to be considered eligible to participate in the VDP, a firm does not have to be already under INT active investigation.[171]

In general terms, to participate, the firm is required to disclose to INT the results of an internal investigation into past fraudulent, corrupt, collusive, or coercive acts in Bank-financed projects or contracts. The firm has also to commit to not engage in

---

[164]ibid, 707.

[165]See Jacqueline C. Wolff, 'Voluntary Disclosure Programs' (1979) 47(6) *Fordham Law Review* 1057.

[166]ibid.

[167]See Tracy A. Kaye, 'Tax Transparency: A Tale of Two Countries' (2016) 39 *Fordham International Law Journal* 1153, 1168.

[168]See 'Update On Voluntary Disclosure Programmes – A Pathway To Tax Compliance' (*OECD*, August 2015) <www.oecd.org/ctp/exchange-of-tax-information/Voluntary-Disclosure-Programmes-2015.pdf>.

[169]See 'Voluntary Disclosure Program (VDP)' (*World Bank*) <http://siteresources.worldbank.org/INTVOLDISPRO/Resources/VDP_web_2009.pdf>.

[170]See 'VDP Guidelines for Participants' (*World Bank*) 8, para 2 <http://siteresources.worldbank.org/INTVOLDISPRO/Resources/VDP_Guidelines_2011.pdf>.

[171]See 'Voluntary Disclosure Program' (*World Bank*) (n 169).

such misconducts in the future and implement a robust internal compliance program, which will be monitored by a Bank-approved compliance monitor for 3 years.[172] Finally, the firm has to cover the costs associated with the program.[173] Where the participant is the holding of a group of interrelated firms, its commitment is extended to the entire entity. In other words, the parent firm is required to ensure that also each of its affiliates fully complies with each and every obligation imposed by the terms of the VDP.[174]

In its documents, the Bank stresses the rewarding nature of the program that is described as entailing a "win–win proposition."[175] As regards the Bank, the program allows INT to gain valuable information about particular actors and schemes worthy of investigation or preventive mitigation, which is also useful in advising national authorities. Moreover, the information gathered helps the Bank in developing more effective ways to counter and mitigate risks.[176] As for the participants, the most significant advantage connected to the program is represented by the fact that, in exchange, the Bank does not publicly debar them for the disclosed misconducts and keeps their identities confidential.[177] Specifically, the Bank highlights that the benefits of the participation include a reduced risk of being the subject of an INT investigation, the avoidance of the potential reputational damage of a public debarment, the opportunity of continuing to compete in Bank-financed projects, the strengthening of the firm's corporate best practices and compliance policies.[178] As a matter of fact, those who participate in a VDP are not debarred by the Bank but subject to "the financial obligation imposed under the VDP Terms & Conditions."[179]

The program provides a severe sanction to be applied in case of violations. In particular, where a participant does not disclose all misconducts voluntarily, completely, and truthfully; continues to engage in misconducts; or violates other material provisions of the VDP, it faces a mandatory 10-year public debarment in accordance with regular Bank procedures.[180] Although it is clear that the purpose of such a provision is to discourage specious disclosures and dishonest behaviors of the

---

[172]The VDO Guidelines provides that "the Compliance Monitor conducts three annual comprehensive reviews and, after each review, submits a Monitoring Report to the World Bank and the Participant. The Participant must cooperate fully with the Compliance Monitor and adopt and implement the Compliance Monitor's recommendations." See 'VDP Guidelines' (*World Bank*) (n 170) 10, para 5.6.2.

[173]See 'Voluntary Disclosure Program' (*World Bank*) (n 169).

[174]See 'VDP Guidelines' (*World Bank*) (n 170) 10, para 5.3.2.

[175]See 'Voluntary Disclosure Program' (*World Bank*) (n 169).

[176]See 'The World Bank Group Integrity Vice Presidency – Annual Update – Fiscal Year 2014' (*World Bank*, Publications) 23 <http://pubdocs.worldbank.org/en/663211449168835106/INT-FY14-Annual-Update.pdf>.

[177]See 'VDP Guidelines' (*World Bank*) (n 170) 8, para 3.

[178]See 'Voluntary Disclosure Program' (*World Bank*) (n 169).

[179]This sanction will not be publicized or communicated by the Bank to any third party. See 'VDP Guidelines' (*World Bank*) (n 170) 8, para 4.

[180]ibid 8, para 3.

participants in the program, the imposition of such a heavy fixed-term sanction raises some concerns.[181] On the one hand, where the severity of the disclosed illicit practices is moderate, the imposition of that sanction may be disproportionate and, as such, unfair; on the other, the rigidity of this rule might discourage the participation of entities potentially interested in disclosing the perpetration of minor sanctionable practices just because the risk is not worth taking. A better option could consist in instructing the Sanctions Board to determine an appropriate sanction to be imposed proportionate to the infringement, possibly providing a specific aggravating factor in case of violations of VDP terms. This is particularly true taking into consideration that the general VDP terms and conditions appear really detailed and complex. For instance, they put the participants under a general duty of disclosure in relation to misconducts perpetrated also by third parties.[182]

6.18 Corporate Compliance Systems

One of the key elements of the sanctions system is the great emphasis that the Bank lays on debarred parties meeting certain integrity compliance conditions before they can once again participate in World Bank Group financed projects.[183] The fact that debarment with conditional release is currently considered as the "baseline" sanction, which should normally be applied to legal entities, is emblematic of such a policy.[184] As a result, the development and implementation of an integrity compliance program satisfactory to the Bank currently represent a principal condition to ending a debarment. The rationale behind such a choice is to place greater emphasis on corporate rehabilitation and encourage sanctioned companies and individuals to adopt adequate and meaningful policies and measures that can effectively help prevent, detect, and generally reduce incidences of fraud, corruption, collusion, and the other sanctionable misconducts.[185]

---

[181]In any case the program terms and conditions clarify that the participant will not be deemed to have violated the agreement where an individual has deliberately violated the firm's policies for his/her own benefit and took actions to conceal or delay the discovery of such actions, provided that the firm notifies the Bank of the misconduct and takes all appropriate measures to address it such as an appropriate disciplinary action. See 'Voluntary Disclosure Program (VDP) – Terms and Conditions' (*World Bank*, Department of Institutional Integrity, 16 August 2006) 8, I(43) <http://siteresources.worldbank.org/INTVOLDISPRO/Resources/VDPTermsandConditions.pdf>.

[182]Under the program terms and conditions it is specified that the participant "will promptly notify the World Bank of Misconduct involving other firms or individuals of which it becomes aware after the Date of Acceptance of these Terms & Conditions in World Bank-financed or supported projects and contracts, so that the World Bank may take appropriate actions to address such Misconduct." See ibid 1, A(5).

[183]See 'Sanctions & Compliance' (*World Bank*) (n 22).

[184]See *supra* notes 16–18 and accompanying text.

[185]See 'Frequently Asked Questions: Integrity Compliance at the World Bank Group' (*World Bank*) <http://pubdocs.worldbank.org/en/162741449169632232/ICO-FAQs.pdf>.

Antifinancial crime compliance can be defined as the introduction, within an organization, of systematic procedures designed to minimize the risk of corporate misconducts amounting to offenses like corruption, fraud, and money laundering. Such procedures, which are commonly referred to as compliance programs, share with other corporate social responsibility measures the general aim of promoting good corporate citizenship.[186] Usually, the adoption and implementation of effective compliance programs could represent within domestic jurisdictions a mitigating factor[187] or a defense.[188]

Within the Bank's sanctions system, the adoption of compliance programs can have a dual function. On the one hand, under the Sanctioning Guidelines,[189] the establishment or enhancement of an effective corporate compliance program is expressly included among the voluntary corrective actions that could be considered as mitigating circumstances that may warrant a sanction reduction of up to 50%[190]; on the other, the adoption of certain conditions such as the implementation or improvement of an integrity compliance program can constitute the inherent part of a sanction. Specifically, with both debarment with conditional release[191] and conditional nondebarment,[192] the Bank might impose such conditions to encourage the respondent's rehabilitation or to mitigate further risk to Bank-financed activities.[193] In such cases, the sanction will be respectively lifted or not applied only where the legal entity demonstrates that it has met the conditions set by the SDO or Sanctions Board.

The decision whether the compliance condition set by the Bank have been satisfied lies with the Integrity Compliance Officer (ICO). The role, which has been established by the Bank's Integrity Vice Presidency (INT) in September 2010,[194] consists in monitoring integrity compliance by sanctioned companies and

---

[186]Over the course of the last decade, these programs have acquired increasingly importance especially in the United States where, thanks to the adoption of the so-called pretrial diversion agreements, the prosecuting authorities commonly requires firms to alter their governance structure or the way in which they conduct their business operations. See Jennifer Arlen and Marcel Kahan, 'Corporate Governance Regulation through Nonprosecution' (2017) 84 *The University of Chicago Law Review* 323, 325.

[187]For instance, in the United States, the Sentencing Guidelines recognized the adoption of compliance programs as the *sine qua non* for receiving leniency upon conviction as of 1991. See Michael Goldsmith and Chad W. King, 'Policing Corporate Crime: The Dilemma of Internal Compliance Programs' (1997) 50(1) *Vanderbilt Law Review* 1, 3.

[188]For instance, in the English legal system, under s.7 of the Bribery Act 2010 it is a defense for a commercial organization to prove that it had in place adequate procedures designed to prevent persons associated with it from undertaking such a conduct. See Costantino Grasso, 'Peaks and troughs of the English deferred prosecution agreement: the lesson learned from the DPA between the SFO and ICBC SB Plc' (2016) 5 Journal of Business Law 388, 391.

[189]See 'Sanctioning Guidelines' (*World Bank*) (n 1) V(B)(3).

[190]See *supra* notes 74–78 and accompanying text.

[191]See *supra* notes 16–26 and accompanying text.

[192]See *supra* notes 27–30 and accompanying text.

[193]See 'Sanctioning Guidelines' (*World Bank*) (n 1) II(A).

[194]See 'Sanctions & Compliance' (*World Bank*) (n 22).

deciding whether the compliance conditions established by the SDO or the Sanctions Board as part of a conditional nondebarment or debarment with conditional release have been satisfied.[195] In order to perform such a duty, the Bank's Sanctions Procedures give the ICO the power to impose on the sanctioned party requirements "as may be reasonably necessary."[196] The procedures also comprise a merely illustrative list of requirements, which includes obligations such as periodic reporting by the sanctioned party, the appointment of an independent monitor, external auditing, and inspection of the books and records of the sanctioned party.[197] In particular, the matter is regulated by section 9.03, which provides that where one of the abovementioned sanctions is imposed, the ICO shall contact each sanctioned party to advise them as to the requirements for meeting the conditions, including the adoption or improvement and implementation of an integrity compliance program.[198] The sanctioned party may then submit to the Bank an application setting forth arguments for, and evidence of, its compliance with the requirements set by the ICO.[199] The deadlines are set by the Sanctions Procedures, which provide that the application can be submitted

> No earlier than one hundred and twenty (120) days prior to (i) any deadline for compliance with conditions for non-debarment under sub-paragraph 9.01(b) or (ii) the last day of the minimum period of debarment under a debarment for conditional release under sub-paragraph 9.01(d), but no later than any such deadline for compliance with conditions for non-debarment under sub-paragraph 9.01(b)[200]

It is also provided that the application has to include, *inter alia*, a detailed report on the sanctioned party's adoption or improvement and implementation of any integrity compliance program agreed with the ICO; details relating to remedial actions taken in response to the misconduct for which the sanctioned party was sanctioned; and any other misconduct detected during the period of debarment or conditional nondebarment.[201] Upon receipt of the application, the ICO has to determine whether the sanctioned party has complied with the conditions for nondebarment or release from debarment.[202] Such a decision has to be based on the arguments and evidence set forth in the application and any other factors that the ICO might consider relevant.[203] The Sanctions Procedures establish that the sanctioned party has to cooperate fully with the ICO and, in particular, has to allow him

---

[195]Under the Bank's Sanctions Procedures it is expressly established that the Integrity Compliance Officer has the right to monitor compliance by each sanctioned party with the conditions for release or nondebarment. See 'Sanctions Procedures' (World Bank) (n 6) Part A, 9.03(b).

[196]ibid.

[197]ibid.

[198]ibid Part A, 9.03(a).

[199]ibid Part A, 9.03(c).

[200]ibid.

[201]ibid.

[202]ibid Part A, 9.03(d).

[203]ibid.

or her to access all the relevant books and records.[204] Although the Procedures expressly provide that the ICO shall begin its review within 30 days after receipt of the application, no term is fixed for its conclusion. As a matter of fact, the Procedures just make it clear that the ICO shall conclude such a verification and make the related determination "as soon as practicable."[205] Some concerns arise from such an absence, which could potentially lead to unfair deferrals of the release. The Sanctions Procedures also provide for a system of basic guarantees in the event that the ICO reaches a determination of noncompliance. Specifically, such a decision may be appealed by the sanctioned party submitting a request in writing to the Sanctions Board within 30 days.[206] Then, within 90 days after receipt of such appeal, the Sanctions Board has to decide whether or not the Integrity Compliance Officer committed an abuse of discretion in the determination of noncompliance.[207] In this regard, the Sanctions Procedures offer a definition of "abuse of discretion" specifying that it occurs when the decision

> (1) lacks an observable basis or is otherwise arbitrary, (2) is based on disregard of a material fact or a material mistake of fact, or (3) was taken in material violation of the procedures set out in this sub-paragraph 9.03.[208]

Finally, the Sanctions Procedures cover the case of "default by the sanctioned party," which occurs where it fails to timely submit an application with respect to conditions for nondebarment or for release or fails to fully cooperate with any verification of compliance conducted under the procedures.[209] On such occasions, it is provided that the sanctioned party is not considered as compliant with the relevant conditions for nondebarment or for release and that such a determination is not subject to any further review.[210]

In order to offer companies guidance on how to foster good corporate behavior through the introduction of effective compliance programs, the Bank has issued the Integrity Compliance Guidelines. In particular, these Guidelines illustrate the basic requirements that a sound compliance program should include. Among other things, they highlight how companies have to prohibit misconducts in a clearly articulated and visible way; create and maintain a trust-based inclusive organizational culture that encourages ethical conduct; foster individual responsibility of all employees; carry out comprehensive risk assessments; develop practical and effective policies and procedures to be used to prevent, detect, investigate, and remediate all forms of misconduct; use its best efforts to encourage all business partners to adopt equivalent commitments; establish and maintain an effective system of internal controls;

---

[204] ibid.

[205] ibid.

[206] ibid Part A, 9.03(e)(i).

[207] ibid Part A, 9.03(e)(ii).

[208] ibid Part A, 9.03(e)(iv).

[209] ibid Part A, 9.03(f).

[210] ibid.

provide and document effective compliance training; promote its policies by adopting appropriate incentives to encourage and provide positive support for the observance of the program, as well as disciplinary measures with all persons involved in misconducts or other program violations; and provide confidential channels for whistle-blowers.[211]

The ICO's first determination was taken on August 15, 2011. It concerned Lahmeyer GmbH, which is a leading international engineering company headquartered in Germany.[212] On that occasion, the ICO determined that the company had satisfactorily adopted and implemented an effective compliance program.[213]

Another example of the application of the abovementioned rules is the one that involved Zoomlion Ghana Limited,[214] a giant in the waste management and environmental sanitation business in Africa that entered into a Negotiated Resolution Agreement (NRA) with the World Bank on September 24, 2013.[215] On September 23, 2015, Zoomlion was released from the Bank's Debarment List because it had satisfied the compliance conditions as established in the agreement. As asserted by the former Chief Operating Officer of the company:

> Change hit the structure of our board, our policies, our messages to staff and our systems. We set up a new oversight mechanism in our main office to monitor and respond to any allegations and in three years provided compliance training to more than 5000 Zoomlion employees, training is ongoing to staff involved in our public-private operations which total 120,000.[216]

---

211 See 'Summary of World Bank Group Integrity Compliance Guidelines' (*World Bank*) <http://pubdocs.worldbank.org/en/489491449169632718/Integrity-Compliance-Guidelines-2-1-11.pdf>.

212 See 'Company' (*Lahmeyer Group*) <www.lahmeyer.de/en/company/about-us.html>.

213 See 'Lahmeyer GmbH Released from Debarment; First Such Determination by World Bank's Integrity Compliance Officer' (*World Bank*, Press Release, 15 August 2011) <www.worldbank.org/en/news/press-release/2011/08/15/lahmeyer-gmbh-released-debarment-first-such-determination-world-bank-integrity-compliance-officer>.

214 See 'Welcome Message' (*Zoomlion Ghana Limited*) <www.zoomlionghana.com/>.

215 Zoomlion Ghana Limited admitted the perpetration of corrupt practices consisting in the payment of bribes to facilitate contract execution and processing of invoices within the World Bank-financed Emergency Monrovia Urban Sanitation Project in Liberia. The company, which entered into a Negotiated Resolution Agreement was debarred for a period of two years. As part of the settlement, the company was also obliged to demonstrate full and satisfactory compliance with the World Bank Integrity standards. See 'Enforcing Accountability: World Bank Debars Ghanaian Company for Sanctionable Misconduct Relating to a Waste Management Project in Liberia' (*World Bank*, Press Release, 25 September 2013) <www.worldbank.org/en/news/press-release/2013/09/25/world-bank-debars-ghanaian-company-sanctionable-misconduct-waste-management-project-liberia>.

216 See 'Compliance at a crossroads' (*World Bank*, Feature Story, 27 April 2016) <www.worldbank.org/en/news/feature/2016/04/27/compliance-at-a-crossroads>.

A question that remains unresolved is the value that will be given, within the Bank's sanctions system, to the determination with which the ICO has acknowledged the adoption and implementation of a satisfactory corporate compliance program in the event that the same company is involved again in the same type of misconduct.

Select Bibliography

Adams, F., *Deepening Democracy: Global Governance and Political Reform in Latin America* (Praeger 2003).
Alldridge, P., 'The U.K. Bribery Act: "The Caffeinated Younger Sibling of the FCPA"' (2012) 73 *Ohio State Law Journal* 1181.
Amar, A. R., 'Sixth Amendment First Principles' (1996) 84(4) *Georgetown Law Journal* 641.
Ambos, K., *Treatise on International Criminal Law*, (Oxford University Press 2016).
Arlen, J., and Kahan, M., 'Corporate Governance Regulation through Nonprosecution' (2017) 84 *The University of Chicago Law Review* 323.
Arlen, J. and Kraakman, R. 'Controlling corporate misconduct: An analysis of corporate liability regimes' (1997) 72(4) *New York University Law Review* 687.
Ashworth, A., *Sentencing and Criminal Justice* (5th edn, Cambridge University Press 2010).
Bassiouni, M. C., 'A Functional Approach to General Principles of International Law' (1990) 11/3 *Michigan Journal of International Law* 768.
Benedetti, M. 'How Multilateral Development Banks invest corruption in their funded projects' in Auby, J., Breen, E. and Perroud, T. (eds), *Corruption and Conflicts of Interest* (Edward Elgar 2014).
Bingham, T. H., 'The Rule of Law' (2007) 66(1) *The Cambridge Law Journal* 66.
Boisson de Chazournes, L. and Fromageau, E., 'Balancing the Scales: The World Bank Sanctions Process and Access to Remedies' (2012) 23(4) *European Journal of International Law* 963.
Canni, T. J., 'Debarment is no longer private World Bank business: an examination of the Bank's distinct debarment procedures used for corporate procurements and financed projects' (2010) 40/1 *Public Contract Law Journal* 147.
Chapman, N. S. and Mcconnell, M. W., 'Due Process as Separation of Powers' (2011) 121(7) *The Yale Law Journal* 1672.
Chemerinsky, E., 'Procedural Due Process Claims' (2000) 16(3) *Touro Law Review*, 871.
Coffee, J. C., '"No Soul to Damn: No Body to Kick": An Unscandalized Inquiry into the Problem of Corporate Punishment' (1981) 79(3) *Michigan Law Review* 386.
Cohen, J. and Sabel, C. F., 'Global Democracy?' (2004) 37 *New York University Journal of International Law and Politics* 763.
Delmas-Marty, M., *Ordering Pluralism: A Conceptual Framework for Understanding the Transnational Legal World* (Naomi Norberg tr, Hart 2009).

The purpose of this bibliography is to give an overview of major commentaries which are directly related to the theme of the book. More detailed references may be found in individual chapters.

S. Manacorda, C. Grasso, *Fighting Fraud and Corruption at the World Bank*,
https://doi.org/10.1007/978-3-319-73824-6

Diez, C. G., 'Corporate Culpability as a Limit to the Overcriminalization of Corporate Criminal Liability: The Interplay between Self-Regulation, Corporate Compliance, and Corporate Citizenship' (2011) 14(1) *New Criminal Law Review* 78.

Dignam, A. and Galanis, M., *The Globalization of Corporate Governance* (Ashgate 2009).

Duff, R. A., *Punishment, Communication and Community* (Oxford University Press 2001).

Folliot-Lalliot, L., 'Introduction to the World Bank's policies in the fight against corruption and conflict of interests in public contracts' in Auby, J., Breen, E. and Perroud, T. (eds), *Corruption and Conflicts of Interest* (Edward Elgar 2014).

Forde, E. L., 'The World Bank's Sanction System As An Example' (2012) 106 *Proceedings of the Annual Meeting (American Society of International Law)* 122.

Giavazzi, S., Cottone, F., and De Rosa, M., 'The ABC Model: The General Framework for an Anti-Bribery Compliance Program' in Manacorda, S., Centonze, F. and Forti, G. (eds), *Preventing Corporate Corruption* (Springer 2014).

Goldsmith, M. and King, C. W., 'Policing Corporate Crime: The Dilemma of Internal Compliance Programs' (1997) 50(1) *Vanderbilt Law Review* 1.

Gowder, P., 'Democracy, Solidarity, and the Rule of Law: Lessons from Athens' (2014) 62 (1) *Buffalo Law Review*, 1.

Grasso, C., 'Peaks and troughs of the English deferred prosecution agreement: the lesson learned from the DPA between the SFO and ICBC SB Plc' (2016) 5 *Journal of Business Law* 388.

Grasso, C., 'The Dark Side of Power: Corruption and Bribery within the Energy Sector' in Leal-Arcas, R. and Wouters, J. (eds), *Research Handbook on EU Energy Law and Policy* (Edward Elgar 2014).

Hovell, D., 'Due Process in the United Nations,' (2016) 110(1) *The American Journal of International Law* 1.

Jensen, M. C. and Meckling, W. H., 'Theory of The Firm: Managerial Behavior, Agency Costs and Ownership Structure' (1976) 3 *Journal of Financial Economics* 305.

Kapur, D., Lewis J. and Webb, R., *The World Bank: Its First Half Century* (Brookings 1997).

Kaye, T. A., 'Tax Transparency: A Tale of Two Countries' (2016) 39 *Fordham International Law Journal* 1153.

Kelley, T., 'Beyond the Washington Consensus and New Institutionalism: What is the Future of Law and Development' (2010) 35(3) *North Carolina Journal of International Law & Commercial Regulation* 539.

Khan, H. A., 'Corporate Governance of Family Businesses in Asia: What's Right and What's Wrong?' (1999) *Asian Development Bank, ADBI Research Papers*.

La Porta, R., Florencio, L., Shleifer, A. and Vishny, R. W., 'Trust in Large Organizations' (1996) no. w5864 *National Bureau of Economic Research* 333.

Laylin, C. E. and Tuttle, A. H., 'Due Process and Punishment' (1922) 20(6) *Michigan Law Review* 614.

Manacorda, S., Centonze, F. and Forti, G. (eds), *Preventing Corporate Corruption* (Springer 2014).

McCormick, C. T., 'The Scope and Art of Cross-Examination' (1952) 47(2) *Northwestern University Law Review* 177.

Motala, Z. 'Free Trade, the Washington Consensus, and Bilateral Investment Treaties the South African Journey: A Rethink on the Rules on Foreign Investment by Developing Countries' (2016) 6(1) *American University Business Law Review* 31.

Nardin, T., 'Theorising the International Rule of Law' (2008) 34(3) *Review of International Studies* 385.

Ormerod, D., *Smith and Hogans's Criminal Law* (13th edn, Oxford University Press 2011).

O'Sullivan, J. R., 'How Prosecutors Apply the "Federal Prosecutions of Corporations" Charging Policy in the Era of Deferred Prosecutions, and What That Means for the Purposes of the Federal Criminal Sanction' (2014) 51 *American Criminal Law Review*, 29.

Parthapratim, C., 'The Effectiveness of the World Bank's Anti-Corruption Efforts: Current Legal and Structural Obstacles and Uncertainties' (2004) 32(2) *Denver Journal of International Law and Policy* 315.

Pech, L., 'Rule of law as a guiding principle of the European Union's external action' (2011) *CLEER Working Papers* 1.
Pinto, A. and Evans, M., *Corporate Criminal Liability* (3rd edn, Sweet & Maxwell 2013).
Pope, N. and Pope, H., Turkey unveiled: Atatürk and after (John Murray 1997).
Quinn, T. P., 'Judicial Interpretation of Silence: The Criminal Evidence Order of 1988' (1994) 26 *Case Western Reserve Journal of International Law* 365
Redmayne, M., 'Standards of Proof in Civil Litigation' (1999) 62(2) *The Modern Law Review* 167.
Reza, S., 'Due Process in Islamic Criminal Law' (2014) 46 *The George Washington International Law Review* 1.
Rodrik, D., *The Globalization Paradox* (Oxford University Press 2011).
Rubin, E. L., 'Due Process and the Administrative State' (1984) 72(6) *California Law Review* 1044.
Sanders, A., Young, R. and Burton, M., *Criminal Justice*, (4th edn, Oxford University Press 2010).
Sarlo, P., 'The Global Financial Crisis and the Transnational Anti-Corruption Regime: A Call for Regulation of the World Bank's Lending Practices' (2014) 45(4) *Georgetown Journal of International Law* 1293.
Schwarz, A., 'Indonesia After Suharto' (1992) 76(4) *Foreign Affairs* 119.
Seiler, N. and Madir, J., 'Fight Against Corruption: Sanctions Regimes of Multilateral Development Banks' (2012) 15(1) *Journal of International Economic Law* 5
Selassie, A. G., 'Ethiopia: Problems and Prospects for Democracy' (1992) 1(2) *William and Mary Bill of Rights Journal* 205.
Shihata, I. F. I., *The World Bank Legal Papers*, (Kluwer Law International 2000).
Strasser, K. A., 'Piercing the Veil in Corporate Groups' (2005) 37(3) *Connecticut Law Review* 637.
Tamanaha, B. Z., *On the Rule of Law: History, Politics, Theory* (Cambridge University Press 2000).
Taylor, H., 'Due Process of Law' (1915) 24(5) *The Yale Law Journal* 353.
Vlastos, G., 'Isonomia' (1953) 74(4) *The American Journal of Philology* 337.
Weissmann, A., and David, N., 'Rethinking Criminal Corporate Liability' (2007) 82(2) *Indiana Law Journal* 411.
Williams, S., 'The Debarment of Corrupt Contractors from World Bank-Financed Contracts' (2007) 36(2) *Public Contract Law Journal* 277.
Winters, J. A., 'Criminal Debt' in Pincus, J. R. and Winters, J. A. (eds), *Reinventing the World Bank* (Cornell University Press 2002).
Wolfensohn, J. D., 'Corruption impedes development--and hurts the poor' (1998) 25(4) *International Journal of Government Auditing* 1.
Wolff, J. C., 'Voluntary Disclosure Programs' (1979) 47(6) *Fordham Law Review* 1057.

MIX
Papier aus verantwortungsvollen Quellen
Paper from responsible sources
FSC® C105338

If you have any concerns about our products,
you can contact us on
ProductSafety@springernature.com

In case Publisher is established outside the EU,
the EU authorized representative is:
Springer Nature Customer Service Center GmbH
Europaplatz 3, 69115 Heidelberg, Germany

Printed by Libri Plureos GmbH
in Hamburg, Germany